P.

THE WORKING TERRIER

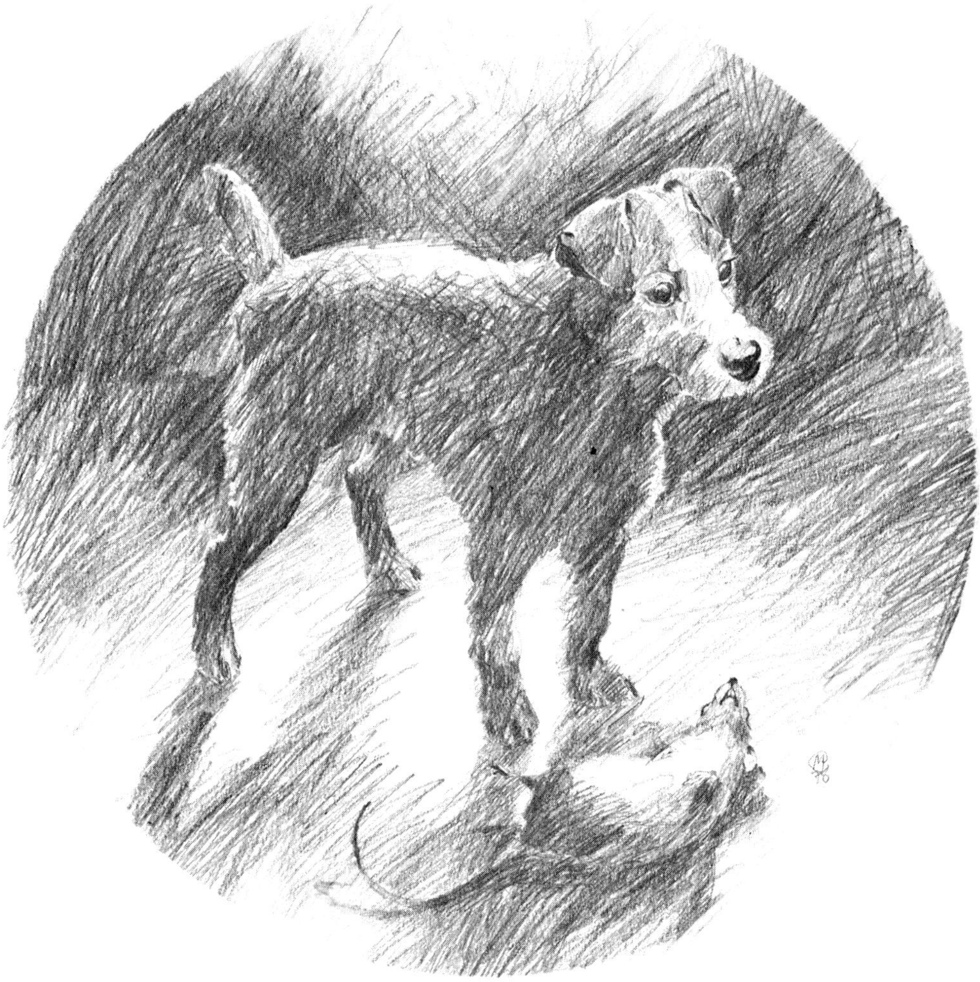

THE WORKING TERRIER

David Brian Plummer

Illustrated by Martin Knowelden

The Boydell Press · Ipswich

© David Brian Plummer 1978

First published 1978 by The Boydell Press
PO Box 24 Ipswich IP1 1JJ Suffolk

British Library Cataloguing in Publication Data

Plummer, David Brian
The working terrier.
1. Terriers 2. Working dogs
I. Title
636.7'55   SF429.T3

ISBN 0-85115-099-3

To Roy Lees – tenth-grade hunter, first-rate friend –
and to Ailsa Crawford of Hamilton Farm Kennels, Gladstone,
New Jersey

Photoset and printed in Great Britain by
Lowe & Brydone Printers Limited, Thetford, Norfolk

CONTENTS

Introduction ... 9

1. THE LEADING TERRIER BREEDS
The Jack Russell Terrier ... 13
The Lakeland Terrier ... 19
The Border Terrier ... 25

2. THE LESS COMMON WORKING TERRIERS
The Smooth-coated Coloured Northern Working Terrier ... 33
Fell Terriers ... 36
Cairn Terriers ... 38
The Sealyham Terrier ... 41
Wire and Smooth Fox Terriers ... 44
The Dandie Dinmont Terrier ... 48
The Bedlington Terrier ... 51
The Irish Terrier ... 54
The Kerry Blue ... 56
Soft-coated Wheaten Terrier ... 57
The Glen of Imaal Terrier ... 58
The Australian Terrier ... 60
The Staffordshire Bull Terrier ... 61
The English Bull Terrier ... 66
The Norwich and Norfolk Terrier ... 68
The Airedale Terrier ... 70
The Yorkshire Terrier ... 72
The West Highland White Terrier ... 73
The Scottish or Aberdeen Terrier ... 75
The Welsh Terrier ... 75
The Skye Terrier ... 77
The Manchester Terrier ... 77
Summary: The Choice of a Working Terrier ... 78

3. THE QUARRY
Entering to Quarry ... 81
The Rat ... 85
Stoats and Weasels ... 99
The Fox ... 105

CONTENTS

The Badger	139
The Scottish Wildcat	161
Mink	167
Coypu	171
The Otter	177
Rabbit Hunting	185

4. **THE CARE AND SHOWING OF WORKING TERRIERS**

Caring for a Working Terrier	193
Leptospirosis	195
Mange	196
Wounds	197
The Fell and Moorland Working Terrier Club	199
Working Terrier Shows	204
A typical show schedule	207
Terrier racing	209
Working Tests and Trials	209

APPENDICES

Jack Russells Working in America *Ailsa M. Crawford*	215
The American Working Terrier Association *Patricia Adams Lent*	222

LIST OF ILLUSTRATIONS

1. 'Tiny', a famous rat-pit dog, who once killed 200 rats in an hour. 14
2. Dai Fish with his Jack Russell ratting team. 15
3. Mick Keighley's noted Jack Russell terrier, showing obvious bull terrier influence. 16
4. Vampire, the author's noted stud dog, whose haul of over a ton of rats in 1977 is probably a world record. 17
5. Grip, Derek Hume's six year old rough-coated Jack Russell terrier. 18
6. Lakeland terrier: Mr Nixon's Ch. Watlands Weapon in 1962. (Photo B. Thurse) 20
7. Lakeland terrier puppies need early breaking to ferret. 22
8. First fox: Border terrier Ch. Gaelic Coffee. 26
9. Early Border terrier puppies – note 'houndy' ears. 28
10. Janette Smith with one of the unregistered strains known collectively as Border/Lakeland. 34
11. Northern Working Terrier erroneously known as the Patterdale – note obvious bull terrier influence. 35
12. A Fell type terrier showing obvious Bedlington influence – note 'linty' coat. 37
13. Joan Hancocks' noted working Cairn terrier. 39
14. Two working Cairns belonging to Joan Hancocks with a haul of foxes. 40
15. Sealyham terrier. (Photo G. Ryder.) 42
16. Early terriers: note native black and tan terrier. A print of 1809. 45
17. Early fox terriers, from a mid nineteenth-century engraving. 46
18. Wire-haired fox terrier: Mollie Harmsworth's Ch. Bengal Emprise Ellerby. 47
19. Smooth-haired fox terrier: Mollie Harmsworth's Ch. Bengal Ashgate Quadrille. (Photo Lionel Young.) 48
20. Dandie Dinmont terrier: E. A. Oldham's Ch. Warkworth Wavewrack. 49
21. Bedlington terrier: Ch. Stanolly Scooby-Doo. 52
22. Irish terrier. (Photo Monty.) 55
23. Kerry Blue terrier, Ch. Binate Blue Mist. (Photo Anne Roslin-Williams.) 56
24. Soft-coated Wheaten terriers. 57
25. Glen of Imaal terrier Killarney Princess. (Photo Bord Failte.) 59
26. Early Bull terriers, drawn by Vero Shaw, 1881. 62

7

ILLUSTRATIONS

27.	Staffordshire Bull terrier, Ch. Rapparee Renegade.	63
28.	English Bull terrier, Ch..Foyri Electrify.	67
29.	Norwich terrier, Mrs Monckton's Ch. Jericho Gold Sovereign. (Photo Sally Anne Thompson.)	69
30.	Airedale terrier, Mrs J. Averis' Ch. Turith Adonis.	71
31.	West Highland White terriers, Alvermar Alida and Alvermar Anna-Katrina.	74
32.	Early Welsh terriers before 'improvement' ruined the breed.	76
33.	Welsh terrier, Kingpin.	76
34.	Manchester terrier, Ch. Black Sensation of Laureats. (Photo Dog World.)	77
35.	Dai Fish's famous pack in the early days.	133
36.	Two bobbery packs: above, c.1914, below, a bobbery pack today.	135
37.	Dog and badger; an engraving of 1815.	149
38.	A lurcher provides a useful partner to a terrier team: the author's lurcher Burke retrieves a hare flushed by terriers.	155
39.	The Fell and Moorland rescue service in operation: above, digging out, below, a successful ending.	200

INTRODUCTION

There have been terriers for as long as man has been troubled by foxes and badgers. Terriers are, by definition (Latin, *terra* = 'the earth'), required actually to go into the lairs of subterranean vermin and either bolt them or dispatch them *in situ*. Most books on the history of dog breeds give elaborate details of how the terrier was created, but such statements are largely hypotheses and, though interesting in themselves, have no place in a book on the working terrier. All breeds of dog will go to ground if the holes are big enough. Many fox hounds disappear down large badger setts if given half a chance, and often become trapped there. All man had to do was breed a dog small enough and plucky enough to get into the lairs of the fox and badger and do their work – and, quite simply, these dogs would be referred to as terriers, dogs of the earth. I will offer no other data on the history of the terrier as I believe quotes from Stonehenge, Turberville and even the inevitable *Master of Game* to be totally out of place in a book intended to have a highly practical bias. Few people read these useless quotes anyway, and usually skip the chapters on history of dogs to get on to the 'meat' of the book. As I intend this book to be purely on the working of terriers, let us dispense with their highly dubious origins and get to the 'meat' forthwith.

I

The Leading Terrier Breeds

THE JACK RUSSELL TERRIER

Broadly speaking, the most commonly worked breeds of terriers are the Lakeland, the Border and the newly standardized mess of canine strains known collectively as the Jack Russell. As the most popular type of working or hunt terrier is the Jack Russell, I will begin with the description and use of this the most variable of breeds.

In the year 1814, an Oxford undergraduate called John Russell, who was walking through the village of Marston in Oxfordshire, bought a terrier bitch from the local milkman. The terrier, who was called Trump, became the founder of the famous strain of working terrier known throughout the West Country as the Jack Russell terrier. The bitch was broken-coated, white in colour with tan eye-patches and a shilling-sized spot near the base of the tail. Russell's terriers were required to bolt foxes for his hounds, not to slay them underground, so this West Country parson avoided using bull-terrier blood in dogs as outcrosses to his strain, for such dogs were invariably so impetuous and hard as to rush in and kill or cripple rather than bolt the fox. It was said that Russell held all smooth-coated terriers as suspect as he believed (probably quite rightly) that such dogs were produced by crossing with bull terriers at some time in their history. There is some doubt as to whether Russell actually bred a strain of terrier, for he was a noted dog dealer and bought and sold any terriers that took his fancy. After he died, few people were especially keen on keeping this particular strain alive, so to all intents and purposes the bloodline passed into extinction.

What are today popularly called Jack Russell terriers are certainly not descended from the dogs of John Russell. Many breeders claim to have the original bloodlines (always descended from the inevitable Heinemann's Jack or suchlike), but without any form of registration or proof, such claims are outlandish and ridiculous and should be treated as excellent sales gimmicks and nothing more. But having debunked the 'Jack Russell strain' legend, we should try and discover what the dogs who masquerade under the title of Jack Russell terrier actually are. To do this we must, as Dylan Thomas says, 'begin at the beginning'. The original British terriers were most likely merely curs of no exact type, probably looking rather like rough-and-ready cairn-type terriers. They were reputedly black, tan, or black and tan in colouring, and so unstandardized that no two districts produced the same type of terrier. These terriers were probably quite useful for keeping foxes and other vermin under control, but in the early eighteenth century two events occurred that completely altered the appearance of the working terrier.

The first was the colonization of the country by the brown rat, *Rattus norwegicus*, which, when well established on our shores, bred at such a rate that not only did it become a major social problem but also the sporting quarry of the poor. At the rear of most seedy country pubs in big cities was a rat pit into which dozens, sometimes hundreds, of rats were tipped, and where a terrier was required to kill as many as possible in a set period of time. Rats are ferocious creatures in spite of their small size, and they bite with great savagery. Most terriers would see off a few rats, but to tackle a hundred, or in some cases even a thousand rats, required a very courageous dog indeed. Now the old English terriers were probably well able to kill a few dozen rats, but for the big-time stuff a different type of dog was required, for dogs had to be very game to set to and kill a hundred rats. Subsequently, most breeders of sporting terriers took to crossing the native terrier with what was the gamest breed known to man – the

'Tiny', a famous rat-pit dog, who once killed 200 rats in an hour.

Dai Fish with his Jack Russell ratting team.

English bulldog. Bull and terrier hybrids dominated the rat pits – dogs so valiant that Henry Mayhew, author of *London Labour and the London Poor*, said they were better with a hundred than a dozen rats. The sporting bulldog of the time was largely white-bodied or pied, and so, by dint of crossing these with native terriers, smooth-coated, white-bodied terriers began to appear. One such dog, a hybrid between a bull and terrier bitch and a bulldog sire, killed a thousand rats in fifty-four minutes – a rat every three seconds, and an incredible feat by any standard.

The second event that was to alter the appearance of the working terrier was the popularizing of the ignoble sport of badger drawing or baiting. This cruel, pointless and rather ridiculous pastime involved a badger being chained inside a barrel. A dog was required to rush into the barrel and drag out the terrified badger. As soon as the badger was dragged clear of the barrel, some lunatic rushed forward and bit the dog's tail, whereupon the dog released his grip and the badger rushed back into the barrel, whereupon the whole stupid game began again. A dog was deemed winner if he drew the badger a certain number of times or succeeded in drawing a badger a number of times in a given time. Badgers defend themselves mightily, and a dog had to be remarkably tough and strong to succeed in this form of sport. The native English terrier was a plucky little dog, but was hardly suitable for it. To produce the correct type of animal for the job, he was crossed with the bulldog. Nearly every noted badger-

THE LEADING TERRIER BREEDS

Mick Keighley's noted Jack Russell terrier, showing obvious bull terrier influence.

drawing dog was bull-blooded, as a glance at Alken's well-known prints of the sport show.

Thus the white-bodied hunt terrier evolved, but although these dogs were fearless, they were also mute, for the bulldog ancestor simply waded into his opponent and held a deathlike grip. Bulldog crosses seldom give tongue, preferring to tackle their prey and put in the deadly bite. It is, of course, nearly impossible to dig to a mute dog that has gone to ground. Furthermore, most bull-blooded terriers do not bolt their foxes but simply close with them and kill or cripple them. Thus other breeds were brought in to ameliorate the hardness and produce a dog that was both valiant and vocal. One of the more common ways of producing such a dog was to cross the very hard terrier with a tiny pocket beagle. The Earl of March, in *Records of the Old Charlton Hunt*, quotes a poem of unknown authorship on the subject of terrier breeding:

> Let terriers small be bred and taught to bay.
> When foxes find an unstopt Badger earthe
> To guide the Delvers where to sink the Trench

THE JACK RUSSELL TERRIER

> Peculiar in their breed to some unknown
> Who choose a fighting biting Curr who lyes
> And is scarce heard but often kills the Fox
> With such a one bid him a Beagle join
> The smallest kind my nymphs for Hare do use.
> That Cross gives nose and wisdom to come in
> When Foxes earth and hounds all bayeing stand.

Thus the Jack Russell terrier came into being – very heterogeneous and mongrelly in appearance, but in no way inferior for such a mixed ancestry. At the time of writing, few strains of Russell breed true to type, but, in 1975, the Jack Russell Terrier Club of Great Britain was formed by the dynamic Roma Moore of Exeter, and perhaps this club will help to produce a more even type of terrier without ruining the working qualities of the breed. Even so, the working-terrier man should adopt the attitude that handsome is as handsome does, and it is fair to mention that, despite their mongrelly appearance, few hunts use any other type of terrier for the task of bolting fox.

The 'Standard of Excellence' for the Jack Russell terrier, as drawn up by the Jack Russell Terrier Club of Great Britain, is still in a state of flux. Basically, two sizes are acceptable: terriers under 11 inches

Vampire, the author's noted stud dog, whose haul of over a ton of rats in 1977 is probably a world record.

Grip, Derek Hume's six year old rough-coated Jack Russell terrier.

and terriers 11 inches and over. The body should be predominantly white with black, tan or tricolour markings. (For some reason, brindle markings are unacceptable, though markings of any sort make precious little difference to the working qualities of the breed.) The tail should be at least 4 inches long; the legs straight; the coat wiry or smooth; the front reasonably narrow – though the most recent draft of the standard states 'strong-shouldered', which is anathema to the working-terrier man.

Whether or not this club will do anything to promote the working qualities of this type of dog, or whether it will merely seek Kennel Club recognition and the resulting increased prices the puppies will bring once they are Kennel Club registered, has yet to be seen. The club would do well to take note of the other breed clubs, such as the Glen of Imaal and the Border Terrier Club, which have encouraged the working qualities of the breeds in which they have an interest to be upheld.

Summary

If one can find a *bona fide* breeder who is breeding the type of Russell one likes, then this type of terrier could be the ideal terrier for the hunter. *Caveat emptor*, however, for at the time of writing every white-bodied street accident with a short tail is sold as a Jack Russell terrier. I must confess that I am prejudiced in favour of this breed as some of my best dogs have been Russells. Two types of Russell exist, the longerlegged terrier, over 11 inches at the shoulder, and the smaller, under 11-inch terrier. Northern hunters favour the taller dogs, as they believe that such animals are more suited to work the larger rocky earths of the north, but few midland hunters favour the leggy type of terrier. Leg length is not really all that important as legs can be and are folded when a dog goes to ground. What is important is width of front and depth of chest, for whereas a long leg can be folded to get to ground, a deep chest cannot. The would-be hunter would do well to avoid corgi-like dogs like the plague.

THE LAKELAND TERRIER

The Lakeland terrier originated in the bleak, hilly fell country, so austere that both man and dog needed to be tough to survive the rigours of the country and the elements. This terrier was bred exclusively for fox control, and as foxes were considered by the hill farmers to be a serious pest rather than sporting quarry, the terrier was required to go to ground and slay the fox in its lair rather than bolt it so that hounds could pursue it. Northern foxes are reputedly larger than their southern counterparts, so a slightly larger type of terrier was bred to deal with them. These terriers were required to live frugally and to work in all weathers, including the sub-zero temperatures common in the rock earths during the winter months. No tougher, hardier breed of dog than the Lakeland ever existed. Stories of their dauntless courage, stamina and so forth are so numerous they would fill a whole book. One noted huntsman from the Patterdale district (the Patterdale is a synonym for the Lakeland) went out on a foray against a noted poultry-killing fox that had plagued the neighbouring farms. The fox was marked to ground in a vast undiggable mound of rock and the terrier put to ground. Eight days later, during which time the land had been covered with freezing snow, the dog emerged, an .eye torn out and very badly lacerated, but dragging with him a 17-pound fox. The dog was wrapped in coats and taken home to a near-by farm, where it lay almost lifeless for three days, but in three weeks had recovered well enough to go to ground on yet another fox. Dogs that were unable to kill a fox, or lacking in courage or constitutionally unsound, were given short shrift by these hill farmers, and through a selective breeding programme that would have delighted the heart of Charles Darwin, the iron-hard, valiant and tough Lakeland terrier came into being.

The Fells were separated by rugged mountainous land that tended to limit travel. Thus the number of Lakeland-type sires found in the Fells was often limited. A noted dog – noted for his courage and working ability rather than for his appearance – would be used on numerous bitches in one fell district, and thus stamp his type into the terrier population in that particular district for several generations. Thus each fell tended to produce its own type of terrier – a type of dog which might be quite distinct from the dogs in the neighbouring fell. While tinkers and gipsies brought in new blood from time to time, and Bedlington terriers were certainly used as outcrosses, these Fell terriers (see also pages 36–38) were usually very carefully bred, and dogs from the outside world (particularly white-bodied dogs) were treated with suspicion.

Lakeland terrier: Mr Nixon's Ch. Watlands Weapon in 1962. (Photo B. Thurse)

Early Lakeland hound packs were trencher fed as a rule, each farmer or hunter taking his own hounds to the meet, and thus the terriers were never kennelled with the hounds, as were the Border terriers, who undoubtedly share a common ancestry with the Lakeland terrier. It was this fact that probably helped to cause the divergence of temperament between the fiery Lakeland and the more phlegmatic Border terriers, for the Lakeland terrier, with its fractious and aggressive nature, did not live long when kennelled with a pack of hounds weighing 60 pounds apiece. Lakeland terriers were strictly loners, sharing the fireside with their northcountry masters and encountering hounds only on hunting days. Thus fractiousness and fiery temperament were not deemed too severe a fault, providing, of course, the dogs were just as game below ground when fighting their lawful opponent. The modern Lakeland terriers still retain this fiery and often quarrelsome disposition.

Early Lakeland terrier breeders bred their dogs exclusively and entirely to hunt fox, and these dogs were usually unsuitable for hunting the more formidable badger. Not that these terriers were in any way lacking in courage – far from it, the antithesis is true. Lakeland terriers who encountered badger in the rock earths usually waded in and endeavoured to kill Brock. The result was not entirely to the hunter's liking, for the badger, besides being double the weight of the terrier and invulnerable to its bites, is a ferocious biter. Badgers usually commit mayhem on any dog foolish enough to 'mix it' with them. What is needed in a badger-hunting dog is an animal that has discretion and learns to stand back from the quarry and to bay. This is entirely foreign to the nature of the Lakeland terrier, and the result was both obvious and unpleasant. John Winch and Cyril Tyson of the Fell and Moorland Working Terrier Club, two present-day authorities on the working Lakeland terrier, confess to being decidedly unhappy about using Lakeland terriers for badger digging as their incredible courage often brings them to grief. Several Lakelands I have trained have taken some frightful poundings from badgers – poundings that a dog not so hard would have avoided.

In 1921, the Kennel Club decided to accept this valiant terrier into its folds and the scruffy and ugly Lakelands underwent a transformation, emerging a few years later as a smarter, neater, far more attractive dog. Fox-terrier blood was introduced to produce a greater reach of neck and a short coupling. Winch believes that Irish terrier blood was also bred in during the time of the metamorphosis, for many Lakeland terrier breeders, including the incomparable Willie Irving, kept a few Irish terriers on their premises. Welsh terrier blood was also introduced at this time, and within twelve years of the

Lakeland terrier puppies need early breaking to ferret.

founding of the Lakeland Terrier Association, a smart 14-inch black-and-tan red grizzle or blue-and-tan fox-terrier-type dog had been created out of the scruffy Fell terrier.

There are many who believe that this beautification ruined the working qualities of the Lakeland. Geoffrey Sparrow, in his *The Terrier's Vocation* (1939), agreed that one hunter stopped working Lakelands when they became indistinguishable from the Welsh terrier (they certainly resemble the Welsh terrier closely enough). The strains of Lakeland untouched by Kennel Club influence are thus now known collectively as Fell terriers. Though the addition of southern terrier blood was thought by many to have taken the edge off the working Lakeland, the reader should not imagine that the Kennel Club-registered Lakeland has had the working instinct bred out of it. John Winch, of the Fell and Moorland Working Terrier Club, has hunted both the unregistered Lakeland and the smart, improved Kennel Club variety, and finds that both work extremely well, even in adverse conditions. Even a few hunts have used show stock Lakelands and been very successful with them.

Cobby, of the South-West Wiltshire Hunt, once told me of a very good-looking blue-and-tan bitch who worked four seasons with a neighbouring hunt. She was a little too tall for the country – an

11-inch dog is about right for that area – but when she could choose her earths, she went in like a tigress. She once swam nearly a hundred yards up a flooded drain to do battle with the fox, and stayed well in bad conditions. By her fourth season, however, she had become so hard that it was unwise to use her since she invariably killed rather than bolted her fox. Cobby mentioned that this bitch gave tongue well when at both fox and badger, though I have personally not found this to be the case with Lakelands. I have trained both types of Lakeland, and while I have found that both are hard and eager to enter, they have all within two seasons become so mute that they are impossible to dig to.

Some five years ago, I trained a pedigree Lakeland dog to working certificate standard. He had been sired by a Crufts winner, and frankly I expected a rather nesh, silly, statue of a dog to result from such breeding. I could not have been more wrong. He killed rats like a fury at six months old and entered to fox before his first birthday. This dog found little difficulty in killing foxes, but became so mute that I dared not use him in deep earths. I once put him into a one-eyed earth that couldn't have been more than a few feet deep – or so I thought. For a few minutes he gave tongue like thunder, but the barking became so distant that it was obvious that the earth was a great deal more extensive than I had anticipated. At last the barking ceased and we waited. After about eight hours, night fell and we decided to dig to the dog. I put in a noisy bitch who found immediately and we began to dig. However, the dig took four days, and we eventually unearthed the Lakeland, who had eaten a good portion of the fox but was frightfully bitten. Without the help of the bitch, it would have been impossible to dig to such a dog – a problem, for I dislike putting two dogs to ground in the same earth for reasons to be explained later. The Kennel Club dogs might not be quite as hard as the original Fell-type terrier, but still take some beating for sheer guts.

Whether one considers buying a Lakeland from a Kennel Club strain, or simply from a Fell strain, the following type is the most suitable:

Height: up to 14 inches. There is a tendency to breed very tall Lakelands today, but a dog above 14 inches will find difficulty in getting to ground in small earths.

Weight: 16 to 18 pounds. The famous 1 pound to 1 inch standard, supposedly set by John Russell, is ridiculous; a 14-pound 14-inch terrier would be emaciated.

Backs: should be short. A long back is a weak back, and a short-coupled dog is usually very agile. There is a tendency for hunt-show judges to award prizes to longbacked exhibits, particularly in the north – this is a grave error.

Heads: should be short in the muzzle and very strong, for the Lakeland is required not to bay at its quarry but to kill it. Fine muzzles and poor biting muscles do not help in this task. It is, however, very difficult to breed a fine narrow-fronted Lakeland with a powerful head. I like powerful-headed dogs, and I would prefer to sacrifice just a little narrowness in the chest to produce these heads. Winch is not so worried about fine heads, as foxes are killed by a throat- or neck-hold rather than by a straightforward bite, so perhaps a powerful head is not all important in a fox-killing dog. Even so, a weak head is not to be desired.

Fronts: should be narrow. A 'shouldery' dog is at a great disadvantage when getting to ground – as I have stated, legs can be folded, chest and shoulders cannot.

Before leaving the Lakeland terrier, I should mention the so-called Border-Lakeland cross. These are rarely the result of crossing a purebred Border with a pure-bred Lakeland, but are merely black-and-tan rough-coated terriers of dubious ancestry – some probably descended from the old English terriers that predated the modern breeds. Many are very useful indeed. One strain, bred in Lincolnshire, is quite incredibly good to both fox and badger, and will give tongue well when against his quarry. Do not despise dogs because they seem to contravene the Trade Descriptions Act when advertised as Border/Lakelands. 'What's in a name?' should be the motto of any terrier man, and many of the black-and-tan terriers are ideal for the job.

Summary

If the reader has suitable earths and does not consider hardness to be a fault in a working terrier, then the Lakeland terrier would be an excellent choice of dog. Most are inclined to be fiery and quarrelsome, so provision for their disposition has to be made when considering kennelling arrangements. They are, through their keenness and enthusiasm, ideal 'first terriers' for the beginner, for they enter very well and easily.

THE BORDER TERRIER

Though the Border terrier and the Lakeland share a common ancestry, they are, personality-wise, as different as chalk to cheese. Border terriers owe their name to the fact that they were used to bolt foxes for the Border Foxhounds. Several artisan hunters also used these dogs to exterminate such vermin as foxes, badgers, polecats, and sometimes even the formidable Scottish wildcat if one strayed too far south. Many books suggest that the Border terrier owes its origin to a now extinct breed of terrier and the Otterhound, but, apart from the fact that the Border terrier works very well in water, there is no indication that Otterhound blood has been used in its make-up. The Border terrier is, in fact, simply a terrier bred for hundreds of years in an isolated district that has developed a distinct type.

Over the years, the Border terrier seems to have been relatively unaffected by the show craze. He remains much the same as he was when the Kennel Club began to take an interest in him. Rawden Lee, in his famous book *The Terriers* (1894), has an illustration of three dogs that are undoubtedly Border terriers. He refers to them as Reedwater terriers, which was at that time a synonym for the Border. This terrier has changed remarkably little in the eighty-odd years since the book was published. It was indeed fortunate that the committee which drew up the standard for the Border terrier in 1920 consisted of working-terrier enthusiasts, not show-breeders out to establish a pretty little dog suitable only for a household pet. Everyone who sat on the committee which drew up the standard was keen to maintain the working qualities of the terrier. The Border Terrier Club can rightly claim that theirs is the only breed of terrier where champions can still be workers. Club shows do, in fact, run classes for 'Borders' who have working certificates, and these classes are usually fairly well attended. Working certificates are signed by masters of foxhounds or otterhounds, and state that a dog is game and has worked in conjunction with a hound pack.

A glance at the Border terrier standard will suffice to show the reader that the dog is in no danger of being ruined by the show craze. The Border terrier is essentially a working terrier; it should be able to follow a horse and must combine activity with gameness.

Head and skull: head like that of an otter and moderately broad in skull with a short, strong muzzle; black nose preferable, but a liver- or flesh-coloured one is not a serious fault.

Eyes: dark, with a keen expression.

First fox: Border terrier Ch. Gaelic Coffee.

Ears: small and V-shaped, of moderate thickness and dropping forward close to the cheek.

Mouth: teeth should have a scissor-like grip, with the top teeth slightly in front of the lower, though a level mouth is quite acceptable. An undershot or overshot mouth is a major fault and highly undesirable.

Neck: of moderate length.

Forequarters: forelegs straight and not too heavy in the bone.

Body: Deep and narrow and fairly long, ribs carried well back but not oversprung since a terrier should be capable of being spanned by both hands behind the shoulder.
Hindquarters: racy, loins strong.
Feet: small with thick pads.
Tail: moderately short and fairly thick at the base, then tapering; set high and carried gaily, but not curled over the back.
Coat: harsh and dense with a close undercoat. The skin must be thick.
Colour: red wheaten grizzle and tan or blue and tan.
Weight and size: dogs, 13 to 15½ pounds; bitches, 11½ to 14 pounds.

What an admirable standard for a working terrier! It is to be hoped that the breeders of the Border terrier will not deviate from their standard of excellence.

Border terriers were invariably kennelled with hounds, and so a spiteful, quick-tempered terrier was undesirable. Any fight involving several hounds and a terrier would quickly result in a very dead terrier. Thus a terrier with a placid temperament was evolved by the northern huntsman. Few present-day Borders are keen to pick a fight, though most will give a very good account of themselves when provoked to battle. Furthermore, Border terriers are rarely spiteful with people. I have judged hunt shows for twenty years, and have never been bitten by a Border terrier, though my knuckles have frequently been damaged when examining other breeds.

However, this seemingly most perfect of terriers is not without its faults. Many Borders enter with exasperating slowness. A puppy of most terrier breeds will usually be keen to kill rats by the time it is six months old. Borders are often still remarkably juvenile at this age, and sometimes take an interest in rats and small fry when they are well over a year old. This is often most disconcerting to the tyro terrier man, who will often wonder what is wrong with his terriers and perhaps go as far as to sell the bewildered animal to a pet home, only to find, two months later, that the dog has become a raging tiger, tackling all before it. Borders are not usually really suitable as first terriers, neither are they suitable dogs for people who want instant or rapid success. However, once a Border has decided that it is ready for work, it is usually excellent, though great patience is sometimes necessary when entering a Border terrier.

Some huntsmen refuse to use a Border because its colour resembles that of a fox, and hence a dog emerging from an earth covered with fox scent can be chopped and killed by hounds. This does indeed sometimes happen, but hounds that kill a Border terrier are usually just as keen to worry a white-bodied dog. True, a trigger-happy gunman may

THE LEADING TERRIER BREEDS

sometimes shoot a Border, believing it to be a fox, but hounds are not so stupid and soon learn the difference, At one time it was common practice to kennel a coloured terrier with foxhounds, but this is not really necessary. Even greyhounds – not a breed particularly noted for its perspicacity – quickly learn the difference between a coloured terrier and a fox.

Another quality which does not commend the Border terrier to the average huntsman is the fact that the Border is one of the most sensitive and easily ruined of all terriers. Many will refuse to work if smacked or shouted at. One very valiant bitch that I once owned, bred

Early Border terrier puppies – note 'houndy' ears.

from the incomparable champion, Eignwyre Enchantress, wet herself when anyone shouted at her, yet she stayed for days to fox, badger or otter, and suffered terrible wounds without so much as a whimper. Borders do not recover easily from early mishandling. Lakeland puppies often get over traumatic experiences quite easily, but a Border is often permanently ruined by severe mishandling. If the Border Terrier Club requires a motto, may I suggest that *Festina lente* – 'Make haste slowly' – would be a good one. No terrier is more easily ruined, but, conversely, few terriers reward patience and persistence so much as the Border terrier.

It is all the more curious that many hunts which use Borders frequently reject them after two or three seasons as they become very hard. Many almost timid Borders develop into raging tigers to fox when they are about three years old. Some become so hard that they refuse to give ground to a badger, and suffer greatly as a result. This may be a fault in the genetic make-up of the breed, or perhaps just a fault in entering brought about, as Lucas believed, by too early starting to large quarry, or, as John Cobby believed, by allowing a young adult to become badly bitten by a fox during its early hunts. Some terriers quit after a beating from a fox, others become so decidedly anti-fox that they tend to kill rather than bolt them. Jim French of the Cotswold Hunt believes that hard dogs can be made more suitable for fox bolting by working them to badger for a spell. I have had little success with this method, for, like Lucas, I find dogs that are worked regularly to badger tend to knock a fox about quite a lot.

Cobby believed that only certain strains of Borders were guilty of the sin of fox-slaying, and he avoided using noted stud dogs which tended to produce such lethal offspring. Again I do not believe this to be true. Some of the dogs bred by Cobby were often quite lethal with foxes, so perhaps his strain only worked properly when handled by the right people. Cobby was certainly an expert on entering a terrier – as he was on training a hound. His death left a gap in the working-terrier world. Cobby actually stopped breeding his noted line of Russell-type terriers (dating back to Nimrod Capell's dogs, and so useful that Joan Begbie used quite a lot of these dogs to create the famous Seale Cottage Jack Russell Terriers) to breed Border terriers, so perhaps he may have been right about using the correct strain of Border.

Lucas mentions that, prior to 1930, some hunters were very careful about avoiding particular strains of Border. Many were famous for being mute and overhard, even during the 1930s. Tom Evans of Blaengarw used many of these early Border terriers, and he, too, was of the opinion that the wrong strain was practically useless. Even if one does not object to this hard type of terrier, nothing is more annoying than a mute terrier who silently thrashes his prey below ground, giving no indication of his whereabouts to the anxious diggers. Personally, I have trained a great number of Border terriers for various people and I have found them a very useful breed indeed. I trained dogs from both the Future Fame bloodline, and also dogs from the Deerstone strain, and found them incredibly good workers when entered properly and given a chance to prove themselves.

Border terriers are quite often crossed with other breeds of working terrier in an attempt to produce the ideal working dog. Border/Russell crosses are quite common, and quite a few Jack Russell terriers have ottertype heads and flexible bodies as a result of a Border terrier ancestry. As I have already said, few of the supposed Border/Lakeland hybrids are descended from pure-bred Border terriers, or even from Border terriers at all, and few breeders actually cross Border with Lakeland to produce the ideal working terrier. Some twenty-five years ago, Sealyham to Border terrier hybrids were fairly commonly advertised, particularly in South Wales. I have seen a great number of these dogs, and all were useful. Most entered far more readily than the pure-bred Border terriers, and they were absolute demons to work. They are rarely bred today, however, and have probably been absorbed by some of the strains of Jack Russell terrier.

Summary

If the would-be hunter is prepared to wait a considerable time for his terrier to start work, if he has the patience and a great deal of time and tolerance, if he can take the ridicule of others with a grin, then the Border terrier may be the ideal dog for him. If he is impatient, keen to make an early start with his terrier, enthusiastic about premature entering, then he should avoid the Border like the plague. Many Border terriers will start work fairly early – the strain used by the Zetland Foxhounds is reputedly an early starter, and quite excellent workers at that – but a great number of Borders are late starters and take a good deal of persuasion to start work. If the breed is sensibly entered, however, there is no finer hunt terrier available. They are usually tractable and valiant, and make excellent ratting terriers, particularly in watery places, for most Borders swim like fish.

II

The Less Common Working Terriers

The Smooth-coated Coloured Northern Working Terrier, Erroneously Known as the Patterdale

In the last twenty or so years, a new breed of working terrier has emerged and started to breed relatively true to type. This dog is erroneously referred to as the 'Patterdale', which is really a synonym for the Lakeland, though that name is rarely used in Kennel Club circles these days. It is usually 12 to 14 inches at the shoulder, smooth-coated, tan brindle or black in colour, with an enormous biting jaw. The legs are usually straight, and although the tendency today is to produce rather shouldery specimens, many are quite narrow-fronted. Most have good pendulous ears, but a few prick-eared specimens occur from time to time. Some ten years ago, this type of dog was winning well among the hunt terriers in the Midlands, and was one of the more popular dogs in the Border/Lakeland or cross-section. In recent years, its place has been taken by pure-bred Borders and rough-coated Lakelands, but this type of dog is still very popular among working-terrier men in the north of England and also in South Wales.

As I made clear in the Introduction, I am always loathe to speculate on the ancestry of a breed, since most speculations are at best just educated guesses. Frankly, the origin of this dog is still a bit of a mystery. Tyson, one of the founder members of the Fell and Moorland Working Terrier Club, refers to them as smooth-coated Fell terriers, but Winch, President of the same club, and no doubt an authority on the northern working terrier, says that as a type of dog it is practically unknown in the Fells. Many have heavy jaws that indicated bull-terrier ancestry, and some, in fact, exactly resemble the small fighting bull terriers that were reputedly bred and fought in Bloxwich at the turn of the century. Perhaps Lakeland and Border blood has been used to refine this type and to create straight legs and narrow front, but this, I confess, is pure guesswork.

Nigel Hinchcliffe, chairman of the Pennine Foxhounds and breeder of an excellent strain of black, smooth-coated terrier, believes this type also has the blood of an unregistered breed called the Lancashire heeler in its veins. Hinchcliffe's dogs all seem to breed remarkably true to type, and the ones I have seen have all been exceedingly game and useful. Whatever has been used in the ancestry of this dog, the resulting animal has an attractive, smart and workman-like appearance. Although the ancestry of the breed is in doubt, what is certain is that no harder,

Janette Smith with one of the unregistered strains known collectively as Border/Lakeland.

tougher breed of terrier exists. There are few of the breed who are not noted fighters, and most have a very low flash-point.

At a time when I frequented hunt shows I used to avoid standing close to one of these formidable terriers. Bill Brockley of Etwall once showed a few of these terriers, but stopped breeding them because of the frightful kennel fights they became involved in. Dog v. bitch fights were fairly common, and whatever the breed used to create its massive biting head, it also endowed the dog with a disposition to go with the jaw. Most are lethal to fox and rush in for a hold, mangling the fox rather than bolting it. My own Patterdales were as deadly as Brockley's were, and also became dreadfully damaged through badger digging. They were very difficult to dig to as they simply waded in for a hold, releasing only when an opportunity arose to put in a more lethal bite. I used one on a badger dig near Conisbrough, and after an hour at badger he resembled a saw-mill accident, with both ears torn off and three throat wounds that exposed the oesophagus and most of the neck muscles. As ratting terriers they are excellent, though I found my own perhaps a trifle lacking in nose. It was nearly impossible to rat more than a pair of these dogs together as a dispute over the ownership of a rat often resulted in a ferocious fight.

Bray of Kirkby Lonsdale bred some excellent-looking dogs of this type which were also extremely gutsy working dogs. Quite recently I saw an advertisement in *Exchange and Mart* for dogs of Bray's strain, the appraisal for which went that they would not give an inch. If one requires a terrier to go into ground and kill a fox, then this type of terrier is ideal. The strain is very popular among the hunters in the South Welsh coalfield, but noted terrier men like Jim French of the Cotswold Hunt and Malcolm Haddock of the Meynell Hunt are not very keen about using them to work with hounds. The Meynell terrier man states that though the dogs enter early to fox, some as early as six or seven months if the terrier man is foolish enough to try his terriers at such an early age, they are much too hard for the type of terrier required for the midland hunt terrier man.

Few of this strain seem to be able to be taught to stand back and give tongue, although Nigel Hinchcliffe states that most of his learned this knack in their second season. I used a tiny dash of this

Northern Working Terrier erroneously known as the Patterdale -- note obvious bull terrier influence.

type of dog in the creation of my own Jack Russell. My stud dog, Vampire, was out of a bitch that was the granddaughter of one of Bray's dogs. I found that the massive jaw of this type of dog had also been inherited by my own Russells. Furthermore, my own strain has inherited the early entering qualities of these terriers. On the debit side, for three generations I have been troubled by fighting through the introduction of this blood, and I lost a considerable amount of nose as a consequence. As time goes by, these problems are in process of resolving themselves.

Summary

This type of dog is far too hard for the midlands and southern hunts. The dog is, however, ideally suited for the hunter who regards foxes as vermin and is not particularly worried whether the fox bolts or is killed underground.

FELL TERRIERS

Fell terriers are a mixed bunch. In fact the term is usually applied to any Lakeland type terrier that is not immediately recognizable as a pure-bred Lakeland. Many are black with silky top-knots which indicate that Bedlington or allied blood has been used in their creation. Quite a few of these terriers are very tall. One blue-black dog in Monmouthshire measured 17 inches at the shoulder, but was so narrow-chested it could struggle through a 9-inch pipe. These dogs are a very variable type, but all have as common denominator a great deal of courage. It seems likely that this type of dog was the progenitor of the present-day Lakeland terrier. Many photographs of early Lakeland terriers prior to the Kennel Club recognition would be instantly labelled as Fell terriers today.

Though I have only trained one of these terriers, I have worked with several, both in Wales, where they are reasonably popular, and in northern Lancashire, where some very useful strains are bred. Few are used in the midlands, for reasons I shall explain later. Most enter to fox at a fairly early age, and many are extremely good at working foxes in tight places, for most are very narrow-chested. On the debit side, some of them are very hard and most have a tendency towards

A Fell type terrier showing obvious Bedlington influence -- note 'linty' coat.

being mute. Furthermore, the very narrow-chested terrier usually has a weak head with very poor jaws in proportion to the overall size. Most Lakeland and northern hunters have some heretical views about jaw size. The general opinion is that a dog does not require strong jaws to dispose of a fox, for most of the fox-killing dogs kill by a strangling action rather than by simply crunching the fox with strong jaws. As I have stated, I am not entirely happy about this theory since I tend to favour terriers with strong jaws, even if they gain a little in chest width. I have judged a great number of Fell-type terriers with jaws that have at some time been broken by foxes. Nevertheless the average Fell-type terrier is usually not so aggressive as the Lakeland and is certainly less fiery than the so-called Patterdale.

Summary

This is the ideal type of dog to work and kill foxes in rock piles and tight-roof earths. Their value in bolting foxes, which is what most hunts need them for, is a bit limited on account of the fact that they tend to be hard. They are useful dogs to introduce into Jack Russell terrier stock which has become too chesty. Some very nice northern Jack Russell terriers owe their present shape to a liberal dose of Fell-terrier blood, and one noted winning Jack Russell terrier was a white-bodied puppy from a mating of two black Fell terriers that had bred relatively true for generations.

THE CAIRN TERRIER

Cairn terriers are a very ancient breed of dog. Many consider them to be the most ancient British earth dog. James I of England (VI of Scotland), feeling perhaps a twinge of patriotism, sent to his native land a request that six earth dogs (probably of the Cairn type) be sent as a gift to some French terrier enthusiasts. Scotland and the north of England are indeed justly famous for their courageous little terriers.

Early photographs of Cairn terriers show a dog not dissimilar to our present-day show Cairn. The coat was perhaps a little more scruffy and less profuse, the backs somewhat longer and the early type of dog perhaps a little higher on the leg, but the modern Cairn seems practically unaffected by the show craze that has mutilated and ruined so many useful terriers. The word cairn is, of course, a Scottish word for a rock pile, and the original dogs were bred to work and flush out vermin that had taken refuge in such inaccessible places. Present-day Jack Russell breeders who state that only long-legged terriers are suitable for working these rocky borrans would do well to examine these early cairn terriers, the largest of which would not have measured 12 inches at the shoulder, to realize that quite small terriers, providing they were agile enough, could work these rock piles.

The late John McCleod, a former gamekeeper in the Grampians, stated that an unregistered Cairn-type terrier was used by most keepers and hunters well up into the 1920s. His own Cairns were scruffy but useful, and worked well to fox, otter, badger and wildcat. Tess, his veteran terrier and mother of some of his best work dogs, took over two hundred foxes and seventy badgers during her lifetime. At the age of two and a half, she entered a rabbit earth that held a Scottish wildcat that had just kittened in an enlarged section of the warren. After a struggle which lasted for over an hour, Tess killed the cat and dragged out the body, but in the struggle lost an eye and had both ears bitten off to the head. She recovered from this mauling and went on to live to a ripe old age. McCleod told an interesting tale of the death of the bitch. She was senile and sat most of her time looking into the fire with one rheumy eye. John had put her granddaughter on a lead and was leaving to dig out a fox that had an earth near his cottage. As he left, Tess staggered off to join him and died half-way down the road. It was a fitting ending for the old warrior to die in harness.

Few Cairn-terrier breeders in Britain specialize in breeding dogs for work, for, as Rawden Lee once said, not many show breeders are anxious to have their valuable dogs knocked about by a fox or a badger. While one sympathizes with this attitude, it is sad that show breeders seem to breed exclusively from stock that has positively no working instinct, thereby reducing a noble and useful terrier to the rank of a lap dog. Mrs Mawson of Leeds once owned quite a few working Cairn terriers that had entered to fox, and some of her dogs had obtained working certificates from masters of foxhounds, so there are specimens of the breed which preserve the working qualities of their rugged ancestors. Jeff Burman of Grimblethorpe, Louth, once hunted a pure-bred pedigree Cairn to badger, and was delighted with its performance. He bred several litters from this bitch, mating her to a dog which was a noted ratting Cairn, but had, I believe, seen no work below ground. Certain Cairns often make excellent ratting terriers, as their

Joan Hancocks' noted working Cairn terrier.

jaws are still good enough for the dog to inflict a powerful bite – an essential feature in a good ratting dog. Joan Hancock of Sutton Coldfield has some very useful ratting Cairn terriers which not only work and kill rats well enough, but also have the ability to predict which way a rat will bolt. She has also been able to test her dogs' ability at heavier quarry.

In the United States they seem to make better use of their Cairns than we do. A recent issue of the *American Working Terrier Association Gazette* tells how Peter Shea of New Boston fosters the working instinct of his Cairns. 'I emphasize hunting potential in my advertising', he states. His dogs apparently win well at the American Kennel Club shows, and also work well, but the United States has few of the restricting laws that we have in Britain, and working trials on live quarry probably increase the show breeder's interest in the working ability of their pets. Perhaps a working certificate scheme similar to the one put forward by the Border Terrier Club would increase the English Cairn breeders' interest in the working ability of their dogs.

My own experiences with Cairn terriers have not exactly been favourable. I once trained and hunted a litter sired by the beautiful champion Oudenarde Midnight Chimes – a handsome terrier that

Two working Cairns belonging to Joan Hancocks with a haul of foxes.

was winning well at the time. All the litter entered well to rat by the time they were eight and nine months old, but the majority of the litter remained slightly nervous and edgy about the banging and clumping about normal in a typical rat hunt. They were slow to go to ground on fox, and were what Cobby described as spade-shy, coming off the fox when the diggers came near to them – a bad fault at fox, and certainly fatal at badger, which soon digs in. Cairns are also difficult to control in number, a fact which Jocelyn Lucas notes in his masterpiece, *Hunt and Working Terriers* (1931). On the whole, I was not particularly impressed with the litter of Cairns I trained, but this could be put down to a personality clash rather than to a failure of the breed. I am naturally a boisterous, extrovert person, and some terriers do not respond to owners with this type of temperament. I am quite prepared to accept that these Cairns might have worked better if trained by somebody else.

Summary

As a companion dog and hunter of small quarry, the Cairn has its uses. Some make excellent hedging and rabbiting dogs. Few breeders of Cairns work their dogs, however, and the slightly nervous disposition and intractability of most Cairns does not make them very good prospects for working heavy quarry below ground. I hasten to add, however, that many people do not share my opinion of the Cairn. Perhaps this is indeed a breed which retains much of the workmanlike shape of a true terrier and which needs exploiting. Some criticize the Cairn for having pricked ears that reputedly get bitten off when at quarry – though this is, of course, an old wives' tale, since prick ears are normally held back tight to the head when any terrier engages its quarry.

THE SEALYHAM TERRIER

The Sealyham is a relatively modern breed of terrier, in spite of the Reverend William Williams's poem which opens, 'As old as the hills is the Sealyham'. The Sealyham was bred by John Tucker Edwardes for the sport of badger digging. Many books claim that the Welsh corgi was the starting point of the breed, but, like so many theories

Sealyham terrier. (Photo G. Ryder)

regarding the origins of terriers, it is pure hypothesis besides being slightly absurd. The cobby shape was probably derived from the sturdy white-bodied terriers that already existed in Pembrokeshire before Edwardes was born. The creator of this useful breed was prepared to admit that the pedigree of his best sporting dogs had been known for over a hundred years. Edwardes probably crossed his dogs with the working north country Dandie Dinmonts, and then brought in a particular brand of bull terrier called the Cheshire terrier to increase the strength of the jaw in the dogs. The original Sealyhams levelled out as rather leggy dogs, mid-way between the Sealyhams of today and a fox terrier. One often sees rough-coated Jack Russell terriers that are almost identical to the Pembrokeshire dogs bred in the district of Sealyham.

Edwardes was a hard master and he perfected his strain of badger-digging dogs by rigorous selection and, sadly, very rigorous premature culling. At a year old, his sapling puppies were taken out to a gamekeeper on the Edwardes estate. They were tested on a live, wild, hob polecat, dragged in a wire cage until it had reached a state of pungence and terror. The dogs were then encouraged to rush into the cage and drag out the screaming, biting, fury, and those who showed the slightest tendency to be wary of the polecat were immediately put down. This was a rather hard and, frankly, most unfair test for a yearling puppy which, given time, might have made a very valiant terrier. Edwardes probably realized the error of his ways, as the following story may indicate. He had given one of his tenant farmers a puppy to walk – a condition of tenure on Sealy Ham estate at one time – and the farmer grew fond of his charge. Edwardes tested the puppy and found it lacking, but the farmer begged the puppy's life. The farmer took the sapling home and it grew into a superb badger dog. Edwardes was eventually forced to pay a pretty penny to buy it back.

The breed was bred exclusively for badger digging, but they were very versatile dogs indeed. Gladdish Hulkes hunted a pack of lightly built Sealyhams in the New Forest, and their quarry was primarily stoat. Jocelyn Lucas bought the pack from the dying Gladdish Hulkes and used them as some of the foundation stock for his famous Ilmer strain Sealyhams. Lucas's stories of hunting Sealyhams make fascinating reading (he wrote for the *Field* Magazine under the *nom de plume* 'The Lad'). He hunted his Sealyham pack to all manner of prey, including otter, stoat and rabbit, but he, too, used them primarily as badger dogs. Lucas succeeded in resisting the show craze which produced heavy, cloddy dogs, too slow to be of much use, and continued to breed a game and useful type of terrier. His famous stud dog, Ilmer Jack, was a little too large for the ideal fox-hunting terrier for he weighed 24 pounds, but he was mated to many hunt-terrier bitches and produced some very useful offspring. Many hunt terriers of the Bedfordshire district still display this Sealyham ancestry, perhaps as a result of Lucas's liberal use of his stud dog.

Sealyhams of the type favoured by Lucas – light, leggy and agile – were highly popular in South Wales during the 1930s. One pair in Maesteg is supposed to have accounted for a thousand rats in one night – a stupendous feat. Most of the noted rough-coated terriers of South Wales – and some very valiant dogs were bred from these terriers – had obvious Sealyham ancestry. A curious fact about these terriers which were so common around the head of the Rhondda and adjacent valleys, was the fact that sometimes a puppy resembling a tan-and-white Dandie Dinmont was born in some litters, and as I have stated, Edwardes probably used Dandies in the early days of his breeding programme.

Few people use Sealyhams today, however, though Lucas's strain is still worked by quite a few hunters. The show craze has practically ruined this attractive breed, for the modern Sealyham is a heavy, cloddy, overcoated animal, and most unsuitable for the task of going to ground. Some specimens are more suitable for a day on the hearth rug than one in the hunting field. An interesting breed has, however, emerged from crossing the Sealyham with the Norwich or Norfolk terrier. The result, referred to as the Lucas terrier (after Sir Jocelyn Lucas), is a very handy rough-coated little dog resembling an old-type Sealyham. Most are a little heavy-coated for my liking, but the ones I have seen are very plucky and agile. They are reputedly excellent ratters, for they have some of the agility of the Norfolk or Norwich, and a fairly strong head from their Sealyham ancestry. A few are worked to heavy quarry, and apparently acquit themselves reasonably well.

Summary

There are still some strains of working Sealyham around, but they are few and far between. It would be foolish to recommend the modern show Sealyham to any hunter since the breed is now almost totally unsuitable as a working terrier.

WIRE AND SMOOTH FOX TERRIERS

These were the most common hunt terriers at the beginning of the century. Many strains were actually prefixed with the names of a hunt, for example, the Belvoir Ranter. The origin of the dog is a little obscure, but most books venture a speculation. The most common opinion is that it is a result of crossing the Old English white terrier with black-and-tan terrier, similar to some of the early Welsh terriers. A more likely explanation is that it was a result of crossing the native British terrier with a bulldog-cum-bull terrier type of dog. John Russell was a pioneer of the rough-coated fox terrier, and was against the bull-terrier cross as it produced too hard a terrier. Few fox-terrier breeders, on the other hand, could resist crossing their dogs with bulldogs or bull-terrier types to produce heavy jaws and great courage in the offspring. Undoubtedly some beagle blood was brought in, as is indicated by hound markings on the modern show winners.

Rough-coated terriers were not as popular during the middle of the nineteenth century, and it was this type that John Russell did much to promote. They are now, of course, far more popular than their

Early terriers; note native black and tan terrier. A print of 1809.

THE LESS COMMON WORKING TERRIERS

Early fox terriers, from a mid nineteenth-century engraving.

smooth counterparts. The turn of the century saw the decline of this attractive animal as a working terrier and its rise as a popular show dog. Rawden Lee gives a hint of the way the breed was going in his cryptic comments in *The Terriers* volume of his major work, *History and Description of the Modern Dogs of Great Britain and Ireland* (1890-94), and also in his monograph *A History and Description with Reminiscences of the Fox Terrier* (1895). Already the breed was becoming a show animal, far too valuable to allow it to go to ground.

Gradually, long, elegant heads were bred in – heads so elegant and weak that a fox would break the jaws of such a dog and a badger would smash them like matchwood. Stiff stifles were bred in to create an elegant look, and today few fox terriers are suitable for the job for which they were originally bred. The wire-haired fox terrier in its untrimmed state now looks like a sheep, and its coat has now been increased to a ridiculous length. I have in front of me a photograph of champion Dusky Reine, an early wire-haired fox terrier of 1889. What a shame the show breeder has not retained this useful type. Such a dog would acquit itself well against any fox, and its jaws are certainly strong enough to hold a badger.

Some fox terriers are still worked. Bill Brockley of Etwall hunted a very useful fox terrier (smooth) about twenty years ago. It was a useful fox dog and did well at badger, but it was not a show-type animal, and had a rather larger head than the classic-bred fox terriers. There is a tendency today to mate smooth- and wire-haired fox terriers to Jack Russell-type terriers to produce narrow-fronted, straight-legged dogs to win at the hunt shows. I see little to commend this practice, and the Jack Russell Club of Great Britain has passed a resolution that any dog showing indications of having such hybrid ancestry shall be ineligible for registration in the advanced register of suitable breeding stock. This is an excellent ruling, as the crossing of these elegant show dogs with the genuine working-type Russells will do nothing to help the breed.

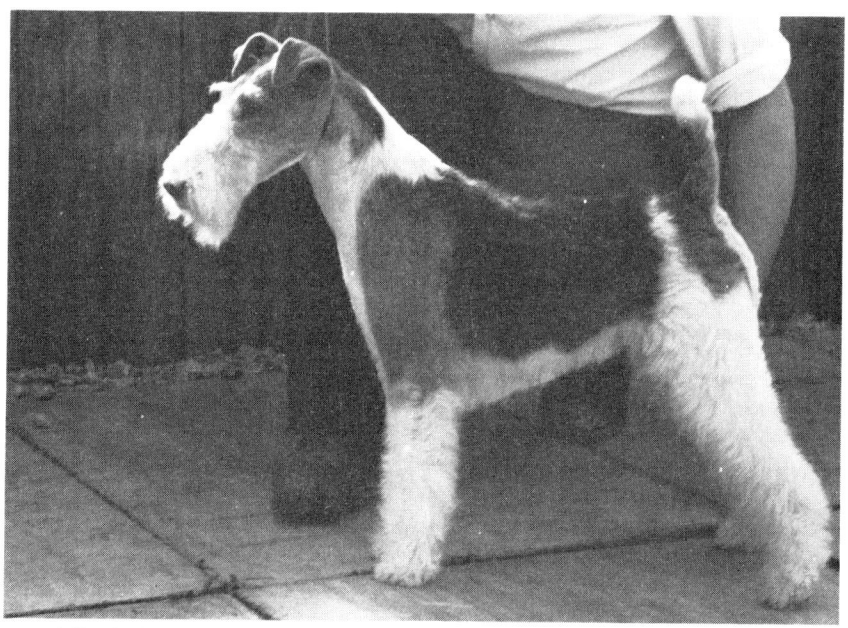

Wire-haired fox terrier: Mollie Harmsworth's Ch. Bengal Emprise Ellerby.

Smooth-haired fox terrier: Mollie Harmsworth's Ch. Bengal Ashgate Quadrille. (Photo Lionel Young)

Summary

Hardly a suitable breed to work heavy quarry any more. Many make useful ratting terriers. Sometimes suitable specimens can be found that really will work quite well, but few breeders go out of their way to produce work dogs.

THE DANDIE DINMONT TERRIER

What a fascinating little dog is the Dandie Dinmont Terrier! I can do no better than quote John Winch in a superb article, published in the 1976 edition of the *Fell and Moorland Working Terrier Magazine*, as to the history and origin of this strange-looking breed.

This breed of terrier got its name after the publication of Sir Walter Scott's novel, *Guy Mannering*, in 1814, but it had been bred

THE DANDIE DINMONT TERRIER

for at least a hundred years prior to this on the border. Some say it was a rough-haired terrier crossed with another hound, but the best theory is that it was a rough-haired terrier bred by farmers and noblemen in the Border district and was of pure descent from the earliest dogs. The Dandie and the Bedlington were closely related with the same courage, hanging ears and top-knot. Lord Antrim showed two dogs out of the same litter in 1870. He won with one in the Dandie class and gained a distinction in the Bedlington class with the other.

Piper William Allen of Holystone was born in 1704 and was the celebrated hunter of otters and foxes. He was offered a farm by the Duke of Northumberland in exchange for his dog, Hitchin – he refused. By 1820 the Duke of Buccleugh and the Duke of Northumberland, the Duke of Roxburgh and every gentleman or tinker and farmer between Alnwick and Edinburgh was breeding Dandies. The Dandie Dinmont Club was founded in 1876 to preserve the characteristics of the breed. The original Dandies had to have a strong head, a broad skull and a domed forehead and there had to be a soft top-knot of silky hair and the eyes had to be round, hazel and intelligent. The teeth had to be very strong and out of proportion to the size of the head. The body had to be long, strong, flexible, the tail short, the forelegs short and very

Dandie Dinmont terrier: E. A. Oldham's Ch. Warkworth Wavewrack.

muscular, the back legs longer and set well apart. The size of the Dandie had to be between eight and eleven inches to the top of the shoulder, from fourteen pounds to twenty-four pounds in weight, the best weight eighteen pounds, and the colour had to be either pepper or mustard.

The Dandie was the *crème-de-la-crème* of workers. Captain Edwardes imported Dandies into his kennel to shorten the legs of his Sealyhams about 1860. He considered the Dandie at the time to be the ultra sporting terrier. The Sealyham of today often carries the top-knot and thereby some Jack Russells have been bred away from it. The Dandie was the progenitor of the Border terrier. Rawden Lee tells us of a dog show that was staged in 1860 in the north, and two or three fox terriers were shown and won all the prizes. They were supposed to be good at badger, fox and fighting. That night some Committee Members visiting the show produced a semi-tame fox and all the terriers ran away from it. Someone produced Sir Douglas, a Dandie who was benched a little distance away. He grabbed the fox and almost killed it on the spot before he could be choked off.

The Dandie was a weasel like dog with a seemingly large head. There is no more difficult dog to breed to comparative perfection because of its shape. The modern Dandie may not work, although someone, somewhere, is sure to have one that can be seen to work, but it had a glorious pedigree of work and has influenced the Lakeland via the Bedlington, the Sealyham directly, the Border directly and the Russell through the Sealyham. Gainsborough painted one in 1770 into a picture with the 3rd Duke of Buccleugh and Arthur Wardle continued the tradition in 1890.

Whether or not this breed is still a useful worker is in doubt. I know few people who breed, let alone work, this curious little terrier. I believe a Miss Nightingale of Rutland once bred some useful Dandies and put several out to keepers where they worked both fox and badger. Some good reports were obtained as to their courage and working ability.

Summary

In spite of its formidable jaw, the Dandie can scarcely be regarded as a force to be reckoned with as a working terrier. I find them far too slow to suit my requirements, and their very shape indicates a fundamental lack of agility that is essential in working terriers.

THE BEDLINGTON TERRIER

The Bedlington shares a common ancestry with the Dandie, and is also closely related to the Border and the Lakeland terriers. Both Dandies and Bedlingtons were used by gipsies and artisan hunters for the sport of badger baiting, fox digging and the occasional dog fight. The gipsy breeders, who lived outside the law in the Rothbury Forest area, bred these terriers that, according to Rawden Lee, looked like a lamb and fought like a lion. He adds that when two fought each other, only one walked away from the scene of battle. The courage of the breed was almost legendary. An American terrier man once sent to England for a hard terrier. He was sent a particularly plucky type of fox terrier with a cryptic note to say that, if the dog was not hard enough, he would have to buy a Bedlington.

Again, whatever it was that went into the genetic make-up of the dog is largely conjecture. The oft-repeated story of otterhound blood being introduced into all northern terriers does not stand up to critical examination, though, curiously enough, all northern terrier breeds (with the exception of the Lakeland) seem very much at home in water, and it was this disposition that probably gave rise to the theory that they had otterhound blood. The common-sense dog fancier would do well to ask himself why any terrier man would consider crossing a small terrier with an otterhound standing perhaps 25 inches at the shoulder. Bedlingtons share this affinity to water, and a Bedlington once won third prize in a contest designed to test the life-saving qualities of various breeds of dog, when the contestants had to dive into the water and drag out a dummy. (It is only fair to add that the first prize was won by a Newfoundland bred exclusively for watery tasks of this nature.) The itinerant families who bred them probably wanted a dog who was not only valiant but versatile enough to go to ground on a badger or fox, tackle otter and be fast enough to take a rabbit or so. With such high standards as guidelines, the original Bedlington came into being.

Other breeds were probably introduced later on. In the 1800s, a group of nail makers from Staffordshire moved into the district around Bedlington, bringing with them the fighting bull terriers so beloved by Black Country sportsmen. Some of these were reputedly crossed with the Bedlington, adding additional fire and guts to an already potent canine cocktail. Stories of the courage of these early dogs are legion. Ainsley, a noted Bedlington terrier breeder of long ago, owned a particularly game Bedlington dog which, in addition to being a

Bedlington terrier: Ch. Stanolly Scooby-Doo.

show dog, was famous for its prowess at badger digging. One day, at harvest time, an Old English sow attacked a small child in a cornfield. Piper, Ainsley's famous dog, then aged fourteen, drove off the sow before it could do any damage. At fifteen years old, this old dog reputedly drew a badger from an earth after the beast had trounced several younger dogs matched against it.

The Bedlington and the Dandie were once classed as the same breed, but the show craze was to produce a hiatus between the two types. The Bedlington was crossed with whippets and other breeds to produce a racier, more attractive dog, while the Dandie breeders set about producing a more low-slung animal. Perhaps the Bedlington lost a little of its guts and fire through the liberal admixture of whippet blood, but even present-day show Bedlingtons are still very plucky and keen to do battle for the smallest insult. A visit to the Bedlington ring at a championship show will convince any sceptic that the Bedlington is still quite a ferocious fighter.

Many hunters still work the Bedlington, though Sparrow, in his fascinating book *The Terrier's Vocation*, expresses horror at the way the show breeder has altered the dog. Most Bedlingtons make useful rabbiting dogs, for their coats are capable of withstanding the effects of thorns and nettles. Many hunters cross the terriers with greyhounds and whippets in order to produce lurchers endowed with some of the terrier's pluck and tenacity together with the speed of a greyhound. At the time of writing, the most popular lurcher types have strong indications of Bedlington ancestry. As rat hunters, Bedlington terriers are certainly useful dogs, for their whippet ancestry gives them the added agility so useful in a ratting dog. Their readiness to take to water also serves them well when ratting a river bank. Few, if any, Bedlington terriers will show the white feather when entered to quarry like fox or badger, but whereas they are valiant to a fault, they are also, in common with a great number of working terrier breeds, usually mute, preferring to attack and do battle with their foes rather than give tongue. Another failing that has to be mentioned is the fact that the Bedlington's size is against it when it has to go to ground. The dogs measure up to 16 inches at the shoulder, and weigh about 24 pounds, and while this size may be no disadvantage when working hill foxes in rock piles, there are few places further south where one could find use for a dog of this size. I have trained several Bedlingtons, and while I could not fault their nose (which is quite exceptional), their speed or their courage, they were much too large to work the typical midland fox earths.

During my childhood in South Wales, many of the local miners crossed small Staffordshire bull-terrier bitches with Bedlingtons to produce working terriers. The progeny were undoubtedly the ugliest dogs I have ever seen, but they were high in courage if not in looks. Most made excellent ratting terriers, working rats from the banks of the coal-slurry brooks that ran through the valley, but they were of little use as sporting terriers. All were absolutely mute and killed foxes very quickly. This bloodline was not lost as these interesting hybrids were absorbed by the Jack Russell terrier-type dogs being bred at the time. While I believe that it had a deleterious effect on the native working terriers of the valley, making them mute and far too hard, there is little doubt that the assimilation of this blood gave the valley terriers the incredible courage for which they were noted.

Summary

If the hunter lives in a countryside where such a large dog can be used, and if he regards muteness as not too serious a fault, then perhaps the Bedlington is a suitable dog for him. Personally, I have never encountered an earth where such a dog could be used to advantage. As a hedgerow worker and hunter of small fry, the Bedlington takes some beating. It is also a useful starting point for the creation of a plucky, all-round lurcher.

THE IRISH TERRIER

This rugged, rough-coated terrier was bred by the Irish artisan hunter as guard dog, vermin destroyer and fighting dog. Few tougher breeds exist. He was once known by the sporting fraternity as the 'Red Devil', a title that apparently he justly deserved, and generations of show breeding have done little to alter his blind courage. Little is known of the dog's origins, though he probably shares a common origin with the Glen of Imaal, the soft-coated Wheaten and the Kerry Blue. All were bred for roughly the same purpose, the divergences of type only occurring through isolated districts producing their own strains.

As a vermin destroyer, the dog is of some use. I know of two local breeders who hunt dogs to rat and rabbit and speak highly of them. Most will penetrate the most prickly of thickets to eject a rabbit, and will take to water quite readily to catch an escaping rat. Alan Bryant, of Bryant's Rabbit Catching Equipment, also hunts a pedigree Irish terrier and states that the dog is very game and has an excellent nose. He has worked with ferrets and marks every rabbit prior to netting – a most useful rabbiting dog by any standards.

As a vermin destroyer below ground – the legitimate work of the true terrier – the dog is not so useful, however. Like all Irish

Irish terrier. (Photo Monty)

earth dogs, the Irish terrier is a large dog, measuring 18 inches at the shoulder and weighing 25 to 27 pounds. Thus such a dog would find it impossible to negotiate the tunnels of an average fox earth, though he might be able to get into a large badger sett. Our problem does not really end here, however, for while the Irish breeds are nearly all valiant unto death, they also have a well-deserved reputation for being too hard and virtually dead mute. The fact that the were once used for dog fighting probably brought about this muteness, for fighting dogs need to wade in to get a lethal hold rather than bark at their foes. I have seen a few Irish terriers go to ground in badger sets, but I have never heard one give tongue or even bolt a fox. Such a dog, with its death-or-glory attitude, soon comes unstuck when he faces a badger, for Brock quickly disposes of him. Plucky as the 'Red Devil' is, he is no match for an adult badger, any more than any other terrier that tries to tangle with a badger. Thus the use of an Irish terrier below ground is, to say the least, very limited.

Irish terrier blood has probably been used in the creation of other breeds. Many believe it was used in the creation of the once plucky and useful Welsh terrier, and it was certainly crossed with Fell terriers to produce the modern, refined Lakeland. Airedale terrier breeders often crossed their dogs with Irish terriers to get rid of the frightful houndy appearance of early Airedales. Some authorities also believe that small Irish terriers were used in the creation of the Norfolk or the Norwich, but this is very much open to doubt.

Summary

As a companion dog and as a hunter of small fry, the Irish terrier is useful, but, by dint of its size and disposition, it is most unsuitable to perform the tasks of a true terrier.

THE KERRY BLUE

Again, an Irish terrier that was bred as a guard dog, small-vermin exterminator, badger baiter and fighter. This breed is fiery, game and quick to anger. It is a largish, rough-coated terrier with a striking

'Kerry Blue terrier, Ch. Binate Blue Mist. (Photo Anne Roslin-Williams)

blue-black coat. By reputation, they are supposedly the most intelligent breed of terriers, and will adapt to a variety of tasks as diverse as dog fighting and cattle herding. Although ideal for small quarry such as rat and rabbit, their size, like that of all Irish terriers, is against them below ground, for there are few earths where a dog measuring $18\frac{1}{2}$ inches at the shoulder and weighing up to 40 pounds can be used. As with most Irish breeds, they have a reputation for being mute.

Summary

Not really a suitable dog for the working terrier because of its size and weight, but Irish breeders have deliberately kept the working instinct alive by encouraging breeders to obtain the coveted 'Mismeac Teastas' or certificate of dead gameness.

SOFT-COATED WHEATEN TERRIER

Soft-coated Wheaten terriers.

Another hard-bitten Irish breed that is useful as a vermin destroyer above ground. It shares with its Irish cousins the quarrelsomeness common to all Irish breeds, and also the fact that it is too big to get to ground. It is, of course, impossible to recommend such a terrier, which is 17½ inches at the shoulder and weighs in at 35 to 40 pounds, as being of general use to the working-terrier enthusiast. The dog also has a reputation for being mute when it does get to its quarry – hardly a quality to recommend in a working terrier. The Wheaten is also perhaps one of the most aggressive terriers to kennel.

Summary

Small game: probably. Large game below ground: certainly not.

THE GLEN OF IMAAL TERRIER

At one time this quaint and attractive terrier was of great interest to me as I was in need of a heavy Caesar dog (that is, a dog which will grip and hold the quarry at the end of a dig) for my badger-digging team. This is a little-known Irish breed, the coat of which is soft and wheaten, blue brindle or blue-tan in colour. It is a strong cobby terrier that measures 14 inches at the shoulder, but weighs in at up to 35 pounds. It shares a common ancestry with all the Irish terriers, but has not yet been degraded by the show craze. It resembles a rather large, stocky Cairn. Irish breeders and hunters work these dogs to badger (they are far too broad for most fox earths), and also, let it be whispered, for a spot of dog fighting. Their courage is indeed bottomless. Several dogs imported into England have proved to be utterly fearless, and the breed shows no sign of losing its terrier temperament. This is largely due to the small but energetic breed club which has insisted that a dog must hold a coveted certificate of dead gameness before it can achieve high honours in the show ring. This is a lesson which the recently formed Jack Russell Club of Great Britain might well benefit from, to prevent their own working terrier from degenerating into a lap dog.

Some ten years ago, two very valiant male Glen of Imaal dogs were imported into the north of England. They were very game and fractious with other dogs and ever eager to avenge an insult. They were worked a little, and proved to have good noses and a lot of terrier instinct, and though they were not as mute as many

Glen of Imaal terrier Killarney Princess. (Photo Bord Fáilte)

dogs I have worked with, they did not give tongue well enough to justify the title of 'first-class working terrier'. Either through merit, or perhaps through curiosity value, they were mated to a large number of Russell-type bitches and also a few Fell dogs, I am told. The progeny were excessively hard, but without fear.

One of the puppies was sold to a hunter who lived near Conisbrough, Yorkshire. At a year old it entered an earth near an old mine and spent five days fighting and killing a dog and vixen fox that it had bottled up in a blind hole. After a monumental dig by a team of twelve miners, the dog was rescued in a very weak state. One of its eyeballs had been punctured and its face was badly lacerated. So serious were the wounds that the dog died of sepsis and shock a few days later. Perhaps if the dog had given tongue well, it might have been dug out far more easily and hence have remained alive. All the Glen of Imaal hybrids I have seen had very bad fronts and shoulders. Few of these cross-breds are produced today, but the blood lines have probably been absorbed in the cross-bred working terriers around Yorkshire.

For all the dog's courage, it is not without a fault. The fact that it is only 14 inches at the shoulder, but weighs in at over 35 pounds, means that the fronts are far too hefty for a dog bolting fox and that one would find it impossible to enter most of the fox earths of the midlands and south. The breed is excessively hard and correspondingly mute. Most are very reluctant to give tongue when at their quarry, and invariably tackle their foe. This is a liability when digging badger, and will cost the terrier man a pretty penny in vet's fees, for the dog often receives a dreadful mauling from Brock. Some fifteen years ago, I visited a breeder in Ulster with a view to purchasing a pair of these terriers. I found that while they lacked nothing in blind courage and had a total disregard for danger as well as for pain, they were not what I required in a working terrier. However, I have nothing but praise for the breed club that has preserved the working qualities and courage of this magnificent breed.

Summary

As a pure-bred working terrier, the breed has its limitations, but as a 'courage and gameness blood bank' to resuscitate a strain of working terrier, the breed holds out much promise. The work of the breed club must act as an example to breeders of working terriers currently being ruined by the show bug which pays too much attention to the physical appearance of a dog and not enough to its working abilities. For a Caesar dog at the end of a badger dig, it has great possibilities.

THE AUSTRALIAN TERRIER

This lively and attractive breed deserves to be more widely known. Derived originally from the hotch-potch of terriers imported to Australia by early immigrants, it shows obvious traces of Cairn, Norwich and perhaps Dandie blood. These were, and still are, used by Australian hunters to drive out underground vermin, which, though marsupial in type, is as dangerous as British quarry. In the early 1900s, the breed enjoyed considerable popularity, both as a show breed and as a working dog.

One story will illustrate its equal merits in each area. A noted

English breeder was exercising her Australian terriers when one raced off into a deep badger set and began to bay loudly at a boar badger it had bottled up in the corner of one of the holes. His owner panicked and obtained the services of two farm hands, who spent seven hours digging to the dog and his quarry, during which time the terrier had not come out for either air or water. The dog was taken home, washed and brushed, and won its class at Cruft's the following day.

The breed still has the varminty, unruined look that breeders would do well to preserve. It is also a handy size, being 10 inches at the shoulder and weighing only 12 to 14 pounds. Most breeders still eulogize about its working ability to rats and willingness to work a hedgerow. Unlike the Cairn, which is strictly an individual, the Australian terrier works well as part of a team, and since it is not an aggressive dog, it could well form the basis for a first-class ratting pack.

Summary

This terrier has a great deal of untapped working potential. It is a useful-looking dog by any standards, and one that the working-terrier man may do well to explore.

THE STAFFORDSHIRE BULL TERRIER

This incredible canine athlete and gladiator was bred for the ignoble, now illegal, sport of dog fighting. It is the very embodiment of courage, and in spite of its heavy pugilistic shape is amazingly agile. Its origins are in doubt, and three theories exist as to its ancestry:

1. They are the original British bulldog bred on more terrier-like lines.
2. They are fifty per cent each terrier/bulldog hybrids.
3. They are bulldogs with a tiny dash of terrier blood added.

I am inclined to favour the third opinion as many eighteenth-century bulldogs are nearly identical to the present-day Staffordshire or Stafford bull terrier.

This breed was bred by the chainmakers who worked in the

THE LESS COMMON WORKING TERRIERS

Early Bull terriers, drawn by Vero Shaw, 1881.

'dark Satanic mills' of the Black Country. Here, hard times begat hard men, and the workmen kept their dogs for the express purpose of fighting them to the death. As fighting dogs, few other breeds could stand against this powerhouse of muscle that weighed in at 35 pounds plus. Dog fights had strict rules, far stricter in fact than the 'anything goes' rules of the prize ring of that time. First, the dogs were weighed to make sure that dogs of equal size and strength were pitted against each other. Though catchweight contests involving 30-pound bull-terrier dogs against Airedales and other breeds were fairly common in the London pits, the Staffordshire dog fighter fought his dogs according to the strictest rules. A few ounces overweight could, on rare occasions, mean the forfeiture of wager money.

Next, according to some authorities, the dogs were smeared with milk, and an independent taster was invited to lick the milk from each dog to detect whether any bitter chemical had been painted on the dog's fur at the stifle or throat, since such a chemical would prevent the opposing dog from holding a grip tightly. This sickening practice, which is made much of in many books, was in fact rarely followed. The area in which I now teach was the centre of dog fighting, and I have found many friends whose fathers fought these dogs. I have not to date met any dog fighter who can actually remember a tasting ceremony at a dog fight.

The dogs were fought in bursts with short rests between the rounds until one dog was killed or too injured to continue the fight. Sport of this kind required a particularly valiant dog and a particularly nasty owner. Unlike Drabble, who eulogizes over the courage of the men who fought these dogs, I find that people who are indifferent to the suffering of animals are usually faint-hearted themselves. O. Henry, in his famous story 'Theory and the Hound', says that he never yet met a man who was soft on horses and dogs that wasn't hell on people, so perhaps there is something complex in the make-up of a man who will fight his adoring pet to the death. Many bull terriers are highly intelligent dogs, and some learned very quickly to dispatch their opponent by a crippling stifle bite which renders the other dog's hind legs powerless to tug. The smashing of the stifle was a sure sign that the crippled dog would soon be dispatched. Many stud advertisements advertised dogs who were past masters at smashing their opponent's stifles – 'Noted stifle biters' was the usual appraisal of the quality of certain stud dogs.

Of course, the Staffordshire bull terrier was not the only dog used for dog fighting. A heavy, ugly type of dog called the Blue Paul or Blue Poll terrier was popular in the north country. Alken, in a

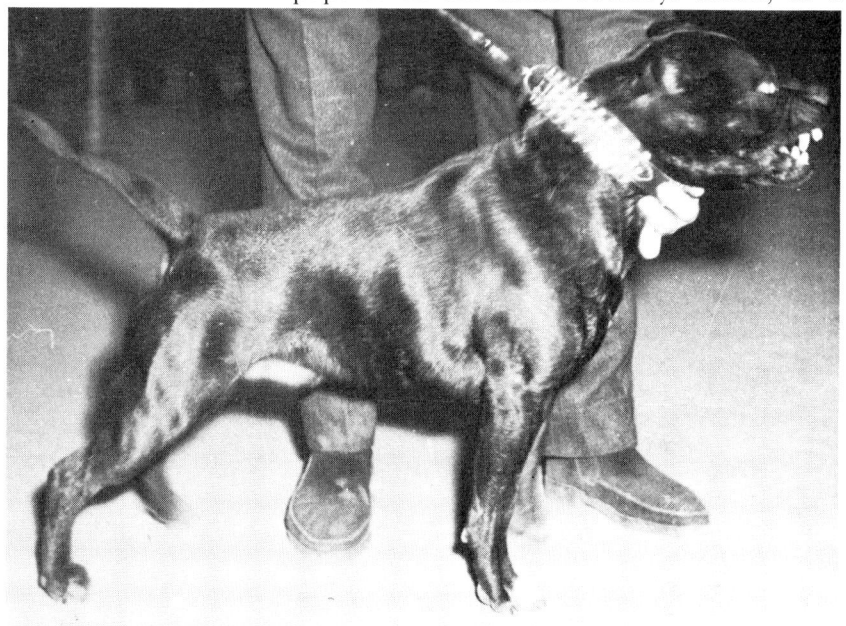

Staffordshire Bull terrier, Ch. Rapparee Renegade.

print of 1820, depicts two rather grotesque specimens at a badger-baiting session. Scotland produced numerous Blue Pauls, probably by crossing some extinct leggy Scottish terrier with the English bulldog. These dogs weighed up to 60 pounds and were ideal for badger drawing and similar inane and cruel activities, but they were so slow and ponderous that the dog fights involving such a breed were not well attended. Gradually the breed fell from favour and into extinction to be replaced by the faster more agile type of bull terrier which eventually evolved into the 'Staffordshire'.

Staffordshire bull terrier types of dog were taken across to the United States, and by dint of crossing with other lethal types of fighting dog, produced the fearsome American Pit bull terrier, mid-way in size between the Staffordshire and the Blue Poll. These dogs are still fought in some American states, and though the practice is illegal, it is fairly well publicized and convictions seem relatively uncommon. A far more useful development of the Pit bull terrier is the mongrelly type of dog known as the Louisiana Cur, a kind of hybrid between a bull terrier and local curs. The star of *Old Yeller* was probably such a dog. These are used as Caesar dogs for hunts on wild boar and feral razor-back swine in the Bayou districts of the Deep South. Such dogs change hands for enormous sums in spite of their mongrelly ancestry, for handsome is as handsome does, and they have the courage of the Pit bull terrier and the sense to stay out of trouble. They are, together with the Plott hound, the most highly rated boar-hunting dogs in America.

Bull terriers were also used in the rat pits so beloved of our Victorian ancestors. Here, a dozen, a hundred, even a thousand rats were tipped into a circular pit and a dog was required to kill the poor creatures in a timed contest. Contests with a hundred rats were quite rare, for good-quality rats could fetch up to 2*s* (10p), and cost the pub owners a pretty penny. Billy, the result of mating a bull terrier to a bulldog bitch, killed a thousand rats in fifty-four minutes, a rat every three seconds. Only bulldog-blooded dogs could stand up to the ferocious punishment such contests involved. Mayhew, in his fascinating eyewitness account in *London Labour and the London Poor*, described the rat pits in detail.

Most were situated behind seedy pubs, and many people, including respectable ladies, brought terriers to these places to test their rat-killing powers. Various breeds competed in contests where a dozen rats had to be killed, but the assortments of Skye terriers, fox terriers, and tiny black-and-tan terriers, one so small that it wore a lady's jewelled bracelet as a collar, were not often used for the bigger contests. For the larger-league stuff, the bull terrier was the dog for the job. Mayhew describes these dogs as 'better with a hundred than a dozen'.

The life of the ratting terriers was usually short. Most rats carry Wiel's disease and sundry other ghastly bacilli, and prior to the discovery of antibiotics, such diseases carried off many a valiant dog. Jimmy Shaw, a 'publican prize-fighter who ran a well-known ratting house', according to Kellow Chesney in his book *The Victorian Underworld*, bought only good-quality farm rats and avoided the evil-smelling sewer-bred specimens in his efforts to prevent his dogs becoming infected. Rat catchers of the time, including the inevitable Ike Matthews, suggested that dogs should have their mouths cleaned with peppermint water to avoid contracting canker, whatever that may have been (probably a staphylococcus infection of the gums). The fact remained that these precautions did little to reduce the death-rate among rat-pit dogs.

As a sporting dog, the Stafford has its uses, though not as an orthodox terrier. Most are far too large to go to ground, and they are invariably so mute that it is impossible to dig to them. Phil Drabble, in his excellent book *Of Pedigree Unknown* (1964), states that the bull terrier of his youth was still an outstandingly good rat killer and had retained the startling speed and crunching bite of the old fighting dogs. What has happened since is that the show craze has produced a heavier, cloddy type of dog that looks every inch a pugilist but is considerably slower than its ancestors. While the jaws remain so strong that any rat unfortunate enough to get bitten will be quickly dispatched, the modern Stafford is too slow for my liking, and I have never seen Staffords or any bull terrier that could match a good working terrier, such as Borders, Lakelands and Russells, in a contest of rat killing. It is not really possible to recommend the Stafford as a working terrier capable of giving his owner an efficient day's ratting, though they will certainly kill any rats they catch.

Many old-time badger diggers used Staffords as Caesar dogs at the end of a badger dig. A Caesar dog is not required to go to ground, but is expected to grip the badger at the end of the dig. Caesar dogs therefore not only have to be strong, but almost totally impervious to pain, for a badger will fight with great fury when cornered. Probably the Stafford has its uses in this direction, for they are not only strong but can take ferocious punishment without giving ground. Old-time dog fighters often lament the passing of the fiery Stafford temperament that spelled death to any other dog moving within lead range. Useful as this quality may have been there is no possible reason why a working terrier should necessarily be spiteful with other dogs. Terrier work often requires team spirit rather than blind aggression, and I know to my cost the problems that can be created by taking an aggressive dog on a dig. I do not lament the passing of this savagery, though the reduction of the agility in the modern Stafford is not to my liking.

The bull terrier has, of course, entered into, and indeed been the foundation of, many working-terrier breeds. Most white-bodied terriers, including Russells and Fox terriers, owe some of their courage and biting ability to the addition of bull-terrier blood in their not too remote ancestry. John Tucker Edwardes, the creator of the Sealyham, mated a distinct type of small white bull terrier, now called the Cheshire terrier, to his Sealyhams to increase their biting power and courage. Both Dandie and Bedlington terriers probably have a strain of bull terrier in their ancestry, brought in by the metal-workers who left Staffordshire for Rothbury and brought with them their fighting dogs. Many Jack Russells have a liberal admixture of bull terrier in them, as the size of the jaw on many modern specimens attests. Too much bull-terrier blood is a disadvantage, however, for the hybrid will almost certainly be too hard as well as mute. Sparrow, in his *The Terrier's Vocation*, suggests that strains of terrier might be improved by adding the occasional dash of bull-terrier blood, suggesting one cross in every ten generations. I feel that few strains have need of such drastic remedies to resuscitate them, and that there are enough heavy-jawed terriers around without having to resort to a bull-terrier cross.

Summary

As a working terrier, the Stafford has its uses, albeit limited. Bull-terrier blood may, however, come in useful to maintain the courage and biting power of a strain of working terrier.

THE ENGLISH BULL TERRIER

This attractive and courageous dog is largely the work of one James Hinks of Birmingham. Hinks was a noted bull-terrier breeder, and he set out to improve the looks of the ugly bull terriers of his day, the type that followed at the heels of Bill Sykes in Dickens's *Oliver Twist*. It is believed that he crossed his bull terriers with dalmatians, greyhounds and some white English terriers, and pro-

English Bull terrier, Ch. Foyri Electrify.

duced the attractive, hard-bitten dog we know today. Many criticized his breeding programme as they said that he ruined the fighting instinct of the dogs by this addition of foreign blood. Once, on his way to a show, however, a fighting-dog man chided him so that Hinks lost his temper and pitted his famous bitch, Puss, against the other man's dog. Puss slew the other's dog and went on to win at the show.

Interesting as its history is, the modern bull terrier is practically useless as a working terrier. They are far too big to get to ground, and a little too slow to be good rat hunters. The same applies to the English bull terrier, and, like all bull terriers, he is reluctant to give voice. They do, however, have some use as Caesar dogs at badger digs, for not only are they still very game, but they are also strong enough to hold a bolting boar badger. I once saw a tremendous bull terrier, fully 70 pounds in weight, used as a Caesar dog by a hunter in Gilfach Goch, Glamorgan. I have never before or since seen a dog soak up as much punishment without flinching as did this cod-headed white dog, who wagged his tail as he was badly chopped by the badger he was holding.

Summary

The English bull terrier has little application as a working terrier, though it makes an admirable guard dog as well as a useful Caesar dog to a badger-digging team.

THE NORWICH AND NORFOLK TERRIER

Once these two breeds were classed as one called the Norwich terrier, but recently the prick-eared type has been classified as the Norwich terrier and the drop-eared varieties as the Norfolk. Apart from the ear carriage, the two breeds are identical. Both are varminty little dogs, as yet unspoilt by the show craze, weighing 11 to 12 pounds and measuring a very useful 10 inches at the shoulder. The coat is rough, red, black-and-tan or grizzle in colour. The origin of this useful breed is a little vague. Many, myself included, believe they are simply native terriers that have been bred to type because of the lack of available and suitable terrier out-crosses. Others believe they are simply small Irish terriers. Certainly the breed has received infusions of working Bedlington and bull-terrier blood in this century, but then most working terriers today have the blood of the bull terrier in their veins. Until the show breeders took notice of the Norwich terrier, he was found almost exclusively in hunt kennels and the homes of hunters. Early dogs were famous for their ratting prowess, and many were bought by Cambridge students who were keen on testing their dogs' prowess in the rat pits.

Lucas speaks highly of the courage of this diminutive terrier. They were utterly fearless and highly aggressive. He tells of the time when someone brought two of them to his kennels, and they suddenly began to fight so violently that they had to be hung on either side of a stable door to break their grips. This tenacious quality, their handy size and ability below ground, probably prompted him to cross them with Sealyhams to produce the useful little Lucas terrier.

As rabbiting dogs, these game little terriers are excellent. I have seen several hunt like a hound and face even the most thorny cover. As ratting dogs they also take some beating, as they are fast and dextrous, and move with surprising speed and agility for such short-legged terriers. I once took a lady who owned a trio of them on a day's ratting trip. Not one of them had ever seen a rat before, but all entered well into the spirit of the game. They killed twenty-nine rats and, sadly, one good jill ferret, for I was unaware of the fact that not only had they never seen a rat, but neither had they ever encountered a ferret. I was, however, most impressed by the ratting ability of this small team of dogs who were at mid-morning entirely new to the game but by dusk were veterans.

It is only since 1932 that the Kennel Club has recognized this useful breed of terrier, and fortunately the standard is so worded as to discourage breeding exaggerations into the type. A sensible standard at the start of the recognition of a dog as a show breed can have a profound effect on the breed's future. The Norwich was fortunate in as much as the early breed club members seemed keen to establish a type of dog that could and would do the job of a true terrier. As a result, they seem to have been changed little by the fickle world of dog fashions.

During the mid 1960s there was an upsurge of interest in the Norwich/Norfolk terrier. So popular did the breed become that several hunt shows put on a class for the Norwich/Norfolk crosses. The Norwich itself did not become as popular, for terriers with prick ears are often

Norwich terrier, Mrs Monckton's Ch. Jericho Gold Sovereign.
(Photo Sally Anne Thompson)

viewed with suspicion by hunting men, the popular theory being that prick ears can become badly bitten when a dog is to ground at fox or badger. In 1968 I took on the training of two saplings sired by a dog from the Gotoground strain. They were aptly named and worked to fox extremely well, finding no difficulty in getting into the narrowest earths. Both were jealous workers, however, and quite difficult to accustom to other dogs being present at a dig. Lucas similarly mentions their reputation for getting into skirmishes with other dogs. This I would regard as quite a serious fault in an all-round working terrier.

The fact that these dogs are small encouraged many people to use them in the creation of other breeds. Lucas, of course, produced the Lucas terrier by crossing Norfolks with Sealyhams, and game little dogs his hybrids are. American breeders also took great interest in the Norfolk, for American grey foxes are smaller than their Old World red counterparts and dig correspondingly smaller earths. Thus a small terrier had to be evolved to go to ground and bolt them. A small Sealyham was imported into the United States in 1911 and was mated to a wirehaired fox terrier; the offspring was mated to a hybrid between a West Highland and a Norfolk terrier. The cross produced the desired dogs: small, wiry and gutsy enough to stand its ground against red or grey fox, or even against raccoon. At 12 pounds the Shelburne terrier was ideal, and it was for a time a very popular working terrier in America. Although mongrelly in appearance, they certainly did the job. The breed never caught on though, and now they are an uncommon sight, even in the United States. I have failed to locate any current breeders of these terriers, despite intensive inquiries among members of the American Working Terrier Association.

Summary

I must admit I like these dogs and feel they deserve to be more popular among hunting men. They are quite spiteful with other dogs, but very good to fox and to small fry; they are also a handy size for most sport.

THE AIREDALE TERRIER

This is the largest of the British terriers, measuring up to 23 inches at the shoulder – so large, in fact, that it can scarcely be regarded as a terrier.

THE AIREDALE TERRIER

The dog was originally bred for ratting along river banks, and also for a spot of dog fighting. The story goes that it was originally created by crossing a bitch bull terrier type with a stallion otterhound called Thunder in an effort to produce a hard-biting rat killer that was very much at home in water. I am deeply sceptical about the supposed otterhound ancestry of every northern terrier, but unclipped Airedales often do look like otterhounds. What is more likely is that the breed came about as a result of breeding from leggy, black-and-tan working terriers. Certainly Irish terrier blood was used to tidy up the appearance of the early Airedale, and the breed no longer resembles the somewhat ugly dogs bred at the beginning of the twentieth century.

As a vermin destroyer, the breed has its uses. They are particularly good ratting terriers, particularly when ratting in watery places. On the other hand, their size is against them when ratting around farms, for example, where a smaller dog is of far greater use. It is, of course, far too large to get to a fox, though I have seen one small bitch get into a badger set, though it was a very tight squeeze indeed.

Against large quarry, the Airedale is quite at home. Many have been used to hunt lion and leopard in Africa and have acquitted themselves well. Several have been used for baboon hunting, and no one can dispute

Airedale terrier, Mrs J. Averis' Ch. Turith Adonis.

the fighting ability of these apes. In North America the Oorang strain produced some excellent dogs that were effective against bear, bobcat, lynx and cougar. Their essential terrier characteristics, however, often prove the undoing of Airedales. Terriers tend to tackle their prey, unlike the Walker and Bluetick hounds normally used on American big game. Ben Lilly, the huntsman to Theodore ('Teddy') Roosevelt on his famous bear hunt (incidentally, the Teddy Bear was invented as a result of the publicity the press gave to this bear hunt), refused to include Airedales in his predator hunting pack. The death-rate in a pack of Airedales used on bears and suchlike must be extremely high. In Louisiana, a strain of Airedale has proved useful in hunting both feral pig and Prussian boar in the creeks and marshes. In 1975, the American periodical *Hunting Dogs* showed such a dog actually engaged in holding a furious and hard-fighting razor-back hog. Some American breeders have also bred useful dogs for flushing coyote by crossing Airedales with Irish terriers. The progeny are attractive and utterly fearless, and will often slay the coyote should it refuse to bolt. Coyote are quite savage fighters, midway between a wolf and fox in size.

Summary

As a working terrier, the Airedale is far too big to be of any use. They may be considered as Caesar dogs at the end of a badger dig, but cannot be recommended as a true working terrier.

THE YORKSHIRE TERRIER

Once this tiny mite was said to have been used as a dog of the rat pits, and many are the books that eulogize over the prowess of these diminutive dogs. Lucas and other writers state that there were before the First World War many Yorkshire terriers which would give a good show at a fox, even a badger. One of Cobby's favourite stories was of being out hunting with the South-West Wiltshire Hunt when the pack put a fox to ground near a vicarage tea party. For some reason or other, Cobby's terrier man had not turned up and one of the ladies offered (by way of a joke) her diminutive Yorkshire terrier. Cobby, who was the epitome of old-time gallantry, accepted the dog and thanked her graciously. He took the dog to the earth, where it promptly flew in and bolted the fox and the hunt continued.

Oh, reader, I bid you beware. This incident took place a long time ago and the Yorkshire terrier has changed considerably since then. The show craze has produced a very small dog that vies with the Chihuahua as the smallest dog in the world. Many books, however, continue to insist that these tiny creatures are still excellent rat dogs in spite of their tiny muzzles and almost atrophied masseter muscles. The writer would suggest that authors who write such drivel would do well to leave the rings of championship shows and for once in their lives attend a rat hunt. The modern show Yorkshire does *not* have the biting power to tackle a fully grown rat.

Summary

Disregard all ill-informed reports. The breed is now unsuitable for the tasks required of a working terrier.

THE WEST HIGHLAND WHITE TERRIER

This attractive terrier is simply a white Cairn, and its origin is quite interesting. Scottish and, indeed, all northern hunters view white-bodied dogs with suspicion. Many equate white colouration with constitutional weakness and cowardice (without foundation, since the white colouration of most southern terriers was derived from their English bulldog ancestors). Hence, when a white puppy appeared in a litter of Cairns, it was given no chance to prove its worth and was drowned at birth. A certain Major Malcolm of Poltalloch decided against tradition to perpetuate these white terriers and produced dogs that acquitted themselves well against badger, otter and wildcat. Malcolm, in his book *The Dog*, states that when at work the dog was frequently outweighed but never outmatched.

It is still a useful Cairn-sized terrier, measuring up to 11 inches at the shoulder, but is also a far more attractive dog than its ancestor. Whether or not the beautification process has ruined the working terrier is open to doubt; they certainly make excellent ratting terriers, for the standard stipulates that the dog should be free-moving and agile. Jack Ivester Lloyd has written in the *Midland Working Terrier Magazine*

West Highland White terriers, Alvermar Alida and Alvermar Anna-Katrina.

that he used one to hunt rat alongside the brooks near his home, and that the dog proved an excellent little worker. Few people work these dogs today, so even if the working instinct has not been bred out, it is given no chance to develop. This is a pity as the dog is ideally shaped for work below ground since it has a narrow front and powerful jaws. I find this dog slightly more nervous than his cousin, the Cairn, but as I have never owned or trained one I cannot comment on its working ability.

Summary

In spite of its useful shape, the dog is seldom seen at work.

THE SCOTTISH OR ABERDEEN TERRIER

This terrier is closely related to both the Cairn and the West Highland white terrier, but, despite its powerful jaws, it has been ruined by the show craze for the work for which it was originally intended. Few, if any, breeders work these dogs. Originally this was a game, agile little terrier with great spirit. Lucas remarks that it might do well to ground, but this was long ago. It has now degenerated into a cloddy, ponderous animal that would be too heavy to work below ground and far too slow for serious ratting. Few rats would survive a bite from these tremendous jaws, which equal those of the Dandie Dinmont in biting power. However, biting a rat is one thing, catching it is another.

Summary

Not in its modern breeding a suitable working terrier.

THE WELSH TERRIER

This attractive black-and-tan terrier, which resembles a miniature Airedale and is often confused with the Lakeland, is not so common as it was fifty years ago. They were originally used to flush foxes for Welsh hill packs and to keep down small vermin. Few are worked today, which is a pity, for many are very game and lack the quarrelsome nature of most terriers. In shape and size, they are practically identical to the fox terrier and have, alas, been caught up in the craze to produce long, elegant, but weak heads. They are said to be excellent ratting terriers, and on account of their reluctance to pick a fight several could be worked together as a team.

Summary

A reasonably useful terrier, but not as useful as the Lakeland, which it certainly resembles.

Early Welsh terriers before 'improvement' ruined the breed.

Welsh terrier, Kingpin.

THE SKYE TERRIER

Though once a useful working dog, it has now been bred into a ridiculously low, heavy and over-coated animal, which makes it unsuitable as a working terrier.

THE MANCHESTER TERRIER

This is probably a very old breed, far older than most authorities are prepared to state. A portrait of such a dog appears in Alys Serrell's book *With Hound and Terrier in the Field* (1904). Once these dogs were famed as ratting terriers, but were reputedly short on courage, even a hundred years ago. Rawden Lee says that while his would nail rats with great speed, they would not tackle a stoat at any cost. It is, however, a very fast, agile breed of terrier, and they may yet make excellent ratters. Few, if any, breeders actually work this breed of terrier to large quarry today.

Manchester terrier, Ch. Black Sensation of Laureats. (Photo Dog World)

SUMMARY: THE CHOICE OF A WORKING TERRIER

The reader will have observed from the first two sections of this book that, though many terrier breeds exist, only a few breeds are worked regularly. Hunt shows usually only cater for Borders, Lakelands and Russells, and any hunter who is considering taking up working terriers would do well to stick to these breeds. If the hunter is looking for something a little different, then perhaps a good-natured Cairn, or a Norfolk, or a Norwich may suffice. He would do well, however, to stay clear of the other breeds of terrier if he decides to take up serious terrier work.

III

The Quarry

ENTERING TO QUARRY

Most terriers will work if given a chance. Some breeds will work more readily and enter more easily than others because of their size, shape and temperament, but, given a fair chance, properly encouraged and not overmatched, every terrier will give a reasonable account of itself at work. The would-be terrier man would do well to disregard the people who blandly state 'such and such a breed is no use', and to remember the dictum that there are no bad dogs, merely bad owners. It is usually fair to say that a man who does badly with Russells will do quite as badly with Lakelands and vice versa. A minor exception to the rule is the Border terrier, which requires a somewhat more careful approach to entering to quarry. Some people fail with this useful breed and succeed with other terriers. I repeat, any terrier properly entered will make a useful hunting dog to rat, fox and badger.

How then should the terrier be entered to quarry? Perhaps the best piece of advice is to be found in the novel *Guy Mannering* by Sir Walter Scott. In this book, which is concerned with life in the north country, there is a noted sporting squire called Dandie Dinmont (a character actually modelled on a noted hunter called James Davidson who lived in Hindlee). In a conversation with a terrier owner called Captain Brown, the squire is asked how he managed to enter his dogs so efficiently; his reply should stand any terrier man in good stead. First, said the squire, I start them on rats, then to stoat, after which I try them to fox and ultimately to badger, after which they fear 'nothing wi' hair on it'. What superb and sensible advice, for Scott besides being an author was also a keen dog fancier. Gradual entering to bigger and more aggressive quarry is far more likely to succeed than taking a terrier from its kennel and entering it straight away to fox or badger.

Basic training should, of course, precede entering. As soon as a puppy is obtained at, say, eight weeks old, the process known as socializing should begin. Allow children to play with him, let him see the traffic, horses, experience various noises and, above all, let him experience stimulating situations. This will allow him to develop his intelligence to the full and make him far more tractable and amenable to discipline. There is an old wives' tale that allowing children to play with a puppy ruins the dog for training. Nothing could be further from the truth. The more contact the puppy has with people, the easier it will be to train. Some years ago a psychologist called Hebb took a batch of four-week-old beagle puppies and divided them into two groups. One group he allowed to play with children and grow up in the household, the other group was fed mechanically and not allowed to see people. At the end of a six-month period, both groups were taken up for training. The socialized group proved playful but tractable, the unsocialized group proved dull, apparently stupid and totally intractable. Puppies reared in large kennels are often unsocialized unless the kennel owner allows his staff to play with the animals as well as merely clean them out and feed them. This is why animals brought up in the house are more trainable than puppies reared in kennels.

Next, lead training is essential for a puppy about to be entered to fox; it needs to be taken to the earths on a lead – not allowed to run free and to vanish into every earth it considers worthwhile. Lead training is a bit of a drag (no pun intended), and will only take a few hours' work, but it is the most essential part of training.

Early breaking to stock is important in all breeds, but it is absolutely essential in an aggressive breed like a working terrier. Nothing bespeaks an amateur more than a dog who, as soon as it is unleashed, makes a bid at sheep, cows, chickens and ferrets. Allow a puppy to be frightened by livestock when it is quite young. Chickens tower over him, causing him to put his tail down and look pathetic, or maybe allow a vicious cockerel to peck him or strike him with its wings. This soon convinces a young puppy that fowl are strictly taboo. Take the youngster among young calves, who will come close to investigate any small animal. Allow him to see an old ewe with her lambs, or better still a veteran ram who knows all about dogs. Do this when the terrier is a young puppy, for an older dog is far more difficult to break to livestock and will retaliate when upset or frightened, a lesson to be learned becoming an insult to avenge.

A young terrier puppy should also be broken to ferret, for ferrets prove useful allies when a young dog is being entered to rat. Break a puppy to ferret, don't wait until the dog becomes an adult. A ferret will probably survive a bite from a puppy, but may well die from a nip put in by an adult dog. Ferrets are strange creatures. They will often recover from savage maulings from rats, but invariably die from a bite from a terrier. Encourage the terrier to develop great familiarity with the ferret. Ferrets are intelligent beasts and often become closely attached to certain terriers. Many will play and cavort with terriers – this should not be stopped. Many terrier men will allow a terrier and ferret to drink milk from the same dish. Encourage such familiarity. A dog that is closely familiar with a ferret, having played with it and allowed it to drink from the same dish, is unlikely to make a mistake as to whether it is ferret or rat bolting from a hole.

Once you have had your puppy inoculated (this is absolutely essential, see pages 193-5) and he is broken to sheep, cattle, hens and other livestock and is feeding from the same dish as the ferret, the time has come to enter him to the first quarry on Dandie Dinmont's list – namely, the rat.

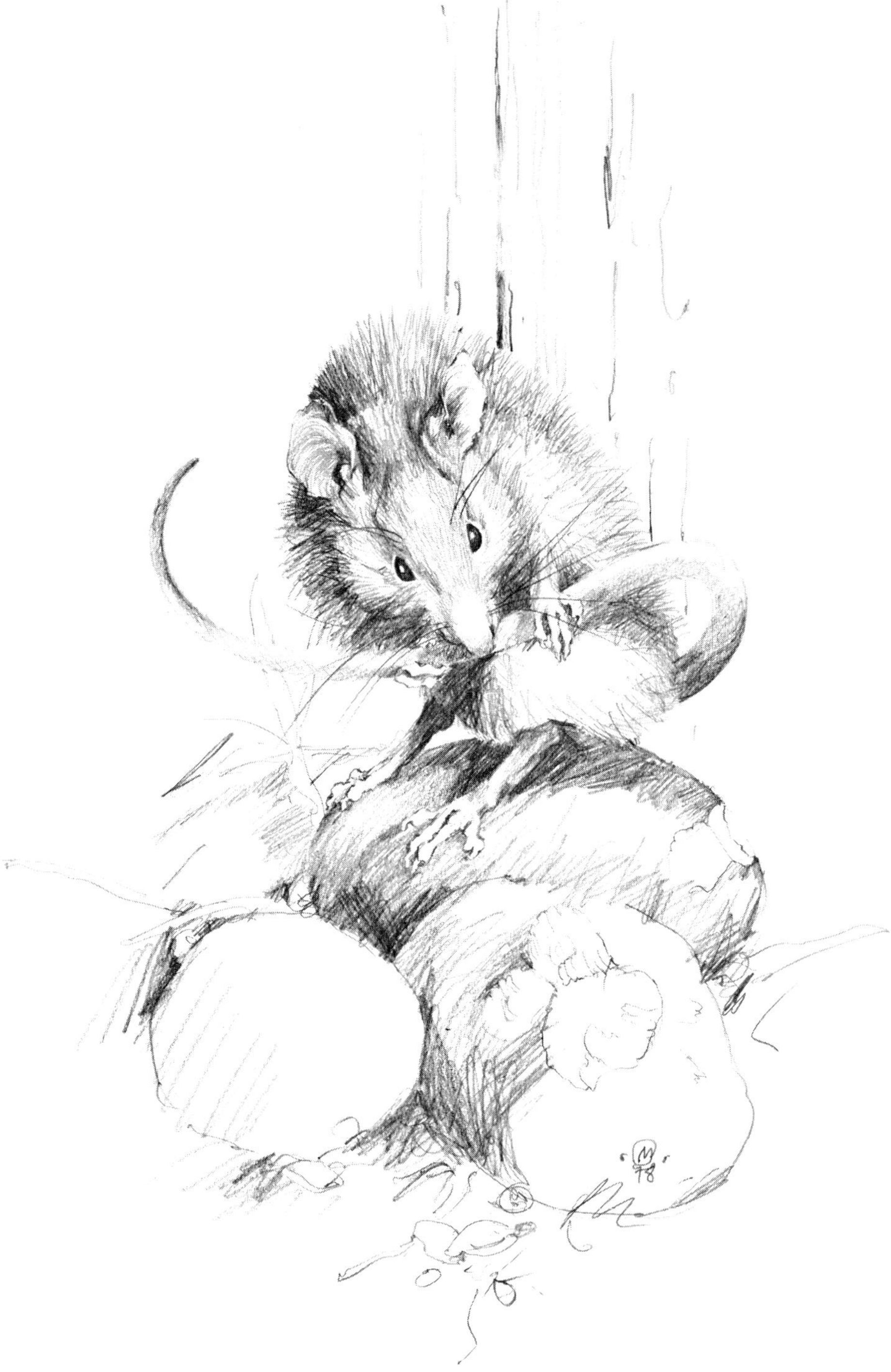

THE RAT

Whyte Melville once said that the best of his pleasure he had with horse and hound. I am a little more plebeian in my attitude and admit that the best sport I ever had has been hunting rats. Jack Ivester Lloyd says that rats are cowardly creatures – how wrong he is. True, most will avoid a contest with a dog fourteen times their weight – quite a sensible act, really – but, when forced to fight, they do so with such dreadful ferocity that, pound for pound, or should I say ounce for ounce, no animal is their equal. A glance at the habits and history of this fascinating quarry is therefore of interest.

Neither the black nor the brown rat is native to this country. Legend has it that the black rat arrived on the ships of the returning Crusaders, but it is probably a native of the Far rather than the Middle East. Here the black rat is still found in abundance, climbing like a squirrel and building its nests of straw, paper and feather in high trees and bushes. The black rat is quite a small rodent, both bucks and does weighing only around 8 ounces. They were probably not particularly at home aboard the ships of the Crusaders, but once on *terra firma* they found the thatched cottages of Britain very much to their liking. I have a feeling that, in spite of much literature to the contrary, the black rat lived in Britain well before the tenth century. Giraldus Cambrensis writes that in Ireland there lived large *mures* (mice). These large mice were almost certainly black rats.

By 1300, however, the black rat was well and truly established in Britain, and in 1383 the rat-borne Black Death hit the country. The plague, which had been in Europe since the time of Justinian, ravaged the country. Fleas which lived on infected rats left their hosts for humans and the disease spread like wildfire. Perhaps if man had understood the plague and its causes he would have made *Rattus rattus* extinct long ago. He did not do so, however, attributing the plague to the miasmas that exuded from the filth-strewn streets of fourteenth-century England. It was not until the second outbreak of plague in the seventeenth century that man began to realize that the black rat might be the vector of the Black Death. Little effort was made to rid the country of the rat, however, but the change in man's hygiene sounded the death knell for *Rattus rattus*. Rubbish was now carted to places outside villages, where hitherto it was merely tipped into the street. Poor old *Rattus rattus*, being from more tropical climes, preferred to dine near to home rather than face the cold, wet journey to and from the midden pile. He could do little else but slowly become extinct. The arrival of his larger, more aggressive cousin, the brown rat, was really the last straw.

Around 1720–60, the brown rat arrived in Britain. European naturalists were expecting him, for he had been on the move out of Asia for fifty or so years. What caused him to move from the steppe lands of Asia is a bit of a mystery. Perhaps overcrowding occurred, perhaps a mutated form, more fierce, more hardy and more carnivorous than the genotype appeared, and thus better endowed began his trip westward. Some believe that he was already in Europe anyway, for Roman temples dedicated to a variety of plague goddesses often displayed small statuettes of brown and black rats. At all events he arrived in Britain – 12 ounces of fighting fury, ready to take on and oust his small black cousin.

He was bound to survive and thrive. He was tougher than the black rat, for he was originally a steppe dweller, able to withstand below-zero temperatures. While he could climb as well as *Rattus rattus* he was at home most places. People referred to him as the ship rat, the Hanoverian rat and the Norwegian rat (he was supposed to have come to Britain on Norwegian ships), and this last name stuck, for his specific and generic name is still *Rattus norwegicus*, the Norwegian rat. Call him what you will, he has an ability to survive which surpasses all other creatures, and once in Britain he was here to stay. I have a sneaking suspicion that should the world be reduced to rubble by atomic warfare, he will be the one creature to crawl squeaking from the radioactive ruins.

He is not particularly choosy about his diet; in fact it is hard to find any food that he will refuse to eat. He can live for some time on vitamin-free fats, surviving by assimilating the vitamins in his body and eating his own excreta. Grain, sewage and even meat in such a state of putrefaction as to make a vulture shudder does not come amiss to *Rattus norwegicus*, and there are few places where he cannot scrape a living. When washed up in the uninhabited islands, he will scrape a living from the coarse beach grasses, and has been known to survive for several weeks existing on candle wax. When food is scarce, he is reluctant to breed profusely, but when food is plentiful – well, his breeding habits put a rabbit to shame.

Rats are born naked and quite helpless. At a week or so a pale grey fur covers the body and the rat remains this colour until it is about five weeks old. At five to eight weeks it becomes sexually mature, upon which the does are mated and the young immature bucks driven from the warren by old veteran bucks. So catastrophic is this action that many young bucks are upset to the point where they are unable to breed and go through life totally celibate. The does, however, are mated by the adult buck rat, and twenty-one days later produce litters of up to sixteen young, though four to six is normal for first kindling does. In Bedfordshire, there is a notion that rats always produce an odd never an even number of young. The reader would do well to forget this notion. During the five weeks before writing this section of the book I dissected 210 dead wild does to test the theory's validity. It hasn't any. One hundred and twenty-four of the does carried even numbers of foetuses, the rest odd numbers. Odd numbers or even, it makes not the slightest difference to the doe, who, immediately after parturition, cleans herself up and goes forth in search of a buck, is served again and the cycle repeated. Dr Jan Hanzak states that no more than four litters of rats are born in a year. I believe this is to be untrue. In warm places, such as warehouses and beneath battery houses, I have taken young grey rats even in mid-winter. The female is bred out and senile at about fifteen months old, but she has left a prodigious number of offspring by the time she has become geriatric. If one pair of rats and all their descendants were allowed to breed without hindrance, their progeny would, in the course of ten years, produce a weight of rats equal to the weight of the earth.

Fortunately, *Rattus norwegicus* has many enemies, and with a little luck you will be among them. Stoats and weasels gobble up young rats, though they give the old patriarchs and adult does a clear berth. Foxes have utilized rats as food since myxomatosis saw off so much of the rabbit population. Man, with staggering quantities of lethal chemicals, cuts an awesome swathe through the rat population. Yet, in spite of all these hazards, the brown rat is actually on the increase, and one thing is certain: he will still be supplying the hunter with sport long after this book becomes an antique curio.

Well, we've described him. Now to catch and kill him. The first piece of advice is: don't enter a dog to rat before it has its permanent teeth. Many puppies will kill rats with their milk teeth, but many are ruined by early entering. Furthermore, never underestimate the fury, speed and ferocity of an adult rat. Many puppies with only milk teeth are ridiculously overmatched by an adult rat and will fight shy of an encounter with such a creature. Rats bite with great force. When hand catching, I usually trap them under my shoes, and I have had several rips in the soles as a result of their bites. Puppies are neither mentally mature enough not nor physically equipped enough to take on adult rats. How, therefore, do we start our terrier on the road to work? There are many methods of starting a terrier to kill rats, most of them belonging in a medieval grimoire rather than in a book on working terriers. The most common method, recommended by nearly every book on the working terrier, is to trap a rat, put it in a barrel and hurl a young terrier in after it, when, with luck, the following will happen: (a) the rat will bite the terrier; (b) the terrier will be angry; (c) the terrier will bite the rat (d) the rat will die; (e) a ratting terrier emerges ready-made from the barrel. Excellent, apart from one small problem – it usually doesn't work. But this is perhaps a minor consideration! Let us examine why the method usually fails, and fails dismally.

Throughout our training we have broken our terrier to various types of stock. He has lunged at livestock, been smacked, experienced pain and associated pain with that which is *verboten*. He has been smacked for chasing sheep – pain/forbidden/sheep left alone. He is now thrust into a barrel with a live, biting, 12-ounce whirlwind who is sure to hurt him. May not the pain/forbidden reaction now occur yet again, and, if so, will he not emerge from the barrel convinced that the rat is yet another creature he is not to kill? It is true that some terriers learn to become good ratters by this method, but the wastage of good dogs ruined by the method must be enormous. It may well work on breeds like Lakelands, which are quick to anger and eager to retaliate, but it spells disaster to the quiet and gentle Border terrier. Moreover, a great number of excellent rat dogs are extremely nesh and reserved. Such ham-handedness as putting them in a barrel with a live rat is sure to ruin them. I once owned a Russell-type terrier that was an excellent ratter. He accounted for 1,126 in one day – a hard act to follow and a harder one to beat. Yet if I so much as shouted at him he would wet himself and become useless for the rest of the day. Such a dog would have been permanently ruined by being put in a barrel with a live rat.

So far very negative. We have discussed how not to train a dog to rat. How, then, *do* we train the dog?

Again, there are many methods. The best is the one vividly described by Drabble in his *Of Pedigree Unknown* and referred to as the 'hot blood method'. The puppy is taken out with adult terriers on a ratting expedition. It is held on a leash while the adults slay rats, and the puppy usually goes berserk with excitement. When it is near mad with excitement, it is slipped at a young rat and, if all goes well, catches it. The rat nips the puppy, who is now so crazy with excitement that it kills the rat. Even this method is not foolproof, however. An older dog kills a rat by shaking it. It is very difficult for a dog to kill a rat by simply biting. A puppy running in on an adult terrier in the process of killing a rat usually grabs the rat's hindquarters and prevents his elder from killing it with a shake. Thus a tug of war involving a live creature occurs, which is very nasty, but more nasty still is the fact that the expiring rat has a chance to do great damage to the adult and puppy before it finally dies.

At the time of writing this section, I was hunting a large poultry farm with a team of terriers. They converged on an unfortunate rat and grabbed it, but the rat could not be killed with a single bite and wreaked havoc on my terriers before it expired. I have seen some terrible wounds inflicted on terriers involved in this sort of scrimmage. It is a very real problem when starting a terrier by working him alongside an older dog. Another problem that can arise through such a method is the failure syndrome. A puppy who works with an adult and sees the adult constantly beating him to the punch, or should I say bite, soon gives up and refuses to try. The moral to be drawn is that as soon as the terrier has learned to kill rats he should be taken out on ratting trips by himself.

So, it's easy if you have a trained terrier ready to hand, but what if you do not have access to a trained dog? Well, all is not lost, but you will need to adopt a process known in rat-hunting circles as 'self-entering'. Terriers which have the run of farms often become demon ratters without the owner having to train them to rat. In their travels they encounter rats, chase them, miss them and finally connect and kill one, and hey presto, a ratting terrier is born! The would-be rat hunter will do well to simulate these conditions. He should take his terrier to a spot where rats abound, preferably just before darkness. His terrier will chase many before it makes a kill, but sooner or later it will make one. Self-entering is an excellent introduction since the dog enters when it is good and ready. It is not spurred on by the efforts of its elders to tasks well beyond its capabilities. It has also learned not to depend on other dogs. It is, however, a very slow method of entering a terrier, but *festina lente* – make haste slowly – should be the motto of the rat hunter.

During the past fifty years, with public health regulations encouraging the cleaning up of the countryside, places to hunt rat have become scarce. Just after the Second World War, the South Welsh mining villages developed what could only be called 'pig fever', for a mass of ill-constructed, dry-wall piggeries littered the hillsides. I did much of my early ratting in these piggeries. These ramshackle buildings, totally unacceptable to the public but a veritable haven for rats, have disappeared and farms in general have become far more tidy. Knackers yards and abbatoirs (which in the time of Henry Mayhew were filthy hell-holes harbouring myriads of huge rats) are now a thing of the past. Nevertheless it is possible to find good rat-hunting locations if you try hard enough. Poultry farms, no matter how clean they are kept, are usually havens for all types of rodents, and I have taken six tons of rats in a year hunting just one of these farms. Most poultry farmers will view your dogs with suspicion when you turn up to ask for permission to rat. They will certainly be alarmed if you attempt to use ferrets, for ferrets are notorious poultry killers. Once you have broken the ice and convinced the owners that you, your terriers and ferrets are not psychopaths out to destroy his livelihood, you will certainly be more readily accepted. Avoid causing any offence when hunting such places, and they will be yours for life. Damage property or slay fowl, and the ratting rights on such a place are soon withdrawn.

Another point about hunting farms. You are ratting for sport. Do not, for heaven's sake, expect to be paid for killing rats. People often ask me how much I get paid for killing the thousands of rats my terriers take. The question is ridiculous. We gladly seek out any new place for rats and hunt them free of charge. If a farmer wished to pay to rid his place of rats, he would certainly do no more than buy a few drums of Warfarin, call in the public health department, who would do the job free of charge, or quite simply pump Cymag down the holes, rather than pay a hunter so much a tail for the rats he kills. Do not expect money for indulging in your sport. Some weeks ago I was approached by the secretary of an up-and-coming working terrier club who was prepared to offer £150 per annum for the sole ratting rights on one particular farm I hunt. I immediately declined to help him, for such places are hard to come by.

If the reader ever gets a chance to hunt a maggot factory, for heaven's sake jump at it. Maggot factories are anachronisms, survivors of a grim and grisly past, living just outside present publichealth regulations. Long may they do so, for they are a positive paradise for rats and, though I would hate to live near one, I have spent some exciting times hunting them. It is nearly impossible to keep such a place rat-free, and literally thousands of rats can be caught in maggot factories. The hunter must, of course, be prepared to put up with the most appalling smell, and accept the fact that the noxious stench will remain on his clothes for weeks. But, if he can accept this, he will certainly find such places well worth hunting.

There are snags. Few maggot-factory owners like people wandering around their property, even if they are there to kill rats. Again, it is far easier for the owner to put down a few hundredweight of Warfarin than to chance having rat hunters talking about the horrors of the place to the outside world. Maggot-factory owners are nearly always fighting running battles with the public health and local pressure groups, who are usually very keen to see their villages blow-fly free. If you can get the ratting rights on such a place, then you will find them more than just worthwhile. I once took a record half a ton of rats in such a place using a team of four men and six terriers. Reader, be warned, however! Such rat-infested Shangri-las are hard to procure, but it is well worth paying £200 to £300 a year to obtain hunting rights in such places.

Though it is not particularly productive, the simplest method of catching rats with a terrier is what is known in rat-hunting circles as 'stalking'. This involves going to a place where rats are feeding out, and quietly slipping the terriers at the unsuspecting rats. The terriers may nail one or two unfortunates, but most will scurry back to their holes and vanish into them. Rats can move startlingly fast over short distances, and, as they know the areas in which they are feeding far better than do you or your dogs, the odds are very much in their favour. Consider yourself lucky indeed if you get half a dozen rats during an evening's stalking.

One place where this sort of hunting is sure to pay off, on the other hand, is in battery hen sheds. These are usually lit with electric lights regulated by time switches, and the lights go off at irregular intervals during the night, for such conditions simulate daylight and encourage the battery hens to feed more regularly and hence produce more eggs. Huge hauls of rats can be taken by quietly entering a battery house and blocking all rat bolt-holes before going back to switch on the lights and slip the terriers. It is a fairly hair-raising activity entering a darkened battery house to block rat holes. Rats frequently scurry over one's hands in the darkness, but rarely, if ever, bite. They are usually too keen on escaping the catastrophe about to overtake them to spend time biting at the hands trying to block their exits. So, back to the doors, on with the lights, and 'let slip the dogs of war'. If you have been diligent in your blocking exercises, the sport will be little short of tremendous, and very exciting. If you have left holes still open, then the sport will be disappointing as the rats escape like greased lightning. Here is a description of a memorable hunt which was held on Friday 6 May 1977, taken almost intact from my diary.

Time: 8.30, and the team assemble at my cottage. Present: myself, Colin Latham, Paul Masters, Joan and Sally Hancocks. Dogs: Vampire, Beltane, Omega (property of Colin Latham and aged seven months), Battle and Blaze (six-month-old daughters of Vampire). We set off and arrived at our venue, a poultry farm six miles distant, as dusk was beginning to fall. Weather: warm, but slightly damp – ideal weather for catching rats out feeding. Shed 1 battery house in total darkness.

Colin and Paul enter the sheds to block all known exits. After they finish we wait ten seconds, put on the lights and Sally slips the terriers free. Bedlam breaks loose. Rats cascade from the trays, darting for the escape holes, most of which are blocked. Several scamper through two holes overlooked by Colin, but Omega, his seven-month-old puppy, kills two before they can escape. Elsewhere, Vampire is creating havoc with the hordes racing back from the holes Paul has blocked. Vampire grabs a rat but, before he can kill it, Beltane rushes in and seizes the head – a deadly situation as Vampire cannot shake the rat to kill it. Beltane receives a four-inch rip inside her mouth. Sally and Joan are killing several with their sticks and driving more back under the trays. Battle and Blaze are on their first ratting venture and are standing petrified in the corner, obviously bewildered by the whole proceedings. Rats race past them, but Battle makes only a half-hearted lunge at them. Too early to write either of them off. Their great-grandfather was equally slow at starting, and he made an excellent ratting terrier. All rats have now escaped or been killed, so Paul totals the number of dead and bags them. Total – 32.

On to Shed 2, which is still lit by electric light – a difficult spot to try. Doors open, dogs down. Three small greys escape through unblocked crack in floor, but both Battle and Blaze are quite keen on trying to catch them. It is nearly impossible to 'rat' in a well-lit battery shed for not only will few rats feed in such conditions, but it is nearly impossible to block exits in brightly lit sheds. Total – nil.

Shed 3 – complete darkness, poultry near lay. Paul and Colin down sheds to block exit. Obvious rats feeding as scurrying noise in trays indicates. Allow a full minute for blocking. On with the lights – a myriad is feeding, and they race off the trays to the safety of their holes. Paul and Colin have worked well and all holes are blocked. Vampire and Omega nail three before they can scarcely leave the trays. Battle and Blaze join in and rag an old buck Vampire has killed. Must encourage this – creates enthusiasm. Another scampers down from the trays and Sally and Joan nail it with a stick. Beltane is bleeding very badly from the mouth wound, but is still killing rats very quickly. Must put her back in van or else she is going to be quite a mess. Battle and Blaze have chased a large doe into a corner, and it is screaming and feinting at them. Omega runs in and shakes the rat and Battle and Blaze join in the attack. Battle leaps back with a bite on the nose and then furiously attacks the rat. Colin and Paul are now poking the manure beneath the trays. Another crop of rats dives from the trays and the dogs are on them fast and furious. Both Battle and Blaze are now furiously attacking a large buck rat that is standing on hind legs and menacing them with his teeth. (This was the biggest rat of the night, a monster weighing over a pound in weight.) Battle snatches at the rat and receives a nasty bite under her eye but, infuriated by the wound, starts shaking the monster – Blaze joins in the kill. Cry halt, gather up the dogs, total up the rats, check for wounds. Total – 64.

Shed 4 – lights on. No rats feeding.

Shed 5 – an empty battery house, recently vacated. Sport incredible after rats were poked out of the empty cages. Both Battle and Blaze are entered well and are hunting like veterans. Total – 47. Really exciting hunting, but exit holes were well blocked so a little like shooting ducks in a barrel.

Next shed – well lit. Two rats bolt into walls. Total – nil.

Shed 7 – excellent sport, very fast, very furious. Dogs bitten quite badly through face. Vampire receives a bite near his eye-socket, which swells so rapidly that the eye becomes closed. Blocking done badly, however; in spite of a valiant effort by Sally to prevent rats escaping, we lose nearly a hundred. Total – 16.

We load up the dogs and head for home, taking our rats with us to use as ferret food. We examine the dogs. Vampire, with one eye closed, has several other bites on his face, also one bite beneath the jaw so deep it has pierced the jaw-bone. Beltane's mouth has a four-inch rip and the cheek muscles are now badly swollen. Omega is practically unbitten. (A very deep, narrow bite overlooked and festers very badly in a few days. Rat bites are very nasty, as the incisor teeth of a rat spread out as the rat inflicts a bite.) Battle and Blaze have minor damage and will not need antibiotic treatment. We dose Vampire and Beltane with two tablets of oxytetracycline before putting them away in their kennels. (Beltane was decidedly ill after the hunt.) Rat bites should always be treated immediately after a hunt.

A very successful hunt. Total killed – 159. Time taken – 28 minutes.

Of course, to get large hauls of rats it is first necessary to persuade them to leave the security of their holes. This can be done by gassing them out with carbon monoxide and petrol fumes, created by running a car with the choke out and piping the fumes from the exhaust into the rat warrens. It can also be done by flooding them out (only really successful in places with impervious floors, such as concrete-floored sheds), or, best of all, by using ferrets. No working terrier man should be without these valiant and useful creatures, and every terrier should be completely broken to ferret while still a puppy.

Ferrets are probably domesticated European polecats. I say probably, for the history of the ferret is dark and shadowy to say the least. Little has been written on these fascinating creatures until recently, and now a spate of literature, including my own *Modern Ferreting*, has appeared. For rat hunting, the jill or female ferret should be used, the hob or male ferret usually being too large to get down the average rat hole. The rat hunter should keep several jill ferrets, for he will surely need them. Rats are not the natural prey of polecats, and, after a while, a jill ferret will receive a very bad thrashing from a rat and realize that rat hunting is not all beer and skittles. Henceforth she will refuse to enter a rat hole, and will even bite the hands of those who are trying to get her to tackle this formidable rodent. Do not force her – let her go to a rabbit hunter (she will still be useful for bolting rabbits) or put her aside to breed. Some jills take terrible poundings and still come back for more, others will quit as soon as they realize the rat's fighting potential. Rat bites invariably fester and are so deep that they frequently rip the eyes out of a ferret. I have yet to see a rat kill a ferret, but I have had literally dozens die as a result of the sepsis introduced by rat bites. Clean rat bites with disinfectant and antibiotic ointments and your casualties will often recover.

This is as good a time as any to deal with the scourge of rat hunting: the dreaded 'rat catcher's yellows', or Wiel's disease. This deadly bug is carried by about half the rats in Britain, and the rat does not need to bite someone to infect him. A person has only to put his hands where a rat has urinated to become infected. The symptoms of the disease are jaundice, rapid loss of weight, and death – all within a short time after infection. Treatment is long, very protracted and frequently unsuccessful. The reader would do well to realize that if he hunts rats he stands an excellent chance of developing the disease, and that the disease is more often than not fatal. During the time of the famous rat pits, as Mayhew mentions, several families who lived in the notorious London rookeries made substantial livings by providing live rats for the pits. Chatton, a philanthropic doctor who practised among the tenants of the rookeries, remarks in a letter to his sister on the high death-rate among these families – and the reader must certainly realize why. Every animal, except the rat, can become infected with the disease, and the disease is just as deadly in any species. Dogs, particularly ratting dogs, are often infected, and, if not inoculated, die from Wiel's disease, or leptospirosis as it is often called. Inoculation is an absolute necessity, for not only can an uninoculated dog become infected, he can also transmit the infection to other dogs as well as to human beings. Inoculation is a 'must' for anyone who intends to hunt regularly. I am literally amazed that many working-terrier men pay a huge price for a working dog and then refuse to inoculate it. This is simply to throw money down the drain. The life of the rat-pit dogs, who were not, of course, inoculated, was extremely short, for the peppermint mouthwash advised by experts to be a prophylactic did little to counteract the deadly virus. Inoculate any dog – but most of all a rat-hunting terrier.

The time has now come to weld the trio of man, dog and ferret into an unbeatable rat-hunting team. The ferret is so tame as to allow the owner all manner of liberties. The dog is so completely broken to ferret that it will eat and drink from the same dish, and is beginning to kill rats with a degree of enthusiasm. We are ready for our first hunt. We find a place where rats abound by the signs – the holes are well used, lumps of food are found jammed in the holes as the rats have tried to carry it to their nest. Excellent – we know there are rats about. We approach the rat warren quietly; silence is an important part of ferreting. The holes are fairly obvious, but we clear away the grass (gently and silently) and find many half-hidden bolt-holes. We now take a small handful of dried grass and insert it in the bolt-holes (again quietly), placing it gently so as not to prevent the rat getting out of the holes. So far, so good. We now position our terrier and, with a silent gesture, bid him be still. The ferret is taken from the box and inserted into the hole. The atmosphere is electric. The jill sniffs the edges of the earth and her tail fluffs like a bottle brush – a good sign by any standards. She lashes her tail from side to side and enters the hole to meet her adversary. Beckon the dog to watch the hole. There is a scuffle below ground, and a squeaking. Our jill has nailed a baby grey – watch out, the doe is bolting. She is nabbed and shaken by the dog – and followed by three young greys, all of which escape. A successful start.

The ferret emerges, fresh from battle. She is now behaving in a decidedly unusual manner. A gentle lamb of a ferret went in – a tiger has emerged. Don't pick her up – it's dollars to doughnuts the most tranquil jill ferret will bite after such a tussle with a rat. We have arrived at a difficult situation. The terrier is flushed with excitement and is awaiting another rat. The ferret has emerged furious and triumphant after her kill. Beware squalls. The terrier may lunge at the ferret, the ferret retaliate with a bite, and the result – a very dead ferret and a ruined terrier. Many ferrets are killed by excited terriers. Hold back the dog and allow things to calm down. You may miss a rat or so, but maintaining the relationship between dog and ferret is more important.

On, then, to the next warren, but here we encounter our next problem. Doe rats with young capable of running about will usually bolt with the young – a sort of devil (or ferret) take the hindmost. A doe with newly born, helpless babies is another matter. She will stay with them to the bitter end, and will often fight off the jill as she creeps up the earth. I have been attacked by rats only three times: one was a demented buck and the other two were does with newly born young. Our ferret noses the mouth of the rat warren and sniffs cautiously, as if aware of the danger within. She lashes her tail and creeps slowly down the warren. All hell breaks loose and the terrier's ears cock to listen to the carnage. The jill creeps out backwards; don't – I repeat, don't – put her back again. You will certainly lose the use of the jill if you do, for she is no match for a doe with a litter of blind, naked youngsters who is prepared to defend her family with her life. Leave her, or dig her out if you must, but do not try to put the jill ferret into this particular rat warren again.

Rat hunting is super sport. I thoroughly enjoy it. The Duke of Beaufort once said: 'There are only two sports – fox hunting and ratting, and ratting is a damned good second.' I, for one, would place rat hunting well before fox hunting, for rats are so numerous that a 'dead' day's sport is most unlikely. It is estimated that above 50 million rats live in Britain alone. Some purists object to rat hunting as not being a terrier's true work, terriers being required to go to ground by definition. Others dismiss the rat as small fry, unworthy of attention. Oh, most foolish of men! You really don't know the rat. He is a valiant, brave and fearsome fighter, albeit only weighing 12 ounces. And to hunt rat in number, a dog has to have guts a-plenty to endure the formidable bites of this game little animal.

Thus, sadly, we leave my favourite sporting quarry and move to the next on Dandie Dinmont's list – the stoat.

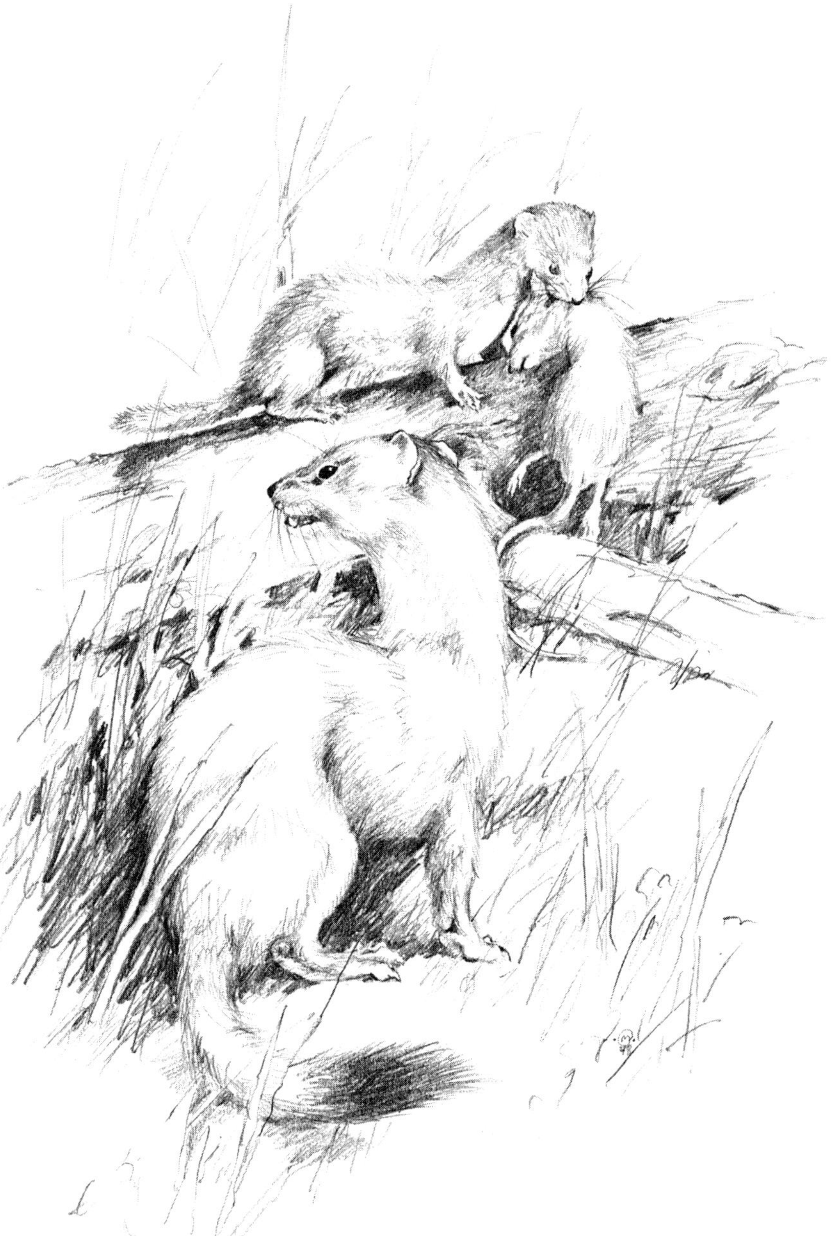

STOATS AND WEASELS

Stoats, weasels, ferrets, polecats, otters, badgers, mink and martens belong to the same family – the *Mustelidae*, which have as a common denominator a courage far in excess of size. No group of animals excites such admiration from the naturalist, nor such hatred from gamekeepers, as do the mustelids. At some distant geological era they shared a common ancestry with bears, but the phlegmatic disposition one associates with bears is totally lacking in the *Mustelidae*. Nursery stories justly depict them as red in tooth and claw – murderers, albeit valiant murderers. Kenneth Grahame's *The Wind in the Willows* describes the stoats who take over Toad Hall as behaving like a crowd of football rowdies, and European legend credits them with a supernatural intelligence beyond that of man and other animals. The polecat, one of the most foetid of the mustelids, holds the same position in European legend as Brer Rabbit in Joel Chandler Harris's Uncle Remus stories, and besides being an arch 'wide boy', he is also ranked as an incredibly dextrous thief. Maybe such legends have some basis in fact, for the ferret, the domesticated polecat, owes its name to the Latin *fur* – 'a thief'. All the mustelids are reputedly highly intelligent, though I would question placing the ponderous, ursine-looking badger among the ranks of the animal intelligentsia. Drabble's excellent book *A Weasel in My Meatsafe* (1957) gives a fascinating account of the domestication of various members of this valiant and intelligent family.

Stoats and weasels closely resemble one another, and to the uninitiated they may appear to be the same animal. They are, however, quite distinct. Weasels are considerably smaller, the adults measuring only 9 inches from head to tail, while the stoat is roughly the size of a jill ferret. Both are reddish brown in colour (though some stoats have greyish tinges to their coats), but the stoat invariably has a black tip to its tail. In the far north, both of them turn white in the winter, and the pelt of the white stoat, known commercially as ermine, is extremely valuable. At one time, ermine pelts with the black-tipped tails, which even in winter remain black, were used to trim the robes of office of judges and peers of the realm. Today few furriers are interested in the pelts of stoats and weasels, though from time to time advertisements appear in magazines expressing interest in small quantities of their skins.

Stoats are regarded as pests by most keepers, for not only does a stoat spell death to the chicks of ground-nesting birds, but the appearance of one on a game estate usually causes such alarm in the game birds that they can leave the feeding grounds. Thus the keeper and owner alike regard the appearance of a stoat on an estate as a sign that there is considerable amount of vermin unattended. Many conservationists state that the good done by a stoat far outweighs the harm, and that keepers would do well to conserve a certain number of stoats on game estates. There is little evidence to support such an argument. When game chicks are plentiful, few stoats will even look at a rat or a rabbit. Furthermore, there is little evidence that stoats will do anything to control the rat population. True, stoats will kill one or two grey rats, but they are usually less enthusiastic to tackle a grown doe or a dominant buck rat. A grown rat is a fair match for any stoat, and although a few young adult stoats will probably chance a dust-up with a rat or so, they learn, and learn quickly, that the fighting ability of a 12-ounce rat will give them a very bad time indeed. Furthermore, although some young rats do undoubtedly get killed by stoats, most baby greys feed fairly close to their mothers and the doe is quick to defend her young from stoats, ferrets and, on odd occasions, cats. Thus I do not believe that the stoats contribute much to the control of rats throughout the country. Weasels, in spite of stories in children's natural history books, are hopelessly outclassed and over-matched by adult rats.

Rabbits provided the main diet of the stoat prior to the coming of myxamatosis. They killed them either by bottling them up in blind burrows and slaying them with the cervical bite in the same way that a ferret dispatches them, or by hunting them above ground. This form of hunting is quite fascinating, for rabbits, as soon as they realize that a stoat is hunting them, quite simply give up the ghost and go into a state of frozen terror, waiting for the stoat to deliver the *coup de grâce*. As the rabbit population declined with the advance of myxomatosis, so did the stoat. In game estates where the stoat had hitherto been regarded as a major pest, they became a rarity. The number of stoats to be seen on gamekeepers' gibbets today are far exceeded by grey squirrel carcasses. This poses an interesting question to the ecologist. Rabbits are supposedly not native to this country, having been brought in by the Romans or Normans, but the stoat has always been with us. On what, therefore, did the stoat exist before the introduction of the rabbit? While it is true that they could live quite well during the nesting season on fledglings, during the winter months they must have had a lean time prior to the rabbit. Two explanations come to mind:

1. The stoat then lived on another type of small mammal that has passed unnoticed into extinction.
2. The stoat was a far from numerous animal before the coming of the rabbit, and the introduction of the rabbit caused an explosion in the stoat population.

However, rabbits are now on the increase again and are rapidly becoming immune to myxomatosis, so perhaps we will soon see an increase in the stoat population.

Stoats, weasels, polecats and martens have always been considered worthy quarry for the hunter, despite their diminutive size. John Tucker Edwardes hunted and baited polecats with his newly created Sealyhams, and several bobbery packs were kept in Wales and the Lake District to hunt stoats, polecats and martens. Gladdish Hulkes once kept a pack of Sealyhams purely to hunt stoats in the New Forest in the days when that area was famous for its large population of mustelids. When Gladdish Hulkes died, this was the pack which became some of the foundation stock for the famous Ilmer Sealyhams strain that Lucas bred.

Many hunters state that terriers are often loathe to kill stoats, not because of their courage and formidable needle-like teeth, but because of their pungent scent glands that explode whenever the stoat is upset or in danger. Certainly some dogs are reluctant to tackle them, but the majority of terriers will, if unbroken to them, slay the far more pungent ferret with great enthusiasm. Drabble gives an interesting account of a stoat hunt in *Of Pedigree Unknown*, and states that his young terrier, Mick, was not particularly enthusiastic about tackling his first stoat. Once dogs have killed them, however, and become used to this quarry, they will hunt them and kill them with some degree of keenness. I have never found any difficulty in getting dogs to tackle stoat. Stoats are also quite fragile creatures, and are easily killed once a terrier decides that he intends to finish one. They are usually far less trouble for a terrier to kill than are large buck rats. A single crunch from an enthusiastic terrier is usually more than enough for a stoat. When I was a boy in Wales I heard much of the fighting powers of the stoat, but I had to rely on second-hand information as the area was devoid of rabbits and stoats. On my twelfth birthday, however, I took my terrier to my uncle's home in Merthyr Mawr and killed four stoats during an afternoon's walk. I was somewhat saddened by the fact that not one of them put up the fight I would have expected from an adult rat.

Stoats are, however, extremely agile, and it is this quality, not their fighting ability, which makes them difficult quarry to hunt. They move with an almost quicksilver fleetness, and thus frequently escape being chopped by the terrier. Furthermore, they make use of any cranny and hole when hard pressed, and can dive into very small crevices at speed. Many times when watching a terrier close on a stoat I have seen them turn in mid-air and escape into minute holes scarcely big enough to house a reasonable-sized mouse. They also climb with the speed and agility of a squirrel and are the very devil to hunt in copses of hawthorn and scrub alder. When pressed, they will simply race up a tree and remain there, spitting and hissing with the fury of a diminutive tiger. Lucas states that all one needs to do when a stoat is treed is shout a few words up at him and he will race down to continue the hunt. I am saddened to find the old master should be writing comments of this kind, for not only would the stoat refuse to leave the tree, but the hunter would appear as something akin to the village idiot standing underneath and shouting 'Come on, Mr Stoat', or similar exhortations.

A stoat put to ground can easily be bolted by ferrets. Most rats run to ground refuse to bolt to the ferret, preferring to make a fight of it below ground rather than face the perils on the surface. Stoats invariably bolt time and time again when a ferret is put in to flush them. Few seem to want to make a fight of it. At first I considered that this was due to their inability to tackle a ferret, a theory I considered incongruous, for not only is the stoat as well equipped for fighting as the ferret, but it is also about ten times as fast. Then, in June 1976, I was ferreting in Alrewas in a rat-infested bank: a stoat ran into one of the rat holes far from the warren and I could not resist the chance of trying my young terrier. I put in a really hard-fighting little jill ferret and held my terrier on the top of the mound. Usually stoats bolt fairly quickly, but this one had obviously backed into a blind end. All hell broke loose below ground, and the stench of exploding musteline scent glands permeated upwards through the gritty soil. After a few minutes my ferret emerged tail first. I reached down to pick her up. She shrieked and struck at my hands, drawing tiny pin-pricks of blood. I soon found out why – her entire face, chest and neck were a mass of tiny pin-holes. At first I considered that none of them was deep enough to be dangerous, so I cleaned the wounds and put her back in her cage. She refused to eat and drink, and although none of the wounds suppurated, my jill died four days later. That disposed of my theory that stoats cannot tackle a ferret.

Stoats are highly courageous in defence of their young. In 1975, John Yates, a local sportsman, found a stoat dragging one of her young to safety. His terrier raced after it and the stoat dropped her baby to commit *hara-kiri* by attacking the dog. Many hunters will tell how they have seen an old stoat leave her pack and turn to attack a pursuing dog. I have seen many such stoat packs. They are nearly always either a very large litter of young or else possibly a late-born litter hunting with their older siblings – for stoats, like ferrets, will sometimes come in season and breed twice a year. When the young are mature, they are usually solitary creatures, only coming together at mating time and leading entirely separate lives for the rest of the year. Still I have seen such stoat packs in mid winter, and Henry Williamson, author of the famous *Tarka the Otter*, talked about such a stoat pack that attacked him one winter evening as he was returning home. Williamson was a superb naturalist, and I have no doubt that he was telling the truth. T. H. White, the falconer and author of *The Goshawk*, once told me that he flew a hawk at a young stoat and the adult rushed to attack the hawk in defence of her young. Surely no animal deserves its name more, for the word stoat is derived from the Belgic word *stotta* – 'bold' or 'brave'.

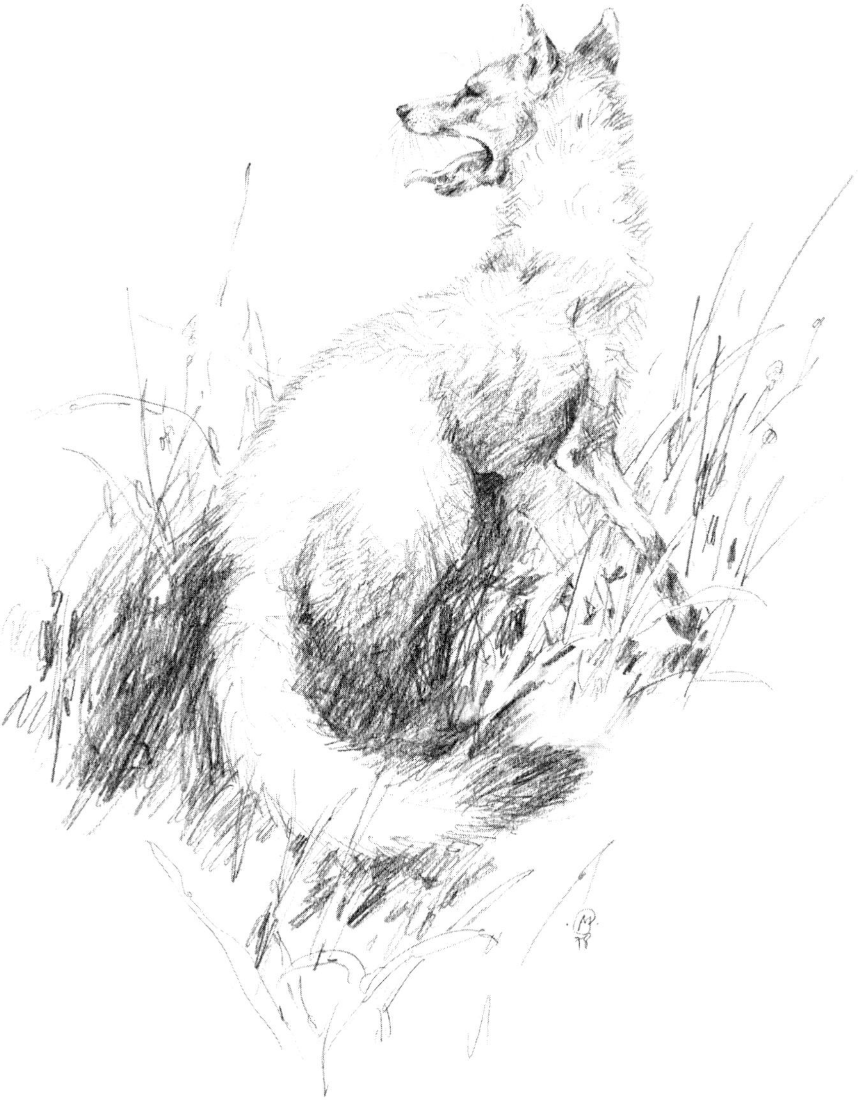

THE FOX

Now that the badger is considered a semi-protected animal (a term to be explained later), the fox must be considered as the staple quarry of the terrier. Foxes are the last of the British wild dogs; wolves passed into extinction around the middle of the eighteenth century, but foxes are as numerous as ever and are rumoured by some authorities to be actually on the increase. Certainly the fox is far more numerous than people imagine. Night-hunting poachers often report spotting foxes in their lamp beams, and policemen working in the hearts of major British cities often remark on the numbers of foxes they have seen at night. Should the much-feared rabies break out in Britain, it is certain that the fox population will have to be drastically reduced, for the fox is a great wanderer and thus capable of spreading the disease over large areas of countryside.

At one time naturalists believed that two species of fox lived in Britain. The lowland districts were inhabited by a heavy, cloddy, mastiff fox, and the hills held a lighter, taller, more rangy species, referred to as the greyhound fox. Recent research has proved this notion totally wrong. The lowland fox may live an easier life than its rangy, ill-fed hill brothers, but both belong to the same species, *Vulpes vulpes*. Some districts are, however, famous for producing heavy foxes. One monster shot near the Worcestershire border weighed in at $28\frac{1}{2}$ pounds – nearly as large as a Welsh working collie – and I have taken many heavy foxes in that district. Leicestershire is justly famous for its fox population, as well as for its well-organized fox-hunting packs, but record foxes are rarely taken in that county. Jim Blake, a noted hunter and judge from Lancashire, states that he deliberately travels to Durham to hunt, as the foxes are considerably heavier there than any district he has put his terriers to ground in in his home county. Tyson, of the Fell and Moorland Working Terrier Club, believes Blake to be correct, and numerous hunters report having taken 20-pound foxes in Durham. The average weight for an adult fox is roughly 14 pounds, and vixens are usually slightly smaller than dogs. One vixen caught near a cricket pitch in Pelsall, however, scaled in at a massive 22 pounds. Smaller foxes are fairly common, particularly in towns, where they live on a somewhat unnatural diet. I once caught a tiny, 6-pound vixen near Newport; the vixen was adult, but very undersized and ill-nourished.

THE QUARRY

Biologically, the fox is classed as a dog, though structurally it resembles a cat. The rib-cage is very shallow – so shallow that it can easily be spanned by a woman's hands. It is also an extremely sinuous animal, and this factor, coupled with the narrow chest, allows the fox to crawl through amazingly small earths and crevices and go to ground in apparently impossibly narrow rabbit warrens. Holland Hibbert, a great raconteur of some years back and a keen fox-hunting man, once told Jocelyn Lucas that he had seen a fox crawl into an earth only two and a half inches in diameter. This, of course, is clearly a tall story. A fox would find difficulty in getting its muzzle into such a hole. Some years ago, however, I was asked to dig out a fox in an allotment in Holmes, a district of Rotherham. The earth smelled of fox and the entrance to the earth was quite large. My terrier bitch, a 9-inch Russell, entered and began to bay frantically. I dug to her and found her barking at a crack between two large blocks – a very narrow hole, scarcely as large as my fist. I began to rate my bitch for rioting on a rabbit. I reached in to draw the rabbit and received a tremendous bite across the knuckles. When I managed to prise open the boulders I found a 13-pound vixen was curled up inside the lair. I would never have believed that a fox could get into such a narrow crevice. Cub foxes are quite fantastic at creeping into very tiny cracks.

Just as size varies a great deal in the fox population, so does colour. Few foxes are exactly the same in colour. A few years ago I hunted fox with Jack Anson, a noted north country lurcher man; my terriers bolted the foxes and his lurchers ran them down and killed them. At the end of the winter we had some 124 pelts, and no two of them matched precisely. Colour is usually a reddish brown, but sandy mahogany red and rust-coloured foxes are common. Many hunts report having killed jet-black foxes, but one so-called black fox killed by John Grant of Leicester was really a red with very thick, dark guard hairs. I have seen many such foxes that have looked jet-black from a distance but on closer examination were found to have black, or near-black, guard hairs. Billy Norton, the South Yorkshire rat catcher and raconteur once told me he had seen pied foxes, and also a pure-white fox feeding on the sewage beds in Blackburn, Rotherham. Grey foxes, or rather brown/grey foxes, are not uncommon and are often caught by hunters working the borrans of Cumberland. Silver and blue foxes are sometimes reported, but they seem to be rather rare. At first I considered such animals to be escapees from fur farms breeding these North American foxes for their glorious pelts, but Locke reports that silver blue and cross foxes are fairly commonly caught in Eastern Europe and Russia, and that these foxes are the same species as our own red fox.

THE FOX

Country legend credits the fox with incredible intelligence. Several noted huntsmen and masters still believe that a team of foxes will get together to elude hounds, the first fox in the team tiring the hounds and then diving for sanctuary in an earth before passing the baton to fox number two, who bolts from the earth taking the hounds after him, only to go to ground where fox number three lies waiting. Scientifically, this does not stand up to examination. First, foxes are solitary animals, so meetings to discuss the order of running are rather unlikely. Secondly, few animals possess any form of altruistic behaviour (except in defence of their young), so the idea of them running in relays is beyond credibility. What is likely is that foxes pursued by hounds or lurchers become frightened and release a scent from their anal glands; the fox then dives into the sanctuary of an earth and startles another fox lying up there. Fox number two picks up the alarm-warning smell, panics and bolts, and so on and so forth. Still, it makes a good story.

Another story indicating the fox's superior thinking power was common in the mining valleys of the South Wales coalfields. A fox infested with fleas picked up a piece of raw sheep's wool in its jaws and gradually submerged itself in water until only its muzzle, still holding the wool, was above the water. The fleas crawled up the fox's back and on to the wool, and the cunning fox dropped the flea-infested wool into the water to emerge flealess from his dip. Even to a half-wit the story must seem a little far-fetched. First, fleas could survive for a very long period on the air trapped between the hair follicles of the fox. Next, the fox would need to be of very high intelligence to adopt such a practice. Lastly, the story is no more than a nursery or old wives' tale.

At one time I thought that stories of foxes leading packs of hounds into oncoming railway trains was equally far fetched. Certainly many hounds have been killed by trains as the hounds chased the fox along the railway lines, but I regarded this as mere coincidence. In 1976, however, I decided to hunt foxes for their pelts again, and used two very hard though not very bright lurchers called Bear and Grip. They took many foxes, but one small dog fox, who fed on some fields near my cottage, invariably headed for the railway to throw them off. He managed to dart in front of moving railway trains so often that it could not have been mere coincidence. I stopped hunting him and went for easier foxes on a near-by estate. One morning, however, I found my Houdini fox near the railway line – he was quite dead and had been hit by an oncoming train. Perhaps he was not quite as intelligent as I had imagined.

Before leaving the subject of the super intelligence that foxes reputedly possess, I would mention that I have reared a great number of foxes in captivity and have not come across one that I could compare with a dog in intelligence. Most are totally unbiddable and resist any form of training. Trainability and intelligence are usually regarded as synonymous in dogs, and if this be so, the fox must be near-idiot. Other factors, such as the almost paranoiac nervousness of the fox, may interfere with training, however, but it would be a very clever animal psychologist who could draw up an IQ test for a fox. The fact remains that Reynard is hunted by all, hated by many, plagued with lethal mange, subject to all diseases, an Ishmael among animals, but in spite of it all continues to survive. Perhaps tractability and intelligence are not always synonymous.

To most town dwellers, whose only contact with foxes is in children's story books, it must appear as if the fox lives exclusively on chickens, ducks and geese. If given a chance he will certainly snaffle poultry, but most foxes are reluctant to go very near human habitation, even after dark. Foxes, like rats, are amazingly versatile creatures and will live on a great variety of foods. First, the fox is not exclusively carnivorous. Even in the wild state, twenty per cent of his food is usually vegetable in origin. Faeces examined in autumn will invariably display traces of corn husks. When I first began research into foxes, I thought that these husks had come from birds which had fed on the corn and thence been eaten by the foxes, but I have since noted that captive foxes will pick off pieces of grain that adhere to the straw used for their bedding.

Town foxes eat quite a lot of vegetable matter – far more than country foxes, in fact. A few years ago some young hunters wrote an interesting article for the Midland Working Terrier Club. They had hunted foxes in the centre and on the outskirts of Birmingham, and had noted the stomach contents of the foxes they killed. Most of the stomach contents consisted of bread and pastry and other farinaceous food, with very little meat of any sort. When I hunted a similar area, I found, in addition to bread waste, boiled potatoes and carrots among the stomach contents. It must be added that few town foxes are in such good condition as country foxes.

Prior to myxomatosis, the rabbit was probably the staple diet of the fox, but when that sickening disease appeared on the landscape the rabbit population came near to extinction and the foxes' dietary habits underwent considerable changes. Foxes were sometimes found in towns even prior to myxomatosis, but since 1953 reports of foxes in such unlikely places as Chiswick, Erdington and central Coventry are now so common as no longer to be of interest to the writers of newspaper articles. With the rabbit becoming a rarity, rats replaced them as the staple diet of the fox, and these are far more plentiful in towns than most urban dwellers would care to believe. It is just possible that country foxes in the first place move into towns to hunt rats. Certainly the faeces samples of town foxes I collected in the three years from 1968 to 1970 all had traces of rat hair among them. Rubbish dumps are often frequented by foxes, as much for the chance of picking up rats as for the edible garbage found there. When I hunted two maggot factories in Yorkshire, foxes were quite often seen hunting in broad daylight, stalking the unwary rat with a cat-like stealth. Lamping men (a term I will make clear below), who hunt and poach the fields around Liverpool, often see foxes killing the rats which come out to feed alongside the rabbits in districts well watered by canals and rivers.

Carrion forms an important part in the diet of foxes. Foxes are often found picking at pieces of birds and animals which have met with death on roads. I live near a canal, and in late spring and summer the roads are covered with frogs migrating from one pool or pond to another, and I have often seen foxes eating up the remains of frogs crushed by vehicles. Meat of any sort has to be somewhat ripe and malodorous before a fox finds it unfit to eat.

At a time when fox pelts were picking up in price – fur fashions are very changeable, and in some years a fox pelt will fetch £15 but in other years will be nearly impossible to give away – I spent a fairly profitable winter lamping foxes with a lurcher bitch I once owned. At first I would deliberately seek out foxes and hunt them with the lurcher, aided by the beam of light produced by a spotlight and a motor-bike battery (hence the term 'lamping'). It was very unprofitable as it was difficult to get within range of the fox at night – close enough, that is, to slip a lurcher at one. I remedied this by tipping waste meat in a fairly late state of putrefaction into the centre of a field and waited near the hedge with my lurcher held on a slip. At regular intervals I would flick on my spotlight to check for foxes. It became a most profitable sport, and I killed a great number of foxes in this way, though it was afterwards necessary to salt the area with paunch and offal for several days before attempting to kill feeding foxes with a lurcher.

Lamping men could pass on to naturalists a great deal of information about foxes and vulpine behaviour (that is, if the reticent poaching fraternity could be persuaded to talk about their adventures). Recently I was lamping with a particularly soft-mouthed lurcher who was retrieving a live, unharmed rabbit to hand. The rabbit began to squeal loudly and a fox ran out to within eight feet of the dog to investigate the squealing.

Fish waste, even in vintage state of putrefaction, attracts foxes. Some time ago I supplemented my pathetic teaching salary by working at a poulterer's and fishmonger's. The fish entrails and heads were waste, and I used to leave piles of the stuff to attract feeding foxes. Mink farms that feed a lot of waste fish often keep a few silver and blue foxes to eat up the surplus fish waste and cereal mix fed to mink. Colin Jackson, a biologist friend who is at present working on a book on some aspects of the British otter, says that otters are very wasteful feeders and will frequently eat only one bite from the back of a large fish's neck; foxes often beachcomb for these carcasses. Some of them are often very maggoty before the foxes find them, yet Reynard finds them perfectly acceptable.

Of course, poultry will be taken if the poultry breeder is foolish enough to leave any of his stock unlocked for the night. Joan Hancocks, a poultry breeder in Sutton Coldfield, often finds foxes hanging around the battery houses in the hopes of picking up a hen or so, or maybe just some carrion from the midden pile. In 1976 I lamped the area for Mrs Hancocks' brother-in-law, who shot fourteen foxes with his rifle, all within a period of a week. Poultry are rarely in danger if locked up for the night in reasonably secure pens. Early in this century, many poultry keepers ran a gamecock with their hens, as they believed that such a cock would protect his harem from foxes. A paragraph from the famous Wright's *Book of Poultry* states that one gamecock actually killed a fox, though I would question the story. A fox is more than a match for any bird weighing a little under 6 pounds. Several breeders of the famous Aseel fighting game swear to the fact that they have seen many foxes driven off by an Aseel cockbird. I have certainly watched swans drive off foxes that are pestering the cygnets.

Only once have I seen evidence of mass slaughter of poultry by fox, though many semi-fictional books on foxes give the impression that this is almost a daily occurrence. It was a September morning in 1969, and a local farmer came to me in quite a state. Some animal had ripped the loose sides from his poultry pen and committed mayhem among his poultry. I went to his farm and saw a scene of carnage that can rarely have been equalled. One hundred and twenty-six hens lay dead, some intact, some merely decapitated. At first I thought the massacre was the work of a badger, but examination of the corpses made it clear that a vixen and her cubs had been the culprits, for many of the dead had the breast meat nibbled off as though a cat had stripped the carcass. The vixen and her cubs had moved from an earth nearly a mile away and taken up residence inside an old badger set. We took the vixen and five cubs from the set that morning.

Few country foxes chance a raid on a poultry pen close to the house unless they are really hard pressed for food. Town foxes are a little more bold and will raid poultry houses even under the noses of guard dogs. A vixen with cubs to support can be a great pest on an estate. One living in Kings Heath, Birmingham, tore down the front of a cattery and killed nine Siamese kittens. This same vixen ripped the front out of a rabbit cage and took the occupant, wiped out a whole 'piggery' of guinea pigs and was an incredible nuisance to poultry and pigeon keepers. It had gone to earth in a very large drain and reared three cubs there. Both vixen and cubs were totally unafraid of dogs, and raided exactly when and where they pleased. The breeding earth was found to be littered with the wings of tame pigeons, poultry and even the remains of some exotic waterfowl obtained from a park about three miles distant.

Hedgehogs are reputedly taken by both town and country foxes, though two tales as to how a fox opens the prickly customer really belong in the realms of folk legend. One story has it that, when a fox finds a hedgehog, he bowls him along until he comes to a brook and rolls the poor beast into the water. Hedgehogs, like all mammals, need to breathe, and so they open up, allowing the fox the chance to savage their unprotected belly. A lovely story, and interesting enough, but I doubt if it has much truth in it. Hedgehogs are found, and a curious and hungry fox perhaps rolls them over in order to kill them. If there is water about, perhaps they fall into it and so are killed, though I doubt if the action is intentional. Another story is that foxes find hedgehogs and urinate on them causing them to open up before dispatching them with a quick bite. I have seen several dogs 'spray' a hedgehog, but I have never seen a hedgehog uncurl or react in any way when sprinkled with urine. Most hedgehogs are literally invulnerable to bites from most mammals. Furthermore, if hedgehogs are so easy to kill, why do they remain so common around the countryside?

In spite of the opinions of many people – there has recently been a spate of controversy on whether or not foxes actually do kill cats – cats may sometimes be taken by foxes. I think cats may be killed when they are asleep, as I imagine a fully grown cat would usually be more than a match for a fox. My siamese female once gave birth to a litter of kittens in an outhouse, and was a veritable terror to my terriers. She once drove off a fully grown dog fox and chased him halfway across the field. Cats are killed nevertheless. My neighbour lost her adult female cat and litter of half-grown kittens to a vixen and her cubs on a hunting spree. I would imagine, though, that a fox would need to be highly desperate for food before he would consider tackling a cat. Cats are veritable demons when cornered and made to fight. I doubt if a fox would chance such lacerations for a mere meal. The kittens so commonly found in breeding earths are usually newly born kittens that have probably been drowned rather than killed by foxes.

Strangely, most carnivorous animals are very partial to cat flesh. Foxes enjoy them and often eat road casualties. Ferrets also find cat meat very tasty.

Contrary to popular opinion, sheep are rarely, if ever killed by foxes. Foxes are reputed to be inveterate lamb killers, but there is no scientific evidence to back up this opinion. Remains of lambs found in and around breeding earths are hardly conclusive proof of sheep worrying. Foxes are very partial to carrion, and there is usually a fairly high mortality rate among newly born lambs, particularly lambs born to hill sheep, who give birth to their young in the most exposed positions. I have no doubt at all that foxes will take dead lambs, and also gobble up the afterbirths of sheep; they may also, now and again, kill an orphaned lamb, but it is as well to remember that a ewe with young is a tough and alert customer. Most would put up such a show of aggression that a bull terrier would be put to flight, and any fox about to attack a lamb would certainly be in for a bad time. As a further indication, may I suggest that the reader takes his terrier or any small dog to a hillside in Wales. The sight of a small dog racing up the hillside will put most sheep into a state of panic. A fox will by contrast walk through a flock of ewes without causing enough concern to stop the flock grazing. If foxes were the inveterate sheep worriers that legend makes them out to be, I doubt if a flock would react to them so phlegmatically.

Before leaving the diet of foxes and passing on to their breeding habits, let me assure the reader that stories of foxes following shooting parties are certainly not among the old wives' tales. They seem to know that not all wounded game is retrieved, and that if they wait patiently they may well be able to eat once the shooting party has retired. Nearly every poacher I have met has stories to tell about foxes following (at a safe distance, mind you) the hunter through woods. A lamping poacher has only to flash his beam around the hedgerows to pick up the saucer-like eyes of a fox watching the nocturnal hunt. Likewise, foxes rob snares. When I first moved to the district where I now live, I snared rabbits to sell. One small vixen was the bane of my life; she would rob nearly every snare I put down and have the audacity to sit on a railway embankment watching me place my snares. I tried many times to catch her, coursing her with dogs and even setting high snares ($1\frac{1}{2}$ fists high, $1\frac{1}{2}$ fists across) along her known runs, but all to no avail. I took other small dog foxes, and one very large dog fox which was bright red in colour, but not the vixen I was after. She would even follow me on ferreting expeditions and snatch rabbit carcasses from the piles I left near the warrens.

Foxes often do this. Moses Smith, the gipsy sage, said that gipsies will urinate near a pile of rabbits to prevent foxes taking the carcasses. I find this an unlikely method of protecting one's kills, as the spot where one has ferreted is usually full of human scent anyway. Thus urination around one's kills may be thought of as both unpleasant and unnecessary, yet Eskimos in Northern Greenland urinate around piles of kills to prevent the small white fox, somewhat tamer than our own fox, from taking kills from the pile.

To the townsman, the fox is a furtive creature, spending most of his time below ground and only venturing forth at night to go on raiding expeditions in near-by farmyards. In point of fact, foxes spend very little of the summertime below ground and much prefer to lie up in brassica crops and corn. It is therefore just a little pointless for the terrier man to put his terriers to ground in the hopes of finding a fox much before the corn is cut. Foxes dig a great number of earths and move from one to another as fancy takes them. Most lowland earths are simply enlarged rabbit warrens, dug out while trying to get to a rabbit. In 1967 I had a very game old bitch called Tiny trapped below ground. She had come upon her fox, killed it, but had been too weak to struggle out of the earth. Consequently my friends and I were forced to dig her out. We spent twenty-nine hours digging through the bank and encountered eight nests of young rabbits during the course of our excavations. Hill foxes frequently disdain digging (there are very few rabbits about to start the earths anyway), and often use piles of rocks as earths. This causes the terrier man a great deal of trouble as such places are virtually impregnable fortresses, and once a terrier is to ground in one it is nearly impossible to dig to him.

In one rock pile in South Wales it is not unknown for a dog to go to ground in this glacial mound and to emerge nearly a mile away. The Lake District has some almost legendary rock borrans where foxes often lodge and breed. Many are so deep that the ice of winter is still found in such earths in late spring. These are very difficult places to work a terrier, and impossible to earth stop when hunting. Not only do such places act as sanctuaries for foxes, but they are also death-traps to terriers whose owners decide to put them to ground in such places. Badger sets often harbour foxes, and litters of fox cubs are often bred in such places. I should imagine that the mortality rate of cubs is remarkably high in such badger sets, for badgers are highly omnivorous and will certainly eat fox cubs.

Some of the very worst earths to dig out are those of foxes who rear their cubs in labyrinths leading off from drift mine shafts. To work these earths using a terrier often results in a dog getting trapped in the most inaccessible of tunnels. One such drift-mine earth in Maesteg has been the death of a great many terriers. Such places often harbour foxes and are a dangerous temptation to any terrier man anxious to try a terrier to ground. Some foxes, on the other hand, seem not to have this earth-digging instinct at all, and nest above ground. I know of three vixens who reared three litters of cubs in gorse patches during 1976. These vixens are probably only successful at litter rearing during mild weather.

City foxes are, of course, very much at home in a variety of situations. I have bolted foxes from beneath the floors of garden sheds, and one vixen actually reared a litter in a disused cellar below a wine shop. Rubbish dumps often harbour many foxes, for not only do such places offer easy digging, but such dumps often furnish the vixen with a great deal of food. Not only carrion, but also rats and the odd unwary seagull are taken by rubbish-dump foxes. I once dug a litter that had been reared in a covered-over gas boiler. Such places are usually fairly well infected with the mange mite, *Sarcoptis communis*. Drains are often utilized by foxes and litters. One litter reared near Kings Heath Bowling Club, Birmingham, were nesting only four inches above the water line in such a drain. Freak rain storms must destroy a great number of cubs reared in such earths.

Before the subject of breeding earths, it would be wise to mention the artificial earth. In hunting country, hunt servants often lay down artificial earths to encourage foxes to breed. These earths consist of a concrete box with a metal lid with a 9-inch pipe leading in and a similar pipe for exit. Many foxes breed in such earths, and are easily dug by artisan hunters out to get a terrier entered. Barry Dainty, once the terrier man for the Warwick Hunt, says that he has taken as many as seven foxes from one such earth. These earths may also often harbour young badgers driven out from their breeding sets.

When a cub reaches eight or nine months old it becomes sexually mature. Every branch of the dog family – foxes, wolves, coyotes and jackals – seems to produce a greater number of males than of females. Few young males find mates during the first year of their lives, for the competition for females is usually pretty fierce. Young males usually live separate and celibate lives, keeping well out of the way of older and more aggressive males. During the mating season, fights between males are a fairly common occurrence, though Ardrey believes that the battle is territorial rather than sexual. Male foxes become fertile during the early parts of December and wander great distances to find mates. Sometimes the obsession with finding a mate is greater than the desire to eat, and the male becomes very thin and emaciated. Recent marking of foxes has shown that a fox wanting to find a mate will wander as far as fifteen miles during one night. In late December 1975 I noticed a great many dog foxes on the move and obviously 'off country'.

Little is known of the mating habits of the red fox, *Vulpes vulpes*. Few people have seen them mate. Cubs are born between fifty-one and fifty-four days after mating. Vixens give births to cubs on the bare floor of the earth. They are born thickly furred, and thus do not suffer from hypothermia through lack of bedding. Vixens will often spend two days below ground when they whelp, and often eat or drink nothing during that time. I once bred a litter of four young foxes, and the tame vixen was very protective towards them for the first days of the cubs' lives. Very young cubs vary in colour, from blue-black to chocolate brown, and this pigment stays with the cub for nearly eight weeks. Fox cubs grow very rapidly, and far faster than dogs of similar size. They are also more precocious than terrier-type puppies. Fox cubs crawl to the mouth of the earth and take their first look at the world at about four weeks old, when a terrier puppy will still be scarcely able to focus.

The vixen finds providing food for her litter a very hard job – a task in which the male takes very little or no part. She usually leaves the breeding earth when the cubs are eight weeks old and takes up residence in a near-by set or earth. She is probably quite sore from suckling, and more than a little fed up with the wild and rowdy games the cubs play. By the time a cub is three months old, he will venture off on hunting trips without his dam. This is the time when fighting becomes a serious problem in litters. In the litters I have reared – admittedly, in the restricting environment of captivity – I have found that savage fights often break out between fourteen-week-old cubs. In the wild, this constant turmoil in the earth results in litters breaking up and going their own ways. They are nearly as tall as a small vixen at this stage, but obviously lack bushcraft. Cubs of this age often get caught up in snares and traps and become road casualties. They are usually tolerated by adult males, but as soon as the male cubs become sexually mature the adult male drives them off territory. This prevents severe in-breeding, for if foxes were not so jealous about territorial guarding, male cubs would invariably serve their own sisters or dams; as it is, they are driven far from the earths. Cub hunting, which starts in September, also helps to split up these litters and ensures that the cubs do not remain in their own territory.

THE QUARRY

In spite of this, however, in times of hardship and stress, fox litters often return to the place of their birth. I have noticed that a terrier put in a well-known breeding earth as late as December may often result in a whole litter being bolted. One noted earth near my cottage, Brough's earth, can be relied on to produce several adolescent cubs during the month of December. Thus we come to the end of our examination of the fox, and perhaps knowledge gleaned from reading the last few pages will make the reader a better hunter. On now to the actual hunting of red fox with terriers.

A puppy is ready to enter to fox when it is ready. This seemingly trite comment is probably the most accurate statement in the whole book. Different terriers are ready to enter at different ages. Lakeland terriers are invariably ready to go at seven months old, displaying all the signs of readiness: namely, aggression towards other dogs and a more than healthy interest in a variety of small animals (tame ones as well, if one has not been diligent about early stock-breaking). Borders may be decidedly silly and apathetic at this age, and in fact well up until they are two years old, but will enter in a decidedly earnest manner. Russells are a mixed bunch generally, and it would be most unwise to generalize about them and their precocity in entering. Lakeland terriers usually have to be restrained rather than encouraged, and this quality makes them an ideal first terrier. Most books suggest that the terrier man should try his terriers to fox when they are at least eighteen months old. Many terriers will enter far sooner.

Sam Towers, the noted Atherstone terrier man, will not consider entering a bitch until she is over her first season, as he equates sexual maturity with readiness to enter. Charlie Lewis of Peterborough, a noted showman and at one time a noted hunter of terriers, is of the opinion that two years is not too old to start a terrier, and only then after it has had experience hunting small fry such as rats and stoats. Brian Forsyth, who does the terrier work for the Warwickshire Hunt at Kineton, and who is a regular font of terrier knowledge, is another who believes in late entry. His noted terrier was an ugly but exceedingly valiant dog, and was very, very late in starting to fox – he was nearly three years old when ready to work to that quarry. From that time, however, the dog was unbeatable and continued to work fox well right up into senility. It would be wise for the beginner terrier man to benefit from the experiences of such a person and not write off a dog that is slow to start. Given a chance, and perhaps time, few terriers will refuse to work. Let the maxim, 'There are no bad terriers, merely bad terrier trainers,' be remembered.

THE FOX

It is, in fact, good policy not to overmatch the youngster at large quarry, but to allow him to burn up his youthful enthusiasm on small fry like rats. I cite a case in point: at one time I bred a very valiant though often mute strain of terrier that might only loosely be classed as a Jack Russell type. These dogs were rough-coated, quite leggy, but very ugly; they were also incredibly valiant, and I have seldom seen their equals for courage. They were a mixture of many game breeds, including Sealyhams, Bedlingtons and perhaps some Dandie Dinmont, and certainly contained some bull terrier. I once bred a litter and was tempted into selling a puppy I fancied. Against my better judgement, I sold him and kept back his less attractive brother. My puppy grew up to be a classic fox dog, though he eventually became so hard that he killed every fox he encountered until he was broken to pieces by a badger. His brother, sold to a man who apparently 'knew all about terriers' was also valiant, and showed such early promise that his owner matched him against a variety of large quarry, including fox cubs, vixens and an old boar badger; this was before the dog was six months old. He was, of course, very overmatched and eventually jibbed. I bought him back at eighteen months old, a shattered, neurotic wreck of a dog, who flinched whenever I would pick up a stick, wet himself whenever I shouted at him. I hunted him for two years before he would even look at a fox earth, and he literally ran away from any carcass that was used to encourage a puppy. The story has a happy ending: I persisted with him and eventually he went well to fox. He became one of the best dogs I have ever owned.

We can assume our terrier puppy is now going well to rat killing and hunting a few stoat, so where do we go to next? We encourage him now to run through a few dry drains, encourage him to enter a few earths. (I must stress at this point that the word 'encourage' does not mean getting a dog into such a state of hysteria that he will race into every hole he sees, furiously giving tongue at everything and anything. Such over-encouragement will nearly always result in false marking, for such a dog will often give tongue in the faint hope of pleasing the owner.) Now we must get him steady to rabbit. No terrier that is meant to hunt fox should even consider looking at a rabbit. Buy a tame rabbit and allow your terrier to see that it is forbidden to chase a bunny. There is method in this seeming madness: rabbits often lie up in the tunnels leading off a fox earth, and terriers will often come off their legitimate prey to bay at a rabbit, unless that is, they are absolute steady with bunnies.

I know of one heart-rending story about a dog that was not steady to rabbit. Alan Peters, a small-time Border-terrier breeder, hunted his dogs to most quarry. We put in his dog, sired by the incomparable Deerstone Destiny, to ground, and deep in the bowels of the earth the dog began to bay. It was a huge earth and nearly impossible to dig. It was a bright, clear Saturday when we started hunting, and a dismal, cold, Friday when we finally dug out the dog. Our team of diggers shifted nearly seventy tons of earth, but his Border terrier had dug on, walled himself in and finally died of suffocation. Two feet further along the tunnel was crouched a very frightened but still alive rabbit. It is indeed a sad tale, and forever after Alan broke his dogs to rabbit. The best Border-terrier bitch I have ever owned was so steady that she would allow a tame rabbit to eat from her food dish, and although she frequently menaced it, she never harmed it. She would run nose down on a fox scent, and not even glance at the rabbits scuttling away in front of her.

If one is intending to work a dog to fox, and exclusively to fox, then it is also wise to break him to badger. This will save you a lot of time, for badgers can be a great time-waster when fox hunting. Not only do they cause the dog to break off baying at a fox, but the sets in which some badgers live are virtual citadels and impossible to dig. Foxes will often bolt from these sets, but badgers will rarely bolt, even from shallow earths. Joan Begbie, who bred the famous Seale Cottage strain of Jack Russell, always encouraged her dogs to regard brock as forbidden, for the sets in her district were deep, rocky and impossible to dig. Cobby also advised breaking his best dogs to badger, though Pickaxe and Pincher, two noted terriers, and both incredible workers, were demons to brock.

Geoffrey Sparrow, in his fascinating book *The Terrier's Vocation*, which tends to be more entertaining than instructive, and Irving and Jackson in their book *The Border Terrier*, suggest that the ideal way to start a terrier to fox is to go out with the hunt and wait until the fox has been run to ground, and then politely ask the master if one might try one's terrier. The short piece of counter-advice to this is – DON'T. A terrier needs an early success to give him confidence for future fox hunts; he needs a fox that will bolt readily, or one that can be dug and killed so that it is his to rag and worry. A driven fox, particularly one that is tired and refuses to bolt, will put up a fearsome fight and easily 'best' any young terrier. Furthermore, when a fox is dug at a hunt, it is killed and thrown to the hounds to worry. Terriers are rarely allowed in on this worry, so the terrier's sense of triumph will be diminished to say the least.

Another point to remember is that the established hunts employ terrier men to bolt and dig foxes. To him it is his job, and he will scarcely relish anyone coming along to waste his time by trying to enter a 'green' terrier to fox that is driven to ground while the huntsman has the unenviable job of holding back the hounds. Few hunt terrier men welcome a tyro terrier at a dig, and few masters will allow you even to try your terrier at this stage of a fox hunt.

By far the best reason for not trying your terrier at the 'gone to earth' stage of a hunt is the human element, and this is the one most commonly overlooked. A terrier should be tried to fox in private, and this stage of a hunt is decidedly public. If one's terrier refuses to enter when a crowd of hunt supporters are gathered around the earth, then the terrier owner is inclined to look a little foolish. Hunt supporters are rarely the kind to spare the feelings of a beginner, and the teasing that follows may well have a sting. A man made to look foolish because of his dog is apt to lose faith in the animal, and any rift in the man/dog bond is to be avoided. For this reason, no terrier man should try his terrier for the first time at this part of the hunt. When Sparrow wrote *The Terrier's Vocation*, it was considered a very wicked deed for a lay terrier man to take out his terrier and dig a fox. Sparrow states that the hunting country foxes should be regarded as sacred, but it is still very bad advice to enter a terrier at a 'gone to earth' part of a hunt, and I wonder whether Sparrow ever entered any of his own terriers by this method. I would certainly advise against it.

The best method of entering one's first terrier to fox is to find a solitary lay hunter who owns a good working terrier or so. Allow his dog to go to ground at a fox, and possibly slip a young one behind him. This method is also full of dangers. First, an old dog will often be peeved if a young dog is allowed at what he considers to be his prey, and he may turn and savage the youngster. Next, a dog working fox needs room to manoeuvre, and this is impossible if a young dog is close to his tail. Lastly, a young dog may get so excited when faced with his first fox that he may savage the hindquarters of the veteran to get at the prey. I have seen tails and vaginas ripped off by puppies driven frantic by having a dog in front of them. I once saw a young Glen of Imaal terrier (a fiery breed) slipped behind his mother in a badger set. All hell broke loose below ground, and we thought the pair had bottled up the badgers in a blind hole. We dug frantically to the roaring (it could scarcely be called barking), and found mother and son locked together in a deadly fight. No badger could be seen. Nevertheless, entering with an older, more experienced dog is an easy and quick way of starting a terrier.

Suppose, however, that the terrier man does not know anyone who is working dogs. Well, all is not lost, even though it is made much more difficult. First, no natural enmity exists between dogs and foxes: it is a state of being that has to be encouraged, and this is a little more difficult when entering a puppy without the help of an older dog. Dislike or hatred of foxes can be encouraged by allowing the dog to rag or worry a skin (it is an old wives' tale that this creates false marking, though it was a popular theory in the Welsh mining valley where I grew up) or the carcass of a fox. Lone terriers should be encouraged to enter known fox earths. More often than not, the earths will be uninhabited, but the terrier man must persist. One day he will come to an earth which does have an occupant, and the very presence of a fox will startle the terrier. In his surprise he may bark. At this moment encourage him by urging him on with shouts of approval. With luck the fox will merely nip him and sow the seeds of enmity. Should your puppy get more severely bitten, it is essential that you dig to your fox, kill it quickly and humanely and allow the puppy to rag the corpse. This will encourage the terrier, for now he has been in on the kill. His beating from the fox has not therefore been in vain. Most terriers will take a terrific hiding from a fox and will not quit provided they can see something for their trouble at the end of the dig.

The worst fault a terrier can develop, so far as I am concerned, is to refuse to come out of an earth when called. While it must be a very bitter experience to quit after winning, I always insist on absolute obedience in my dogs, be they lurchers or terriers. Beware the man who proudly boasts, 'When my dog is down he stays until the fox is dead.' This is absolute madness, and bespeaks an amateur of the first water. Assume that your terrier has gone to ground in an apparently small earth. Alas, as soon as he meets his fox, we realize from the barking that the earth is deceptive, and that it is in reality a disused badger citadel. It is impossible to dig to such a dog. Impossible? No such word – well, not for you. You *have* to dig to him if he refuses to come out when called. Do not plan on going anywhere else for the next few days – you will be digging out a most disobedient dog who refuses to come off a fox. I once dug for five days to rescue a dog which belonged to a friend after it found a fox in a huge earth and refused to come out. It rained, hailed and snowed during those five days, and we took out enough earth to fill in the Mariana trench. When we eventually reached the dog, the fox was another five feet on, unhappy but still alive. I would hate to own such a beast, and though I am often accused of having 'clockwork' dogs because they are stock-broken, obedient and well-mannered, they are always a pleasure to hunt with. It has taken a lot of work to get them to this 'clockwork' level and they well repay the effort.

Here is a piece of advice on digging foxes. Your dog goes to earth and immediately begins baying at his fox. The reflex of many hunters is to start digging away immediately to get to the source of the sound. This is a very foolish action. The fox has probably been surprised while sleeping, and the dog is now harrassing a fox, who is hissing and snapping at the terrier. The fox will move, and the terrier may take quite a few minutes to bottle him up in a blind hole. Let the sound of the baying settle before you start to dig. It is also essential to remember that, should a terrier come out for a breath of air and a drink, it's dollars to doughnuts that unless you put in another terrier immediately, the fox will either leave his blind hole and wander about in the earth, or else he will simply dig in and be a yard further back before the terrier returns to work. A terrier who sticks at his job until called out is a real treasure. (Don't try and buy such a ready-made terrier with these qualities. No one will ever sell you one, whatever the advertisement states.)

A word, now, about the qualities a hunter requires in a fox-hunting terrier. In the north of England, a terrier is required, more often than not, to kill the fox underground. To do this, the dog has to be a fairly tough customer. He must close with his fox and kill him with a throat bite. Most fox-killing terriers tend to strangle a fox to death with throat bites rather than simply bite it to pieces. This is a knack some terriers develop, sometimes without getting badly bitten themselves. John Winch's famous dog, Chanter, a tough but very classy Lakeland with a fair amount of Kennel Club Lakeland blood, is a past master at it and rarely gets bitten. A hard dog is usually a dog who tends to close with his prey and develops this knack of fox killing. Funnily enough, Borders, which are the slowest dogs to enter to fox, often develop and exploit this skill. If this is the skill required, well, many dogs will learn it.

This quality is not welcomed in terriers used in the midlands. In this area, and in the south, a terrier is required, as John Caius said in 1576, to 'nip, bite and make afraid' – in other words, bolt the fox. Fox-killing terriers are usually regarded as a nuisance, and hard terriers are often sold off at a reasonable price in the Midlands. Another reason why few hunters in the Midlands (and even a few up north) object to an iron-hard terrier is that such a dog is invariably mute, for, by dint of the fact that he has obtained a throat hold on a fox, he is unable to bark. Thus it is impossible to dig to such a dog. Furthermore, such a dog usually comes well within range of the fox's formidable carnasial teeth, and usually requires hospitalization after a fox dig, unless he has developed the specific knack of fox killing. Used in conjunction with a hunt, such a dog is useless, since few foxes bolt when a dog of this kind goes to ground, and those which do get out are so badly mangled that they are unable to give the hounds a good run. Most Lakelands are iron hard, as are the newly created smooth brown northern hunt terriers, erroneously referred to as the Patterdale. John Russell was reluctant to use smooth-coated dogs, as he believed they had bull-terrier blood, and that such blood ruined 'the gentlemanly character of the breed'.

Once a terrier has become hard, he is nearly impossible to break from fox killing. The knack is easily learned and rarely forgotten. Sometimes, after a bad beating from a fox, a terrier will learn to stand back and bay, though I have known only one such case. More often than not, a bad mauling causes the dog to become even harder, for he realizes that, the more quickly he finishes off his opponent, the less are his chances of receiving a bad biting.

Nigel Hinchcliffe of the Pennine Fox Hounds does not share my opinion in this. Hinchcliffe breeds a particularly valiant type of black Patterdale dog, with strong bull-terrier influence. Many of them kill foxes and do not give tongue during their first season, but after the first season tend to bay like thunder at any fox they have cornered.

Some advocate trapping a fox in a drain and separating the fox from the terrier by an iron grid, large enough for the dog to get his muzzle but not his entire head through. The fox punishes the dog quite badly, and this is said to teach the terrier to stand back and bay. I am not happy about the method. Not only is it illegal, contravening the laws about baiting animals, it doesn't usually work. Jim French of the Hampshire Hunt believes that working a dog to badger for a year will sometimes teach it discretion. Cobby, however, considered that this usually makes a dog very hard, and Lucas shares his opinion. Cobby believed that entering a dog too young also caused him to become hard, and was of the opinion that the most useful fox dogs were not dogs who were over eager to get at a fox, but dogs who had a great deal of respect for Reynard's biting ability. Such dogs stand back and bay rather than wade in for a tackle.

Pocket beagles were often crossed with various strains of terrier to create the tendency to stand back and give tongue. Frankly, I do not persist with a dog that is too hard and tackles, killing his fox, though I must confess I often breed such dogs. They are usually a bit of a liability underground, as they rarely, if ever, give tongue, and as a rule spend six months of each year recovering from fox wounds. Many learn to kill a fox quickly (and sadly also quietly), without sustaining any damage to themselves, but unless you are living up north, where such a dog is cultivated, then a terrier that is too hard is certainly not as useful as the sensible dog who stands back and gives tongue, thereby bolting the fox.

Yapping dogs are often extremely good at bolting foxes – far better than the iron-hard, fear-nothing type of dog. In my book *The Jack Russell – Its Training and Entering*, I put forward a theory as to why this should be so, and I make no apology for repeating the idea here. Foxes are not aggressive creatures. Most will fight shy of any conflict with a dog and be only too keen to bolt clear from trouble if the coast is clear. At one time, as I said earlier, I caught foxes for their pelts, and though a fox killed by terriers or coursed by lurchers is an exciting event, it does tend to produce a damaged, unsaleable pelt as an end product. When I wanted pelts I simply netted the holes and bolted foxes into the nets with a rather gentle terrier who never tackled, but simply gave tongue like thunder. The fox was then untangled and killed with a sharp blow – no damage to dog or pelt.

Now, as foxes hit the net they behave strangely. They struggle for a few moments and then go absolutely rigid. Their playing possum is not an act, as some people believe, but quite simply a cataleptic fit. The eyes become glazed, and there is little or no reaction to pain. A strong light shone in the eyes likewise produces no reaction. It really is a kind of fit. It lasts only a few moments, after which the fox leaps up and races away. The fit serves a purpose, for it can give the fox a slight advantage when his opponent is baffled by the apparent lifelessness of his victim, but it is still a fit induced by fear. A dog who bays as he approaches a fox lying up in an earth, startles but does not terrify the fox. The fox therefore endeavours to get away from the noisy creature, and thus bolts. A terrier who is too hard, however, races in and thrashes the fox, and the fox reacts by going into a state of catalepsy. The terrier continues to worry the animal, who now comes out of his trance-like state and is forced to fight for his very life. He cannot bolt, and therefore makes a real stand of it.

Some two years ago my stud dog, Vampire (an appropriate name), mated his half sister and produced a most attractive litter. One puppy, a replica of Vampire, was sold to a lady who lived in a flat in Birmingham. It was an unfortunate union of woman and dog, for the woman was elderly and the dog over-energetic. The whole matter came to a head when the dog was a yearling, for he slipped his leash and killed a cat. The old lady brought him back and asked if I would find him a home. He was a beautiful dog, but very wilful.

Vampire and Michael (as the dog was called) hated each other on sight, and there was no peace while the new dog was on the premises. Eventually, Mick Marsh, an amateur keeper and vermin controller from fifteen miles away took him off my hands and the tale now begins. Michael took a matter of a minute or two to learn that fox was fair game, and waded into his first vixen. She thrashed him very badly, but he was a little like Vampire in temperament, and stuck his ground, grunting rather than barking. Mick dug to him with some difficulty, for the dog was dead mute. By the time Mick dug the dog, the dog had killed the fox. Henceforth Michael went to fox with great enthusiasm, and he rarely bolted one. He would tear into his victim as silently as death, and within a few minutes his fox was dead. Mick could only dig out the dog with the aid of a tiny bitch who would bay at any dead animal with the same enthusiasm that she would at a live one. That winter Mick killed forty foxes with Michael and I fed many ferrets on the skinned carcasses. It was not the sort of dog that any fox hunter could use to good advantage, but it does illustrate my point.

A fox does not have to be hurt to leave an earth. I once ran a hare into a drain with a greyhound. The hare hurtled in in a panic, and a fox hurtled out of the pipe equally panic stricken. Ferrets often bolt foxes. One winter I was ferreting a large rabbit warren on the Dyatt Estate in Lichfield. It was during a particularly cold spell, and the ground was frozen so solid that I had to find some way of pegging my nets, for it was impossible to drive a peg into the frozen earth. I made a ham-handed job of fixing the net to stones, old roots and anything else available. The nets might just about hold a rabbit for long enough for me to grab it. I put in my old sandy jill ferret, who trundled into the earth with her usual indifference. The nets exploded: five winter-coated cubs shot out of the earth, casting aside the nets like gossamer.

Lucas mentions one hunt that regularly used a hob ferret to bolt fresh foxes from an earth. Many naturalists have noted that foxes frequently give way to small families of hunting stoats or weasels. Foxes seem anxious to avoid any form of conflict with mustelids. Foxes are easily trundled out by a ferret if they are fresh, and unaware of any danger above ground. If the fox is driven in by a hound pack, lurcher or even terrier, on the other hand, he will be more than reluctant to bolt, and will chop any ferret inserted to bolt him. I once had a useful line ferret killed by a fox who was lying up in a rabbit warren, alerted only by the fact that I had begun to dig to the line ferret feeding on the rabbit.

Dogs often become trapped and buried while out fox hunting.

THE FOX

This statement tends to puzzle the non-hunting fraternity, who feel that just as what goes up must come down, it is self-evident that whatever goes into earth must be able to get back out. Sadly, this is not the case, as many upset terrier men will vouch. The question is, how do dogs get trapped and is there anything the terrier man can do to prevent the tragedy? There is no real answer to the first part of the question. Rock earths are death-traps, particularly rock earths situated in old quarries or glacial mounds. Pit workings, particularly the illicit drift mines dug by strikers during the 1926 General Strike, are places to avoid. Not only are such places somewhat 'out' from the safety regulations point of view; most of the timbers are also rotten, and the roofs always falling in. Moreover, pockets of deadly methane (fire damp) and the even more lethal hydrogen sulphide (stink damp) are quite common. An exhausted dog, breathing deeply and crawling into crevices filled with these gases, is soon in desperate trouble.

Movements in the roofs of these workings cause sizeable cracks in the rock strata – one in Foch Wen Pontycymmer was nearly six feet wide before the rocky roof fell in. Animals such as foxes live in them, and with their sinuous, feline-like bodies can easily negotiate the hazards. A dog, however, finds it difficult to crawl up these crevices, and impossible to crawl back down. Fault lines, particularly when worn smooth and widened by running water, are very dangerous and occur with great regularity in limestone areas. These are impossible places from which to try and rescue a trapped terrier. Sometimes skilled dynamiters are called in to blast cracks wide enough for the terrier to crawl free, but more often than not the weight of the rocks on either side of the cracks resist even dynamiting. A crack that has taken maybe a million years to form is reluctant to yield at a few moments' notice.

Now we must deal with the commonest cause of a terrier being trapped below ground. Foxes are lithe and sinuous, so sinuous that no dog can enter a crevice or hole through which a small vixen has crawled with some difficulty. Forget stories about dogs of fox-like proportions; size and weight may be similar, but the skeletal and muscular structures are very different. Terriers need to dig to reach these foxes, and so they get down to the job with vigour and enthusiasm, both of which qualities are not only highly commendable but also very oxygen consuming. The soil they are displacing must go somewhere, and it usually goes behind the dog. Gradually a wall of soil builds up between the terrier, digging like mad to get at the fox, and the entrance to the earth. Sooner or later this wall shuts off, or limits, the air supply, and the terrier, who has now made such exhausting efforts to get to his fox, quite simply dies of asphyxiation. Often he also suffocates his fox as well, but many diggers have observed that when a terrier is found suffocated, a few feet further on may be crouched a very live fox – frightened, but still alive. How? Well, the fox is not exerting himself so much as the terrier. Therefore its oxygen needs are less, and a creature who leads a subterranean, or partially subterranean, life builds up considerable resistance to bad air and humidity. Autopsies on terriers' corpses can be instructing, though difficult to arrange as terrier men are usually reluctant to have their gallant though dead terrier dismembered. Most die from some form of heart failure rather than from straightforward suffocation. Violent efforts in conditions where the air supply is growing limited often result in cardiac malfunction. Climbers of high mountains and speleologists know how all sorts of cardiac disorders manifest themselves when a man is required to exert himself in places where oxygen becomes rarified.

This is also a good reason for why one should not enter two terriers in one earth, or send in another terrier to find the lost dog. While there are some terriers who do find trapped dogs, these are few and far between. More often than not a terrier sent in behind another results in absolute confusion and finishes up as two dogs trapped below ground. Oxygen is often scarce enough below ground without the second terrier entering to use up more of the precious gas. Furthermore, terriers are not in any way altruistic, and when they do eventually find the exhausted dog, they usually push it into the jaws of the fox in their efforts to reach the quarry. I dislike working two terriers underground in any circumstances. Once a dog is trapped, there is little another terrier can do to help, but a whole lot to hinder.

When trying to rescue a terrier, it is important to keep other dogs silent. Tie up other terriers a few fields away if possible, and keep all clumping about and banging to a minimum. You will certainly need silence to detect any movement in the walls of soil. Often terriers are found only a few feet from the start of a very long dig, separated from the diggers by a solid wall of soil that has completely muffled the barking. Often useful detecting equipment can be made to detect any noise or vibration below ground. Much of this equipment works in the same way as a stethoscope. These home-made pieces often work, and I cannot think why manufacturers have not patented such devices. Surely there would be a market for this equipment.

One useful piece of equipment that has been patented, and indeed improved on, is the electronic locating device. This is quite simply a pellet (inserted into the dog's collar) which gives radio signals which can be picked up on a type of receiver much like a transistor radio. As one nears the source of the signal, the bleeping sound becomes stronger, and as one moves away from the source, the sound becomes much weaker. This device was originally designed for locating ferrets lying up on the kill, but it works just as well on terriers. Early receivers, in addition to picking up the sounds of the transmitter, often picked up the occasional snatches of radio programmes, but the manufacturers have now ironed out these problems. What has not been ironed out, of course, is the fact that such devices have to be carried in the dog's collar, and no terrier man will usually allow a dog to go to ground wearing a collar. Such a dog is in great danger of getting hung up on the roots of trees and strangling himself to death.

How can the terrier man prevent tragedies happening? Quite simply, there is little he can do once the dog has vanished down the earth entrance, for the whole matter becomes a duel between dog and the earth, with only God as Umpire. The only way the terrier man can help is to select carefully the earths into which he will allow his terrier to enter. The first thing the terrier man can do is keep his terrier on a leash until he decides the time is right to slip the dog. This is apparently self-evident, for a terrier running free will usually enter any earth before the owner can arrive at them to net, or station guns or coursing dogs. The fox then bolts well before the owner has prepared himself for the event, and the whole affair is something of a fiasco. Even so, I know of several terrier men who allow their dogs to run free. I am also baffled by hunts who allow a terrier to run with hounds – the hounds reach the earth, the terrier, now more than a little winded, rushes in to the fox, and the whole affair is reduced to chaos in a few moments. Yet many hunts used to breed leggy terriers to run with hounds. It would be interesting to know what happens to the free-running terriers when they reach earths that are impossible to work. A terrier man with a dog on a leash can decide if the earth is workable; with the dog running free, he can make no such choice. I repeat: keep your dogs on a leash until you have decided to allow him to work that particular earth.

Choosing one's earth carefully can also minimize the chances of tragedy. Avoid like the plague deep borrans, pit workings, lead mines and badly faulted outcrops. Certain earths are notorious for trapping terriers, and sometimes they look innocuous from the outside. Earths in pine woods are usually shallow, as pine trees are surface rooting and rarely break up the substrata to any great depth.

Deciduous wood earths should always be suspect, as oaks, and particularly elms, send down roots to great depths, breaking up the rocks below the soil. When such rocks are shattered by tree roots, it is easy for a fox (and particularly a badger) to excavate such holes in the rotten rocks. Such earths spell tragedy to a terrier. Jim Blake of Lancashire tells a tale of a dig in Durham when an established elm tree had to be dug up to recover a terrier trapped in the root-shattered substrata. John Winch, of the Fell and Moorland Working Terrier Club, warns that Durham has some noted 'to be avoided' earths – earths so notorious, in fact, that he puts his head in his hands when he sees terriers being led towards them. Clubs for working terriers are certainly of use, if only to warn tyro terrier people of the location of these 'mission impossible' earths.

It is also well to remember that breeding earths are usually simply excavated rabbit warrens, and that fox cubs often hide in the tiny galleries of the warrens. Terriers digging in to get to the cubs are usually quickly into danger, particularly if the rabbit warren is one of the pre-myxomatosis excavations, for an established rabbit warren is not only frequently vast in area, but often of great depth. In April 1975, which was a disastrous month for the Fell and Moorland Rescue Squad, four dogs after foxes were lost in such vintage rabbit warrens, and the fact that suffocation is usually fairly rapid in such earths is small consolation to the owners of the dogs who perish.

While on the subject of fox cubs, one word of advice. Most fox diggers dig up cubs from time to time. They are appealing-looking creatures, and the fox hunter may well consider rearing them. Don't! Not only do fox cubs carry a pernicious form of scabies, caused by the mite *Sarcoptes communis* (St Leger Gordon believes that this mite causes the death of more foxes than all the hunts put together), which can infect dogs and children, but foxes make damnably bad pets. They are always nervous, suspicious and have a permanently hunted look that smacks of paranoia. They are almost impossible to break to live stock, and when they escape will slaughter poultry with great ferocity. Furthermore, most are fearless of men, having been reared in human company, and will kill poultry under the very noses of farmers. Soon they will cause you notoriety, and although there is little the farmer can do by way of prosecution, the fox, as soon as he goes wild, is classed as feral game. It will cause the terrier man endless trouble and make him unwelcome at most farms. If you dig for cubs, remember that they can be a great pest kept as pets, and dispose of them humanely.

At one time people believed that foxes would hybridize with dogs, and that the resulting progeny would be excellent hunters. Lucas credits the corgi with having fox ancestry. Haagerdoorn goes even further, and in his book *Animal Breeding* suggests that hybridizing dogs with foxes would create a strain of silver fox that had some immunity to distemper. He cites a case where a flat-coated retriever dog served a vixen, and the resulting litter were used to infuse the silver foxes with distemper immunity. Haagerdoorn's claims have now been discredited. Dog to fox hybrids are not only unlikely, they are also impossible to create. Not even under artificial conditions, using artificial insemination, have such hybrids been produced, and although many dogs will tie with a tame vixen, no cubs-cum-puppies have ever been produced.

Taking foxes alive looks very impressive, but is perhaps one of the easiest tasks a terrier man will learn. Taking foxes alive is, in fact, far easier than hand catching rats, and far less dangerous. Should the occasion arrive when you have to dig your fox and wish to take him alive to be released in another district (but *not*, for heaven's sake, to bait to death with terriers), then it is quite simple. Wave a pole across the front of the fox's face – he will strike at it. Drag it away from him – he will tighten his grip still further, enabling you to get a grip on the throat or scruff of the neck and draw the animal from the earth. Now secure it by gripping it across the loins as well as by the neck. The task looks difficult, but is really quite simple. Bag your fox quickly. This will not only allow the poor beast to calm its fears a little, but will also reduce the chances of the terrier man having his hands bitten.

People often talk of the damage from badger bites, but though I admit that the badger is a terrific biter, so also is the fox. I have had many terriers dreadfully mauled by them. Bites on both man and dog should be treated as soon as possible and any household disinfectant will usually suffice. Foxes feed on rats and all manner of carrion, so bites fester unless treated. The neglected bite of a fox can turn quite nasty. I have seen some terriers receive terrific nips and bites from foxes. Fox bites, unlike badger wounds, are invariably inflicted on the dog's face, and some of the bites are very unpleasant indeed. Some wounds will cause the dog's face to swell until the dog is unrecognizable. The swelling subsides in a few days, particularly if the dog is treated with an antibiotic, but until the swelling has disappeared it would obviously be most inhuman to work the dog. Oxytetracycline given internally in tablet form is perhaps the most effective antibiotic, but penicillin is usually quite efficient. Many old huntsmen used to wash infected bites with whisky, which sounds effective but very expensive. Salt water and strong cold tea have little to commend them as antiseptics. Proprietary brands of antiseptic such as TCP, Dettol, etc., are not only effective, but also reasonably cheap. A good tip is to remember that slashes rarely go bad, but punctures can be a real source of infection and often go wrong. (See pages 197–9 for the treatment of wounds.)

Sooner or later, most terrier men will want to try their terrier at a hunt, either to obtain a working certificate or simply to try their terrier in public. Anyone not making trouble or causing offence is welcome at a hunt meet. They are very public affairs, and the meets are usually advertised in *Shooting Times* and similar magazines. Contrary to general opinion, hunt followers are a mixed bunch who came from all walks of life. Being welcome is one thing, but being allowed to try a terrier is another. Some hunt servants will readily encourage a person to put in a terrier when a fox goes to ground; others guard the privilege jealously. If you are acquainted with the hunt's terrier man or master, then the chances are that you will be allowed to try your terrier, but otherwise you may have to go to meets several times before being invited to put your terrier to ground.

If you do attend hunt meets, for heaven's sake avoid telling tales of how many foxes your terrier has killed, or of its deeds of courage at fox. Hunt staff will consider you are simply intent on putting the hunt out of business by wiping out the sporting quarry. Don't boast! It will get you a bad name and make you unwelcome. It is a well-known fact that a man with two terriers and a lurcher can kill more fox than any hunt pack, but hunt meets are social events, not a rabble assembling to create mayhem on the fox population. So if you are a vulpicide (slayer of foxes), shut up about it. It will not help you in any way. A few years ago a man that shot or dug a fox was boycotted by the landowners to the extent where signs proclaiming 'This man shot a fox' were pinned on his gate. Now the powers of the hunts have declined somewhat, and the vulpicide will usually find he is ostracized in a rather quieter way, but ostracized nevertheless. Be reasonable with the hunt staff and the chances are you will get an opportunity to try your terrier.

Working certificates are a bit controversial at the moment. Many people (usually those who do not have working certificates) loudly proclaim, 'Not worth the paper they are written on'. They are, quite simply, pieces of paper, or merely a brief note written by a master, in some cases the huntsman, stating that so-and-so's dog is game and has been entered to fox. To get working certificates for a terrier is not exactly difficult provided that it has been entered to fox. In any case, with training, most terriers will go to ground and give a reasonable account of themselves. Go with the hunt a few times and ask to try your terrier. If he goes well, approach the master at the end of the season and ask him to sign a working certificate. In spite of many comments to the effect that hunt masters are usually so autocratic that they will refrain from signing any form, few will refuse to do so if asked properly. With feeling against the hunts growing day by day, most hunt staff will go out of their way to create good feeling among the hunt supporters. Once you have your piece of paper, apart from the sense of satisfaction it may give, you will also be entitled to show your terrier in the Working Certificate Class at hunt shows – a slightly hollow honour, since most hunt shows should be treated as only a bit of fun.

Hunts are not exactly everyone's cup of tea, but at some point in a terrier man's life he may contemplate hunt service as a living. Beware, the life of a terrier man is hard, often boring and always badly paid. True, he will get a free house, free fuel and free flesh for his dogs, but it is a very tough life. Most terrier men's posts are advertised in a periodical called *Chamberlain's List*, a collection of all hunt staff vacancies for the coming year. Like the now extinct country hiring fairs, most appointments begin on May 1. There will be many applicants after a terrier man's job, most of them under the false impression that all he will be required to do is ride around all day putting terriers to ground. He will be in for a shock.

Master and hunt committee compile a short-list, and select the applicants for an interview. Here each one will be asked his reasons for applying for such a job and his qualifications (not academic, but practical experience in fox digging). The terrier man will be expected to own maybe three to six well-trained terriers, to be in good health and handy with a spade. Most hunt staff are reasonable people with good backgrounds, so applicants with criminal convictions of any kind are not usually appointed. Hunt staffs have to work as a team, so the belligerent, drunken, lazy or thieving personality will not be welcome.

Make no mistake about the work, it will be very hard. During hunting days you will be up at the crack of dawn, but on other days you will be required to work in the kennels, to collect fallen animals (often in a state of ripeness) to prepare the same for feeding, and to valet for the master and huntsmen. If you have been used to working set hours, prepare yourself for the task of not finishing until work is completed, even when it means working well into the night. Many start out on the hunt service ladder, but few survive more than the first year before going back into industry and other employment where the hours are shorter and the work less arduous. If you are suited to hunt service, then it is a very congenial job. Most hunt kennels and stables are happy places. It should be sufficient proof that whole families have for many generations been in hunt service.

THE QUARRY

Your terrier has learned to go to ground and bolt foxes. How will you catch your prey? There are several methods. If you have a terrier and no other equipment, it is possible to block all known holes with wood or stones and dig to the fox your terrier has trapped below ground. Care must be taken to block all possible exits, even the most minute holes, for, as I have mentioned, foxes have very small girths and can get through amazingly small cracks. Provided the earth is not too deep or rocky, then such a method will pay dividends, though it will require much effort to dig out some foxes.

Provided one can persuade the fox to bolt, nets are a useful way of catching them. These are simply large purse nets with very strong draw-lines and made of rather thick twine or nylon. Foxes often bolt into rabbit purse nets, and so long as one is quick at getting to the fox, they can be held. More often than not, however, rabbit nets will be unsuitable for holding a fully grown fox. I once bolted a large dog fox while out ferreting. He flashed into the nets, convulsed slightly and pulled the peg out of the earth. He staggered nearly a mile before actually throwing the nets and getting away. Fox nets are usually more than adequate for holding a fox, and a fox thus netted usually will have an undamaged pelt – an important factor at times when pelts are fetching up to £15 apiece in the capricious fur market. It is also worth remembering that, when the foxes hit the nets, they invariably go into the short cataleptic trance. As the fit is of short duration, the hunter should waste no time in dispatching the fox quickly and painlessly.

Foxes can, of course, be shot as they bolt, though a load of buckshot does little to help the pelt. I dislike guns, and I dislike gun men even more, so perhaps I am a little biased. If more than one fox is present in the earth, the sound of the first bolted fox being shot at does little for the morale of the fox still below ground. Many foxes will slink back into the earth to fight the terrier rather than face gunfire. Furthermore, foxes that are not immediately killed but peppered with gunshot often die prolonged agonizing deaths from sepsis. Foxes are hardly noted for their hygiene, and their earths are nearly all havens for staphyllococcus bacteria. Thus infection of even slight wounds is on the cards. I once caught a small vixen in my snares. She was desperately thin and emaciated. Her hind quarters were simply a mass of suppurating sores caused by a blast of buckshot. Several of the pellets had entered the intestine via the anus, and the bowels were an inflamed peritonitis-ridden mass. She had used her last resources of energy to strangle herself in my snares. I mistrusted gunmen before this – I have thoroughly disliked them ever since.

Lurchers or greyhounds find little difficulty in pulling down foxes, and some kill them very quickly. Most lurchers will kill (even if they

THE FOX

can't catch) hares, and foxes are not a great deal bigger than a hare. Any lurcher with a degree of pluck will tackle a fox, though a dog does need to be at least 22 inches high at the shoulder to kill a fox quickly and cleanly. Lurchers easily outpace foxes, which are a ridiculously easy prey for a good running dog. Bedlington/greyhound hybrids often make excellent fox-killing dogs, for not only does the resulting lurcher inherit a turn of speed from its greyhound ancestor, it also has the guts of its Bedlington parent.

If you intend to kill foxes for pelts, it is advisable to run a fairly big lurcher alone rather than slip two together at a bolting fox. A single lurcher often finds little difficulty in fox killing, but when two tackle fox, it usually results in a tug of war which ruins the pelt. Bull-terrier lurchers are quite common on the Welsh border, and even the heavier reject lurchers (there is considerable wastage in bull-terrier lurcher breeding) are extremely useful fox dogs. The fox-killing lurcher should first be entered to small quarry such as rabbits and hare before being slipped at the more formidable fox. Since there is no natural antipathy between dogs and foxes, lurcher owners may often be surprised and disappointed when they see their dogs refuse to tackle fox. A lurcher should be allowed to see a fox killed, or a carcass worried, so that it comes to regard fox as legitimate prey. Lurchers with a high proportion of greyhound, or other sight hounds, hunt fox with greater enthusiasm than most. Greyhounds will usually tackle foxes quite fearlessly and in spite of stories regarding the inability of greyhounds to hunt by

Dai Fish's famous pack in the early days.

using their noses, a fox is sufficiently aromatic for most greyhounds to follow by scent should they lose sight of him. Greyhounds often suffer foot damage if coursed over rough ground, however.

Gwillym Hardwick of Blaengarw was, in his day, perhaps the finest exponent of the terrier/lurcher combination at fox hunting. He recommended mating a tall collie sire to a greyhound dam and keeping back the strongest of the litter. His lurchers were always kennelled with his terriers and taken out fox hunting at a year old. After being allowed to rag skins, they were allowed to watch a kill, and after the death of the fox, were encouraged to join in the worry with the terriers. The lurchers were then allowed to course a fox and to assist in the first kill, so gaining confidence. Hardwick's dogs were remarkable. When his terrier went to ground, his lurchers would mark the spot under which the conflict between terrier and fox was taking place, even though the sounds were so faint as to be inaudible to the human ear. When the fox bolted, the lurchers bowled him in a trice, and within a few minutes it was all over.

Personally I find greyhounds far from satisfactory at coursing bolted foxes. They invariably degenerate into screaming banshees if a fox pokes out his head and looks to see if the coast is clear – not exactly the best way to encourage Reynard to bolt. Furthermore, it is usually quite difficult to make greyhounds stay close at hand during a fox dig, unless they can be held on a slip. So, for the solitary fox-hunting man, using a greyhound can become a bit of a liability. Lurchers, particularly greyhounds ameliorated with collie blood, are far more tractable, but in the greyhound's favour it should be mentioned that lurchers enter to fox far more slowly than the pure-blooded sight hound.

There are a few falconers who specialize in flying eagles at fox. Although the emperor Frederick II of Germany, author of the famous *De Arte Venandi Cum Avibus*, states that both golden and imperial eagles take fox with almost contemptuous ease, I have not found this to be the case. Eagles have to be fairly sharp set (hungry) before they contemplate a flight of any sort, and need to be nearly famished before they will tackle a fox. I have bolted several hundred foxes for falconers with eagles, but I have never known one catch a fox. The Khirgiz of Southern Russia train a type of golden eagle called the Berkute, and this reputedly will take not only fox, but also the Asiatic wolf. It may be that the Asiatic nomads are far more in tune with their eagles than are British falconers. I have yet to see an eagle keen enough to put in more than a pathetic stoop at a fox.

To round off this chapter on the fox, here is an account of a typical dig based on my diary notes, dated 30 September 1975. Mr Tom Cope of Huddersfield phoned to say he had had several hens taken

THE FOX

Two bobbery packs: above, c.1914, below, a bobbery pack today.

by foxes in the last few weeks. Over a period of ten weeks or so, fifty free-range layers had been killed or damaged by foxes. I phoned four useful diggers, Ian Robertson, Charley Little, Andy Johnson and John Wall, and we met at my cottage at 8.30. For three hours John and his bitch, Spidey, had tried every earth along the soil embankment without success. The weather was inclined to be too warm to encourage a fox to go to ground, and like as not the culprit was lying out in the kale or bracken. At 12.30, Charley Little's dog, Skippy, a big powerful Jack Russell, bolted a vixen from a small copse of alders and the fox was run to ground a few hundred yards from the said wood.

This earth into which it had disappeared was in a railway embankment, but we had permission to eradicate vermin along that stretch of railway track. The embankment was largely black loam and clinker, so would provide little difficulty in digging, but the roots of the scrub oak and alder had matted together to make what at first appeared an easy job into a very difficult dig. We checked every earth opening within seventy yards of the main earth, and blocked with sticks and stones, all the holes that led into the main earth. We then entered Charley Little's dog, Skippy, who found immediately and began to bay, the fox moving around the earth for a good twenty minutes before the baying ceased. Eventually we concluded that Charlie's dog had cornered his prey in a blind tunnel, and we began to dig to the sound of the barking. It was very hard work as the roots had to be severed with short axes before we could dig out the gritty loam. We eventually cut a deep tunnel nearly twelve feet long into the embankment – not really what the railway authorities had bargained for when they had granted us a permit, and I had visions of the 6.35 from Birmingham disappearing into a chasm.

Charlie's dog emerged from the dig for a breather and a drink. His face was caked with mud caused by the earth and grit adhering to the wounds on his face. His face had been bitten to ribbons, several long rips made in the muzzle and one cheek ripped to the gums. Obviously the vixen was in a vantage point and able to rain blows on the dog's face. John Derry crawled into the tunnel and found a vixen peering out from a gap between two rocks. Skippy's head was now resembling a football and the swelling had closed both eyes. To have put him back would have been cruelty, but still we had a vixen to dig out. I crawled in and viewed the situation. Both rocks were enormous boulders and impossible to shift. It was time to give her best and to chance Tom Cope's wrath at further fowl worrying. I could have gone for a gun and shot her at point-blank range, but not one of our team is a gunman and I dislike guns, as the reader knows. John Derry decided to try his bitch, Spidey, whose career as a hunter had been very unsuccessful up to that date. She crawled into the tunnel and began to bay in a most half-hearted way. The diggers were disappointed to say the least. They had dug for nearly five hours and had little to show for the effort. Spidey suddenly went mute and we heard a tugging sound. By some miracle of agility she had caught hold of the vixen's tail and dragged it from the lair. I dispatched the fox rapidly and painlessly.

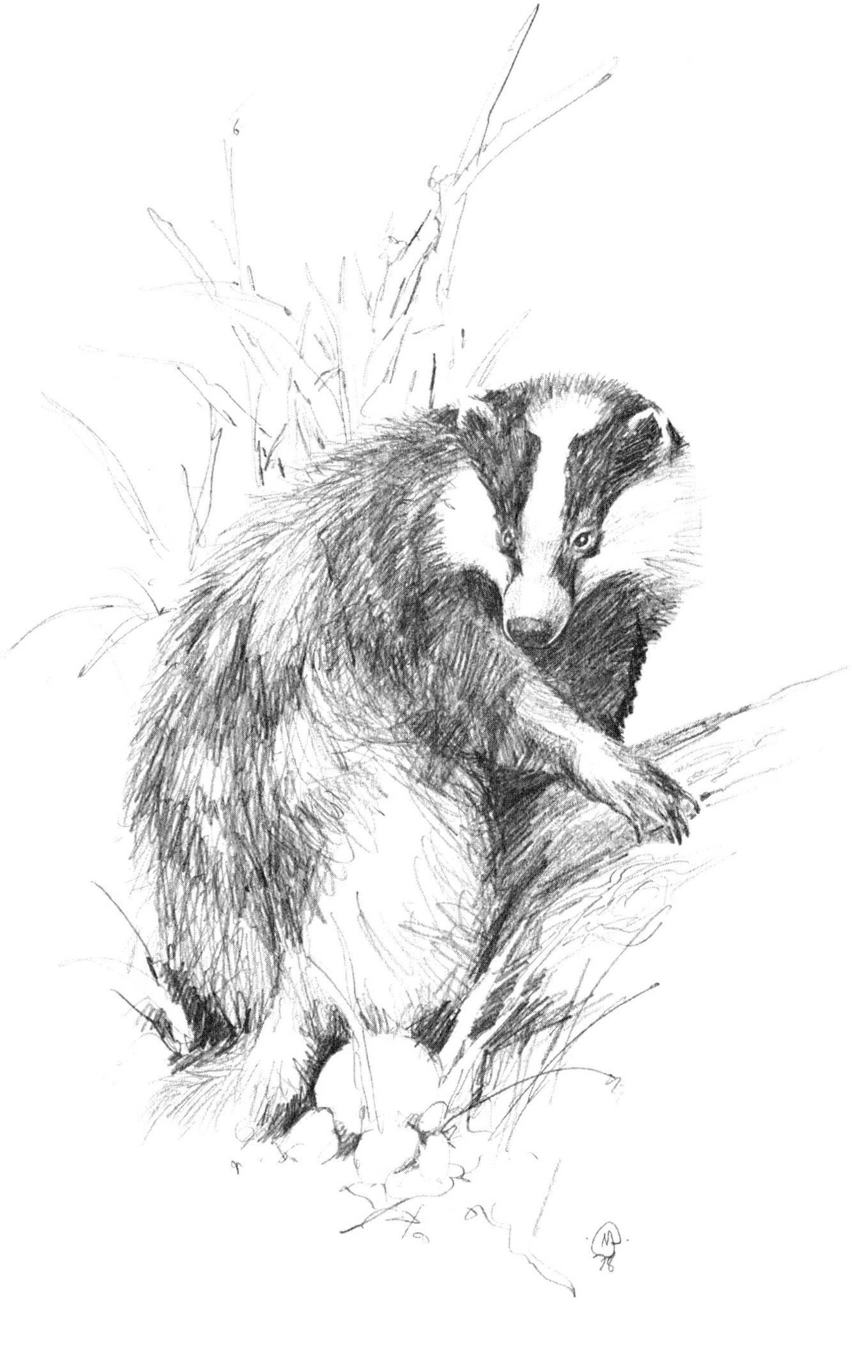

THE BADGER

To the town dweller, whose only acquaintance with badgers must be the prettily written but absurdly anthropomorphic book *The Wind in the Willows* by Kenneth Grahame, the badger must appear as a genial, overweight, erudite old beast. T. H. White in his lovely book *The Goshawk* eulogizes over the corpse of the badger slung across a gate, and calls him the last British bear. In truth both pictures are misleading. The badger is a member of the stoat family, albeit a phlegmatic stoat, streets apart from the quicksilver weasel or the blood-craving polecat, but nevertheless a stoat, and thus a member of the greatest family of pound-for-pound battlers on the face of the earth. He wants no trouble and will not hasten to a fight like his smaller, fiery cousins, but provoke him to fight and seal all escape routes, and he will retaliate with startling ferocity.

He is a natural battler. Built like a tank, his vital organs guarded by strands of leathery muscle and fat, he is damned-nigh invulnerable to a terrier. His bite is almost legendary, and though he cannot bite through a spade blade as some country sages suggest, I have seen him put deep scores in a spade handle. His jaws are very strong and set in such a manner that they will break before they dislocate. The dentition of his mouth resembles the teeth of a 30-pound ferret. He is an anachronism, a relic of the time when bears and wolves strolled abroad in Britain, and he is built to defend himself against such predators that have long since passed into extinction. Such is his might that he has no enemies apart from man, who muddles through an Act of Parliament to protect him, leaves legal loopholes wide enough to drive a horse and dray through, and then issues an edict that the badger is harmful to public health and pumps cyanide gas down his sets. Perhaps he is a relic of the past, but so also perhaps is the sanity of those who concoct our stupid laws.

Sparrow describes him as the Oldest Briton, and he may well be correct, for fossil remains show that Brock was around well before the Irish elk slipped into the peat bog. He is also far more numerous than some naturalists would have us believe. Perhaps he is not as numerous as he was a century ago, when noted badger-digging families sent dozens to meet a grisly and ugly death in the Westminster Pit, but any doubting Thomas needs only to wander abroad at night with a poacher, his lamp and lurcher, to be convinced that the badger is by no means uncommon. He may not be as keen to make his living in towns as is his fellow predator, the fox, but the reader has only to journey through Derbyshire and Leicestershire to see the numbers of dead badgers on roads and railway lines to realize how numerous this fascinating animal is.

One of John Cobby's favourite tales concerns a late-night encounter with a roadside badger. During the early part of the century, an earth-stopper was travelling home late at night on his bicycle, his terrier carried in the pannier at the back. The bicycle suddenly hit a mound and threw the earthstopper several yards, spilling terrier and tools over the road. The mound moved, and suddenly attacked the wheels of the bicycle. He had hit a badger feeding on a rat or a small animal in the middle of the road. After a tremendous scrap involving the hunt terrier and Brock, the badger ambled away, but the bike wheels were too badly buckled to allow the earthstopper to ride the last eight miles home.

The badger is one of the few omnivorous members of the weasel family; martens will sometimes eat fruit, but badgers may go for several weeks on a fleshless diet. I cannot help feeling that it is not by choice, however, for the huge carnasial teeth indicate that Brock is a stoat and basically a flesh-eater. Perhaps his incongruous shape makes him far too slow to catch anything but a crippled animal. It seems likely that his taking to a more omnivorous diet was nature's way of saying, 'Adapt or die!' His adaptability stands him in good stead during crisis times. When myxomatosis struck the rabbit population, most mustelids – the stoats, weasels and polecats – went to the wall. But the badger, phlegmatic and unruffled, continued to maintain its numbers. He is one of the few mustelids not averse to carrion. I live near the famous Broughs Earths, a huge badger set that has been there for centuries. Every summer, hordes of frogs migrate to and from the numerous ditches in Huddlesford and many are crushed by motor vehicles. The badger often spends hours rasping the crushed frogs from the grit of the road surface. I have more than once found cat hairs in the faeces from badger latrines. I would imagine that a cat is far too fast for Brock to catch him, and a cat eaten by badgers would certainly be dead before Brock found him.

In hard weather in late autumn (but not in mid winter), the badgers from our near-by set often turn over waste bins for food, so they must have as catholic a taste as foxes – more so, in fact, for badgers will suffer no loss of condition if the vegetable content in their diet is high, but foxes suffer decidedly when the vegetable content of their food goes above twenty-five per cent. Carrion actually needs to be fairly ripe before Brock finds it unacceptable. I once tipped out a pile of chicken entrails, so ripe that my two lurchers refused to eat them, for my two tame badger sows. They sniffed them for a while, and then ate the whole nauseous mess.

At one time it was thought that, like bats and hedgehogs, badgers hibernated. The fact that they are rarely seen in winter probably gave rise to this theory. Even Geoffrey Sparrow, a reliable enough observer of European wild life, believed that they went into some winter sleep. Not only do badgers not hibernate, they will venture forth on hunting forays even during the coldest weather. Possibly they did hibernate at one time, but from meteorological evidence we know that over the years the British winter has become milder, so the need for a winter sleep and the near cessation of body functions may have lessened in the badger.

Their dietary needs in winter are far more limited than in summer. During the autumn a badger will gorge himself on any food obtainable, particularly fatty or carbohydrate food. Before the first frost he is at his fattest: a rolling obese tank, puffing and panting with exertion. In winter time, the fat is used up, usually fairly slowly, as the level of activity in the badger set is considerably reduced (badgers of record weight – I believe a 50-pound boar has been recorded – are always taken in autumn). Not only is metabolism reduced in winter, but the latrines are used less frequently. Even captive badgers become unenthusiastic about food in cold weather. My own cub, a sow badger, ate practically anything in autumn and her weight went up to 36 pounds. By the end of the winter fasting, during which time even favourite food such as chicken heads was eaten only half-heartedly, her weight dropped by nearly 8 pounds. A great deal of research has yet to be done into the way some animals can reduce their dietary needs during times of hardship.

A great variety of vegetable food is eaten. Bluebell bulbs are dug up and greedily taken. Potato clamps are often raided, particularly in early spring when the badger's ravenous appetite returns. Faeces samples also reveal that quite a lot of corn has been taken, particularly in late summer when playful badgers will often roll the corn flat and probably pick up the grains, though the damage a family of badgers actually do to a field of corn is quite negligible. Farinaceous food is usually much appreciated, and even bread scraps have been taken from my dustbin by cub badgers from our neighbouring set. Frances Pitt, whose amazing book *Diana, My Badger* is a pleasure to read, says that her badgers were besotted by plum cake and would eat it *ad nauseam*. My own badgers would often eat large quantities of bread without loss of condition.

Of course, animal protein is needed to keep a badger fit over a long period of time. Badgers eat considerable quantities of worms and insects as well as small mammals. Rabbits may well be taken – though probably only if they are diseased, crippled or literally senile, for no badger is capable of outrunning a healthy rabbit. Although Brock's eyesight is poor, his sense of smell and hearing is very acute, and he is often able to crown down on top of a very young litter of rabbits. I have also seen rat hairs in the faeces, but for the life of me I cannot iamgine how Brock manages to catch a rat, being not only ponderous, but nearly blind. A healthy rat would find little difficulty in evading such a creature. Hedgehogs are natural victims as they too, are ponderous, slow and nocturnal. People who have thrown live hedgehogs to badgers state that Brock bites straight through the spines. I have no knowledge as to whether this is true.

Northern farmers believe that badgers take lambs. Again, a lamb would have to be very slow, and what on earth is a ewe doing to allow a badger to approach her young? Most ewes with lambs are ready to fight it out with dogs of any breed, and any ewe would certainly see off a badger, who is not particularly interested in receiving a bad butting. I, for one, am doubtful as to whether Brock kills lambs, though he will probably eat dead ones, and I have seen one feeding on an unburied sheep afterbirth one night when I was out lamping with my lurchers.

Badgers are naturally shy of people, so attacks on poultry houses are rare. Once they have decided to raid a poultry house, however, there is little that can be done to stop them. They are the most persistent of creatures when they intend to get into a building, and will rip off planks, tear wire netting and do all manner of damage to get to the poultry. About six years ago I visited a neighbouring farmer's poultry yard to see the damage a fox had done. Six or seven hens were dead and a great hole had been ripped in the side of the poultry shed. The farmer was adamant that the raider must have been a fox, in spite of the fact that no fox could have done such damage – few would even bite through the wood to get to poultry, for foxes are suspicious of any poultry confined in a shed. Still, a fox it was, my friend was certain, and he produced a few reddish-brown hairs that had adhered to the shattered wood round the hole. Reddish-brown they were, but they were not fox hairs; an albino badger (reddish-brown with pink eyes) had raided the pen. I found him two fields away lying up in an artificial earth. Sparrow remarks that one of these was killed at Machynlleth, but such creatures are far from uncommon. Most badger diggers have dug golden badgers from time to time. I snared two by accident only a year ago.

Badgers can be a great nuisance around pheasant-rearing pens, for they find it easy to nose up the pens and gobble the inmates. Sparrow mentions a rather dirty trick he played on a pheasant-rearing landowner when he introduced a family of badgers to an ancient set. Most gamekeepers are reluctant to tolerate a badger near the rearing pens, and even the most passionately pro-badger naturalist can hardly dispute that badgers do take game chicks. Of course, once the pheasants and partridge are able to fly, or even run quickly, the badger can do little damage. He is also partial to game eggs, or any eggs for that matter, even ones in a state of putrefaction. Drabble, in his fascinating book *Weasel in My Meatsafe*, mentions that his badger was not only partial to the contents of eggs, but took delight in munching and eating the egg shells.

Little is known of the breeding habits of the badger. I know no one who has seen them mate. I once took three sows which had badly bitten necks (stoats, ferrets and weasels often mangle the back of the neck of the female when they are mating), but perhaps these wounds were the result of fighting, or of scratching to relieve some skin infection. The gestation of the badger is still unknown, and quite a few people who have kept solitary badgers in captivity state that they have had cubs born to sows six months after their capture. There is a theory that badgers can make a foetus dormant in times of trouble and allow it to continue growing when such times have passed. This 'delayed implantation' has been confirmed by tests, but little is known about why and how it happens. It may occur in humans as well: an obstetrician in the midlands has written a paper declaring that the phenomenon takes place in certain women: a child was recently born to a woman who had been pregnant for eleven months. The child was apparently normal.

Cubs are born on bedding-lined nests in deep portions of the set. They are very thin furred at birth, merely covered with a light layer of bristle-like hair, unlike fox cubs, which are thickly furred at birth, probably because they are born on the bare floors of the earth. In spite of the tank-like shape of badger cubs, they remain blind for several weeks, far longer than do fox cubs. This lengthy period of blindness has its use. Mustelids of all kinds seem totally devoid of any sense of danger when young, and the lengthy period of blindness ensures that they stay well out of harm's way until large enough to deal with any adversary they meet above ground. Every time I handle, or rear, a badger cub, I am always amazed at their strength. The struggle of a young cub at feeding time has to be felt to be believed. Even as babies, they are covered with bands of muscle that can resist a bite from a terrier. It is a curious fact that while dogs (even badger-digging dogs) settle down to the fact of a badger cub being in the house, cats seem to have a distinct mistrust of them, although I once reared a cub by allowing it to suckle one of my Siamese females.

A well-established badger set is a source of wonder. The word badger is derived from the French verb *bêcher*, 'to dig', and badgers are habitual diggers. The set is always being enlarged for some unfathomable reason. Many sets are simply underground cities; enormous areas can be undermined. One set in Conisbrough, Yorkshire, has stretched right under a country lane to emerge four or five yards beyond the opposite side. Near Repton, Derbyshire, a tractor fell into a set and the ground was so undermined that the corner of the field could not be ploughed. The legendary Broughs Earths, perhaps one of the most noted sets in Staffordshire, is literally a labyrinth. Foxes which were hard pressed by the South Staffs Hounds (now disbanded) often made for these earths, and were reasonably safe from terriers once inside these citadels. Often galleries undermine other tunnels and the topmost layers cave in. In one set in Wall, Staffordshire, the structure must be like a multi-storey block of flats. It is situated in an old canal bed, the sides of which rise vertically for about 90 feet. Several layers of tunnels exist in the sets, and the place is a noted death trap for any terrier going to ground in it. I know of at least three terriers that have met their deaths in the bowels of this particular set.

Leicestershire, which is justly famous for its badgers, has some enormous sets. It is no exaggeration to say that in every country pub in the county you will hear stories of badger sets that have held terriers for four or five days. Such places are practically undiggable, unless a terrier traps a badger in a blind hole near the surface. One set, some eight miles from Oadby, is reputed to be several hundred years old and has totally undermined an old house. In a house near my own cottage is a cellar where, if one listens carefully, one can hear badgers digging far beneath the slabs. The entrance to these earths is perhaps sixty yards from the house.

Badgers can shift enormous amounts of soil with their wicked front claws. Some naturalists credit them with being able to dig out a foot a minute in sandy soil, and Sparrow cites an instance where a badger had dug beneath a swimming pool at St George's School, Weybridge. Any terrier man with half a mind will give such places a clear berth when badger digging. All an onslaught in such a place will yield is a great deal of sweat and a badly bitten, or dead dog.

It cannot be too much emphasized that rock sets are absolutely deadly to terriers and should be avoided like the plague. They are usually fairly deep, following the crevices and faults of the rock and quite undiggable. Badgers have to be dug, for they rarely bolt, so putting a dog into one of these rock sets is absolute madness. A glance at the *Fell and Moorland Working Terrier Year Book* of 1975 will give the reader some idea of the problems to be encountered when working this type of earth. Sandy earths are equally dangerous, as the digging of the badger to escape the attack of the terrier may well bury the dog and suffocate him. 'Fox bench', a layer of flint-like ironstone just below the surface and undetectable from above, is perhaps the most deadly hazard. To dig it is hell, and spades and picks grow blunted and tempers very frayed; and a badger is rarely taken on such a dig. Sparrow cites the case of a huge set at Cissbury, near Worthing, where the flints are cemented together with chalk precipitate and resist most efforts to mine it. He goes on to describe how his Border terrier never recovered from a six and a half hours ordeal in this set. My personal nightmare earth is in Lincolnshire, where sandy soil and pine-tree roots prove an absolutely unbeatable combination.

It was almost inevitable that a nation as bloodthirsty as the British should feature the badger among some of their most barbaric practices. Alken, writing in 1820, states that the sport of badger baiting was exceedingly popular in London. Here a bull-terrier type of dog – Alken depicts the now extinct Blue Paul in his drawings – was required to draw the badger out of a barrel. Badgers reputedly survived weeks of this mindless torture and brutality before pining away and dying of sepsis and internal bruising. It was once the greatest boast of bull-terrier owners to have owned dogs that had actually killed a badger, though in past never present tense, you will note. Such stories were invariably untrue. As a boy I saw many fierce duels between dogs and badgers, but never actually witnessed a terrier draw any considerable quantity of blood from an adult Brock, let alone kill him. I once saw a frightful battle between a plucky 40-pound, old type Stafford that had seen off many dogs, and a smallish, maybe 26-pound boar badger. At first it seemed an uneven contest: an agile, aggressive, fast-moving dog against a ponderous, much smaller, animal. Staffords always go for a hold, and this one was no exception. The badger immediately retaliated by three rapid bites delivered with the speed and force of a piston, and the dog reeled back, two teeth and the front of its lips missing. I never saw a dog soak up so much punishment as that one received during the battle that took place in an old coal truck (the usual place for dog as well as for man fights in mining valleys). After nearly an hour the dog was exhausted and had lost a considerable quantity of blood, but the badger, though badly bruised, was not even wounded.

No single dog can actually kill a badger, I am sure. I once bolted a badger when hunting my terrier pack – I had twelve dogs out that day, and most could kill a fox single-handed. In spite of furious efforts, they made little impression on Brock but a great deal of impression on my pocket, for the vet's fees for attending to my damaged dogs were stupendous. Few badgers want trouble, but when unable to run they will put up a staggering display of courage. When I hunt with lurchers at night – the sport generally referred to as lamping – my principal quarry is usually fox rather than rabbit. At one time I hunted a very hard-mouthed lurcher called Bear, a mixture none too judiciously blended of greyhound, saluki and deerhound, with perhaps a dash of collie. She was no spectacular hare dog, but was dynamite on foxes. One night I had had a fruitless run on an estate near Whittington, and was about to return home when Bear moved towards a sound in a near-by copse. She had one motto – if it moved, kill it – and although she was five weeks in whelp I was still hunting her as she had much *savoir faire* at fox killing. This was not a fox, however, but a large, 41-pound badger. A running fight ensued, with me desperately trying to hold the protagonists in the beam of my torch as they crashed and rolled through the wood with Bear trying to deliver a rather futile *coup de grâce*. After about five minutes I decided I couldn't take the damage Brock was doing and killed him with a blow across the snout. Bear looked as though she had been through a saw mill; she was dreadfully mauled and bruised, and lost her litter the next day. Since then I have made a point of breaking any lamp dog to badger, and now my lurchers simply run up, investigate the snuffling ursine shape and return to heel. I repeat: no single dog is a match for a badger.

On the other hand, I have dug to badger to find a terrier baying at a very fresh corpse. At one time it would have convinced me that the dog had slain the badger (even though the body was unmarked), assuming that the dog had gone for a throat hold and strangled Brock to death in the manner by which Fell terriers kill foxes. I now realize that this is not the case. Autopsied corpses of such animals revealed that they died either of asphyxia through lack of air as they dug on, or simply of heart failure brought about by fear and the unaccustomed exertion of a battle with a terrier. These are probably the 'my dog has killed badger' victims, dying from some physiological malfunction rather than from the direct onslaught of a fight. Make no bones about it, Brock takes some killing.

Badger bites are also unique in character. Fox wounds are usually punctures or slashes, and are as a rule inflicted on the faces of their opponents. It is these punctures which invariably go bad when the dog is bitten by a fox. Badger bites are a different matter. Most are pincer bites, and occur below the face and on the neck of the dog. They are invariably delivered with great force, and sometimes do considerable internal damage even though there may be little superficial wounding. Barry Dainty, the one-time terrier man to the Warwick Hunt, lost a very useful dog in strange circumstances during a midnight run at a badger. At the time he ran a small team of terriers at night, marking rabbits in the light of his Land-Rover and running them with a bobbery pack of collies and terriers. One night the pack had a brush with a badger, and his best dog, a hard-bitten, rough-coated, Russell-type terrier, returned to Barry in a very distressed state. There were no wounds, but the dog was dead within five minutes of coming off the badger. The windpipe had been literally smashed by the badger's bite.

In the early 1970s, an action group, probably inspired by the anti-bloodsport brigade, set about trying to get the badger put on the list of protected animals. Various propaganda campaigns were attempted to show the public how scarce the badger was becoming. Not one eminent biologist put his name to the campaign, and no concrete evidence for the dwindling population of the badger was offered. The public in general, however, had never seen a badger and tended to believe in the growing rarity of badgers story. In 1973, however, an Act to protect badgers was passed. It is often said that the law is an ass; this law certainly is. It is, on first appearance, a most stringent Act – fines of up to £200 for each badger caught or killed, prosecution for possession of a fresh skin, and so forth. It is a really severe law until one small point is examined and the whole Act collapses into a rather silly joke.

If the owner of the land on which badgers live decides that the badgers are causing him problems, then he is perfectly within his legal rights to allow someone to dig out and kill or move the badgers. Thus, any landowner giving a terrier man permission to dig his badgers has only to say that Brock is causing him trouble to prevent a charge being brought against the badger diggers. Few people actually poach badgers – a huge hole in the ground is hardly something that can be kept secret for long. Therefore few badger hunters work without permission, and permission from the landowner is enough to get most cases quashed before they get to court. Furthermore, the possession of a badger skin, even in fresh condition, is certainly not proof that the owner has killed a badger. Many badgers are killed in roadside accidents every year. I fed one to my ferrets a matter of a month before writing this, and gave the skin to a friend. Had I therefore committed a prosecutable offence? Such an Act must have been hurriedly drawn up to have so many obvious loopholes. It must also have been drawn up by town dwellers, unaware of country ways.

More recently we have had the brucellosis scare and Brock has been accused of being a carrier for this unpleasant bacterium. Moves are currently afoot to exterminate badgers in selected areas with full government approval – exterminate, not thin out. Pitifully little research has in fact been done on badgers and their connection with brucellosis – pitifully little, that is, on which to base a decision to send a species to extinction. I would be equally interested to ask whether rats, mice, hedgehogs and such like also carry this infection. In our fearfully overgoverned and muddled country, we seem only too quick to accept a bureaucratic decision to rush in and destroy the badgers before suddenly realizing that most wild creatures probably carry this disease. Scientific surveys can meanwhile be made to prove anything that people in power wish them to prove.

Now let us assume you have had permission from the landowner, who is also willing to state that the badgers are a pest on his farm (though it is interesting to ask precisely in what way they can be regarded as a pest). How therefore do we hunt and catch this semi-protected and probably totally bewildered creature, who has alternated between an animal to be protected and one to be ruthlessly persecuted? There are many ways of taking badger, and badger digging with terriers is frankly not the most efficient.

The most effective method is to mark the sets and salt an open space (a large field for preference) with chicken giblets, paunch or what have you. Next, wait until after dark and take a lurcher and a spotlight attached to a motor-bike battery. You will then be able to run your lurcher at the feeding badgers. It is easy meat for a dog with the speed of a lurcher – easy, that is, until he catches up with the badger. Most trained lurchers with experience of badger usually adopt a peculiar method of dealing with Brock, merely rushing in, seizing him and throwing him off balance and then getting smartly out of the way to escape the retaliatory bite. Most lurchers, particularly collie-blooded lurchers, become extremely dextrous at dealing with badgers and avoid getting too badly damaged as a result of these encounters. It is now comparatively easy for the lampers (and there will need to be at least two of you to come up on the protagonists) to catch and lift the fleeing badger by the tail and put him in the bag. But, for heaven's sake, get the dog on a leash before you attempt it. The tailing of a badger is remarkably easy providing you remember to shake the beast to prevent it climbing up its own tail and biting your hands. A dog running loose when you attempt the exercise is a liability to end all liabilities, for you will have your work cut out concentrating on bagging the badger without warning off a dog hell-bent on trying to 'help' you. Once, when I was taking a fox alive, a woman released her hitherto placid little Border terrier, who promptly raced in and savaged my buttocks. Badgers are rarely damaged by picking them up in a lamp with lurchers.

Dog and badger: an engraving of 1815.

Another method is to move quietly round the sets while the badgers are out feeding and net the entrances and exits. A noisy terrier, or maybe a beagle would do as well, can now be slipped and encouraged to hunt the badger, who, sickened by the whole procedure, high tails it for home and becomes enmeshed. This method is recommended in that most plagiarizing of books, *The Master of Game*. Fascinating as it sounds, I have never tried the method, and neither have any of my friends, one of whom remarked in a very practical way, 'Who on earth makes nets to take badgers?' This is a minor consideration, for such nets could easily be ordered from firms who specialize in making heavy-grade fox nets. *The Master of Game*, however, ends its monograph on badger hunting with a curious legend. Apparently it was believed that if a child were to wear shoes made from badger hide from the time when it began to crawl, the child would be able to outstrip a horse at running. This is one story that the author did not steal from Jacques de Fouilloux (the rest of the book quite brazenly plagiarizes other writers' material) and seems to be an invention of the author's own fertile imagination. I can find no reference to the story in folklore, nor can I guess at a reason in sympathetic magic, for the badger is a slow and unwieldy creature.

The fact remains that neither activity is the work of the true terrier, so let us move on to examine the properties of the ideal badger-digging dog. As I have mentioned, the biting power of Brock far exceeds that of any terrier. In the general free-for-all, no-holds-barred scrimmage that takes place when a terrier decides to 'mix it' with a badger, the terrier is bound to come off the worst. John Caius, an oft-quoted, archaic and inaccurate authority, mentions that the terrier's task is to 'nip, bite and make afraid', and this just about summarizes the job of the badger-digging terrier. The ideal dog should stand off the badger and bay to direct the efforts of the digger towards the quarry. If the dog tackles his foe, he will usually be very badly mauled; if he hangs back timidly a yard or so distant, Brock will promptly begin to dig in. Furthermore, the ideal badger dog must be a sticker: a dog that will stay to his badger for a considerable period, not popping out for a breath of air every few minutes. Should he fail to stick at his quarry, Brock will have dug in a few feet further on by the time the terrier returns to the task, or, worse still, have ambled back to another part of the set, leaving the digger the problem of starting all over again.

The badger dog should moreover have a good nose. Badgers, when frightened, dig in very rapidly, presenting the digger with a tunnel filled with loose soil once he has dug down to the dog. A dog that will work such a place and locate Brock through the wall of loose soil is priceless (and quite a few fail in the task, believe me). Hence a dog with an exceptional nose is essential. Another quality overlooked by most working terrier books is voice. A dog that works badger must give tongue like thunder. The dog that is mute is worse than useless, but a dog with a weak piping bark is nearly as bad. Some terriers have very weak voices. Malcolm Haddock once bought a well-bred puppy for work with the Meynell Hunt. It was an extremely plucky little dog, but had only a feeble, falsetto bark. She was quite useless for work below ground.

Here, then is a summary of the qualities to be sought in the ideal badger dog:

1. He should be game, but not foolish enough to tackle Brock head on.
2. He should stay to his badger, giving tongue continuously.
3. He should have a good nose to locate Brock after he has dug on.
4. He should have a good strong voice to guide the diggers; particularly important in very deep sets.
5. As a final qualification, however game the dog may be, he should in no way be neurotic or ultra-excitable. A dog that is slightly neurotic will, when he receives a good drubbing from Brock – and it is part of the education of a terrier to realize the fighting potential of his quarry – sometimes become so fearful of badger as to bay like mad at bedding on which a badger has slept. I have dug to quite a few dogs to find them baying at dried grass.

Dogs that are to be used at badger should become fairly experienced with small quarry before encountering the badger at home. Most of the old badger-digging clubs which flourished in the early part of the century specified that dogs should be worked (and worked regularly) to fox for at least six months before being entered to badger. This enables the dog to become acquainted with working below ground before he meets such a hard-biting creature. There is much to be said for this system of entering. Lucas, an acute observer of canine behaviour, states that he believes that dogs entered straight away to badger, and worked exclusively on that quarry, become disinterested or reluctant to work fox. This is not a universally held view, though I have noticed that dogs worked regularly to badger are more keen on Brock than they are to fox.

I know of one dog, a cross-bred Lakeland, who is an absolute demon to badger, but is not at all keen on working fox. Frankly, I have never found this to be the case with my own dogs. Many breeders eschew the fox and enter straight away to badger. The reasons are obvious: foxes are itinerant creatures and a hunter often can go for several days without finding one at home. Badgers, on the other hand, rarely up sticks and move (though some will when an earth becomes infested with ticks). Thus they are easy enough to find if one knows the countryside. This ease in finding the quarry at home often tempts the terrier man to try his dog to badger before fox. I have entered several dogs in this way, though I much prefer dogs to have a season to fox before entering to badger. Even so, I have never found that a dog really enthusiastic about badger has been reluctant to tackle fox.

Some badger sets, as we have already seen, are very old and often undiggable, particularly when the upper reaches of the set have been vacated and only the large deep tunnels are seeing any traffic. One such set has existed in Etwall, Derbyshire, for maybe a hundred years or so. Originally it must have been a small set on top of a steep clay bank, but now it is merely a two-holed set half-way down the bank, but so deep that it is impossible to dig. Dogs which vanish into its depths cannot even be heard baying. Such places are impossible to dig, though I once entered a small Russell bitch in a deep set in Herring Thorpe and she dragged out an undamaged cub. Avoid undiggable earths, they not only waste time and exhaust the diggers to no purpose, but the chances of losing a dog in such a place are strong. Should a dog become trapped in one of these ancient bankside earths, it is fairly certain to perish. New sets are usually a fair bet, for the badgers will have had little time to excavate deep tunnels. I once took a badger half a mile from where I live. It was a yearling boar, probably driven out from the main earths at a neighbouring farm. The boar was lying in a small earth only four feet long and under two feet of soil; such situations are rare, however, for few badgers are foolish enough to lie up in such exposed places.

The fundamental advice on sets is: choose your digs carefully. Once you have found your diggable set and you have your dogs entered to badger, the time has come to venture on your first dig. For an average badger dig, you will need several dogs. Enter only one at a time, keeping the rest tied up near at hand. There can be a problem here, however. Dogs tied close to the set will bark frantically when they hear their fellows baying at the badger beneath the ground. It may therefore grow difficult for the digger to delve to the exact position of the encounter between the badger and dog. So tie the dogs away from the set. Again, there is a problem. Dogs at at a badger dig often lunge frantically to get to their masters, particularly if the diggers are out of sight. This lunging often results in tragedy, as dogs can be strangled by their exertions. Lucas cites the case of one of his Sealyhams which came to a sticky end in this way. Also, do remember that these dogs are terriers, and terriers in a state of some excitement, so fights break out between them if they are tied close to each other.

There is one final problem where dogs are tied away from the set. The dog below ground has bottled up his badger and is baying at him; he becomes exhausted and comes out for a breather or something to drink; unless another dog is put in straight away (and I mean straight away), the badger either digs in at a surprising speed or, tragedy of tragedies, races further back into his labyrinth. Having to fetch a dog from a distance only increases the chances of this happening.

A good badger dog will not endeavour to tackle his badger head on. Many Lakeland-type terriers at Northern Hunt shows display sign of having done this, that is, teeth and lips torn off. But the dog should be plucky enough to drive back Brock if he decides to move back into the main set. Also, a good badger dog should endeavour to prevent the badger from digging in by giving him a nip or two in the rump when he starts mining activities. As soon as the badger turns, however, the terrier should leap back out of his way and continue baying. As the digger digs closer to the sound of baying, the terrier will need to be extra careful about keeping Brock in position, for as soon as a badger has an indication that the digger is crowding in on him, he makes a valiant attempt to get back to the main set.

Many expert badger diggers advocate using a tough, large dog for the last part of the dig. Sparrow recommends three types of terrier be used on a badger dig: a small, noisy dog with a good nose for finding; a stayer for the main dig; and a hard dog of fair size for the end of the dig. Brian Forsyth, of the Warwick Hunt, is not of this opinion, however, for he believes that the courage of a small dog is often disproportionate to its size, and that a small dog will often try valiantly to prevent a badger getting back into the main set. Forsyth has owned some excellent badger dogs, so perhaps I should be wary of disagreeing with this terrier expert. Personally I have always found that, when a badger tries to regain the main earth, a dog needs all his strength to stop him, and the stronger and tougher the dog, the better. However, Forsyth has certainly owned some cracking small badger dogs.

I once owned a very hard Russell-type bitch called Grim; I say 'Russell-type bitch' with my tongue in my cheek, for she was decidedly ugly and a mixture of a great number of breeds, but she was predominantly white – so, a Russell-type bitch. She was also a demon to work and would take a frightful pounding rather than let a badger get back into the main earth – an ideal dog to have when crowning through to a badger. Some line ferrets will come off the dead rabbit when the spade clangs above them, and some terriers, though they will endure great punishment from Brock, are what is known as spade shy, and at the last second, when the spade breaks through into the tunnel, will come off the badger, who promptly runs back into the set. Grim, on hearing the spade approaching, would go berserk, baying and attacking the badger to keep him in position. I missed her when she died. Such dogs are hard to come by and not easily replaced. The feats that are told by badger diggers are made all the more remarkable by the fact that they take place in the Stygian gloom of a set, against an opponent well equipped to fight in its subterranean blackness.

One often hears hunters state how their terriers drew a fully grown badger from the set. This is a little like the story of a man grabbing rats by the back of the neck: often talked about but seldom seen. If a dog tries to pull out a badger, Brock will clamp his claws into the side of the set, and it will take heaven and earth to shift him, let alone a terrier. Should a terrier encounter a badger in a drain with smooth sides, well, that is another matter. Some dogs develop a knack of drawing their badger out from a drain like a cork from a bottle.

The end of the dig approaches. The diggers now can see the earth-soiled coat of the terrier barking frantically at the piggy face of the badger. Now you've reached him, what do you do with him? First, you hold back your terrier, or get someone to hold him for you, for you stand far more chance of being bitten by the frantic terrier than by the badger. Lucas advises the use of tongs to draw badger; badger tongs being a piece of iron equipment shaped like pincers. With a set of tongs you can grip the paws of the badger and draw him from the earth. Sparrow deplores their use, referring to them as 'horrid implements'. They do, however, save a lot of rough and tumble at the end of a dig and allow the diggers to tail and bag the badger at leisure. The tongs may be cruel (I confess I've used them on wildcat), but I have seen far more cruel methods used. One of these was to drop a wire loop over the poor beast's neck, tighten it and drag it from the earth half-strangled and bewildered. The use of this method of taking a badger merits prosecution.

An equally loathsome method of dealing with a badger is to slip the entire team of dogs on him. Cruel, stupid and also expensive: a badger forced to make a fight of it will slash through the flesh of dogs like a hot knife through butter. He may be killed by the senseless baiting, but he will ruin or even take several terriers with him as he dies. I am reluctant to lend my terriers to other badger diggers for this very reason. Many will allow a dog to take a terrible

THE BADGER

A lurcher provides a useful partner to a terrier team: the author's lurcher Burke retrieves a hare flushed by terriers.

beating just to take the chance of seeing a baiting session – very cruel, and also, I hasten to add, very, very illegal.

So you've taken your badger. What do you do with him next? Many release him elsewhere. Others simply kill him. I am not certain which method is the more unpleasant. Boar badgers tipped out where other badgers have established territory are invariably attacked by the native boars and the fighting is always very fierce, though some sows may be accepted into the set. Many released badgers fail to adapt and finish as road accidents. Some hunters – Sparrow included – believed it is possible to restock old sets satisfactorily. It can be done: I've seen a few badgers resettled. The hunter, however, should ask himself one question: why did the original badgers vacate the set in the first place? If it was because the food supply dried up, then introducing new badgers will only ensure that they die a lingering death from starvation. If disease or tics drove them out (distemper sees off badgers with the same speed as it does stoats and ferrets), then is the virus or tic going to see off the new badgers in turn?

So the hunter kills his badger, quickly and humanely. What can he do with the carcass? First, let me debunk one of the countryside's leading con tricks, oft repeated by gullible town dwellers. Scarcely a week goes by when I do not hear the same ridiculous story with only slight variations on the theme. A town dweller visits a country pub and buys sandwiches from the landlord. The meat is delicious. 'What is this meat, landlord?' asks the townee, delighted at finding the real, long-lost countryside. Landlord emerges, sucking a straw, with corn husks in hair, loudly singing 'The Lincolnshire Poacher' and shouting drunkenly about the merits of well water and cider. 'Badger, sir,' he beams gleefully, putting on his shepherd's smock. Townee goes away extolling to the supermarket supplied world the eating qualities of poor old Brock. End of tale – order another whisky and soda. This same town dweller, who would turn up his nose at the thought of a cesspit or muck cart, has also wandered on to the gipsy site and been offered succulent hedgehogs by peg-making, spell-weaving folk dressed in Magyar costume. Oh my hunters, listen not to such tales of country madness. Badger is decidedly unpleasant to taste.

I am personally omnivorous to the point of needing psychiatric help, but from the culinary morass I have sampled of mole, rats, squirrels and hedgehogs among others, one vile-tasting flesh sticks in my mind as it stuck in my throat for about a month afterwards, and this is the taste of badger. The meat is very nasty. At a time when I was trying every form of food the countryside could offer, I caught and skinned out a large boar badger and took his carcass down to the domestic science room of the comprehensive school where I was then teaching. The hams (always the delicious portion in the townees' stories) were roasted and served up to some members of staff. To the last one, every teacher voted it the most disgusting taste they had ever experienced. It resembled very rank, greasy pork, the flavour of which stayed in the mouth for days – cloying, nauseating and overcoming the flavours of other food. Nicholas Cox in his *Gentleman's Recreation* says that the flesh of badgers is not eaten in England, but is often eaten in Germany and Italy, in which countries it is boiled with pears. Cox wrote in 1677 or thereabouts, and I often wonder whether he really believed that people anywhere actually tried the revolting mess of badger and pear, or was he writing deliberately to goad the said countries into open war with Britain? Badger meat is very nasty.

The skins have a slight use, though no furrier will touch them with a barge pole. They can make hard-wearing rugs if cured properly. Bill Brockley of Etwall had several that saw terrific wear but never seemed to wear out. They do need professional curing, however. The bristles are reputedly much sought after in Czechoslovakia (maybe another Nicholas Cox type of story) for making high-grade shaving brushes, but otherwise Brock's hide offers little as a fur. Early on in this chapter, I mentioned the fairy story that a child shod with badger skin could outrun a horse. I doubt whether you will find a new market for badger hides opening out on this basis.

The fat has certainly had uses in the past. Badger flesh rendered down yields a very thin, oily fat that was much sought after by makers of country simples and witchcraft remedies. One country simple suggests that the fat of the badger be used for alleviating sore throats. It is said that badger fat has the quality of being easily absorbed by the flesh, and many will vouch for the fact that if badger fat is rubbed on the chest, it is only a matter of time before the patient can actually taste the noxious stuff in their mouths. During the reign of James I, who was so obsessed with demons and magic that he infected the whole of Britain with a witch madness, several grimoires (books of spells) recommended the use of badger fat in witch potions. Before attending a Sabbat or gathering of witches, the witches would dissolve tinctures of aconite, hemlock, belladonna or henbane in badger oil and anoint their bodies with the greasy mess. After a short while a state of euphoria resulting from the powerful active drugs in the plants manifested itself, followed by a feeling of weightlessness and finally a deep coma. The dreams that came during the coma were often terrifying. Many Bosch-like creatures flitted through devilish rituals. The climax of the ceremony was the appearance of the devil in the guise of a vile-smelling black dog. The similarity of the witches' experience may have been due to the effectiveness of badger fat as a means of conveying drugs into the system, before the days of pills and injections.

Frankly, badgers have little or no economic value. Curio collectors prior to the 1973 Badgers Act were sometimes willing to pay as much as £1 for skins, but no furrier could even make use of such coarse-haired pelts. There are certainly no profits in badger digging.

Cubs are usually born in spring, and easily reared. Drabble, who is an expert at rearing young animals, states that, provided the baby is kept warm and fed regularly on a milk plus diet, then a cub will certainly survive and, indeed, will thrive. I do not like keeping wild animals as pets, though I have reared several badgers. They make endearing babies and, unlike foxes, become very tame, but are so strong and apparently so wilfully destructive that keeping them in a house certainly presents problems. Mine demolished settees and chairs, and one even dug up the quarry tiles from the kitchen floor. Unlike dogs, they cannot be disciplined or trained, or restrained when some mischief takes their fancy. The cubs slept with my Siamese cat as babies, but once they grew older they gave the cats odd looks that should have sent shivers up feline spines.

I would never again rear a wild animal in captivity. It brought me little pleasure, and the damage done by them, and the misery of having to give them away, was a bit too much for me, I am afraid. Boar badgers can also grow quite aggressive when they reach puberty, and an animal that bites as hard and fast as a badger is going to be a real problem if it decides to turn unpleasant. Last but not least, houses that have held badgers stink for many years afterwards, long after the badger has gone. Badgers are nearly blind, and find their way back to their set by dropping musk, produced by a gland near their anus, every few yards of their way. Thus, though nearly blind, they can scurry rapidly home when danger threatens. When reared in the house, they also drop musk on carpets, clothes and rugs (Drabble tells how they musked his carpet slippers). Such animals are not really suitable for house pets, and nor, for that matter, is any wild animal.

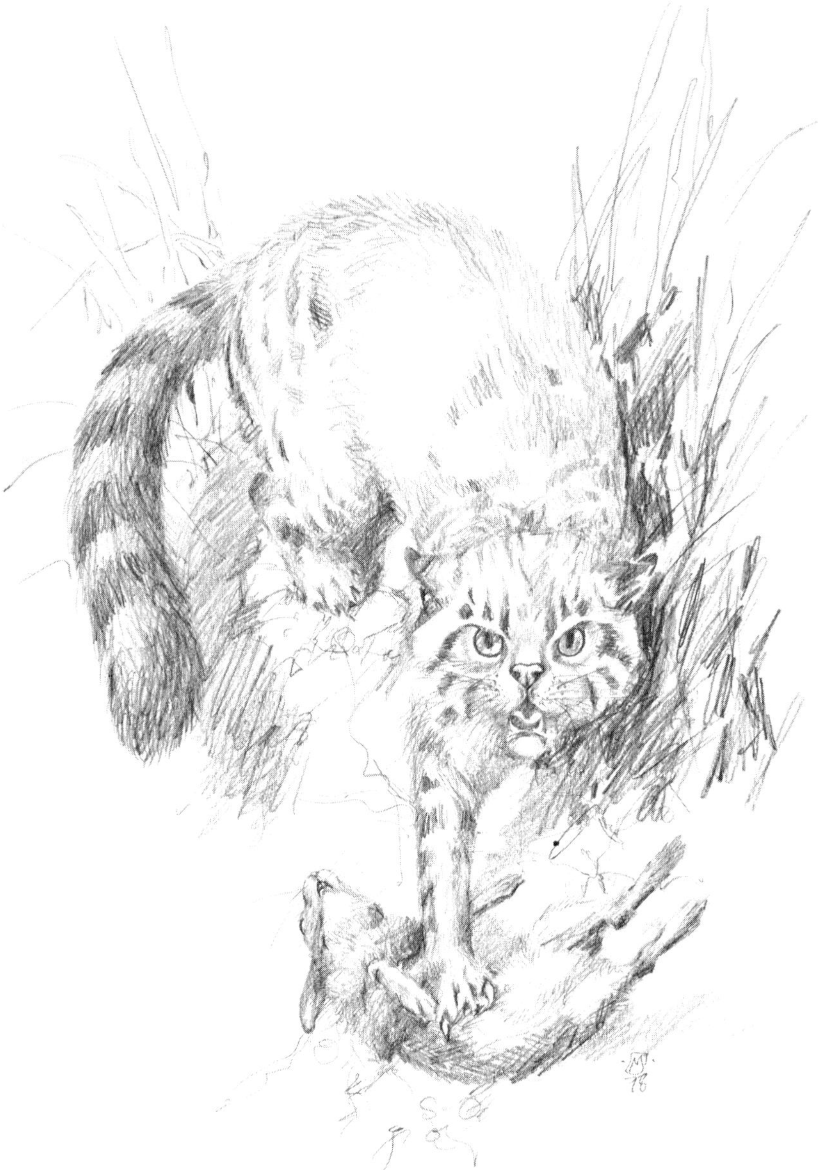

THE SCOTTISH WILDCAT

Few people have seen, let alone hunted, this ferocious creature which justly deserves the nickname of the 'British tiger'. Once this cat lived the length and breadth of England, but its destructive ways and savagery made it an obvious candidate for the extinction stakes in any populated area. Now it is found only in the northern districts of Scotland. Just as the brown rat was reputed to come to Britain with the hated George I, so the wildcat supposedly left England with Bonnie Prince Charlie and the Jacobites. Pure strains are now rare, even in the remote Scottish uplands.

The European wildcat is, however, found throughout Europe and some parts of Asia. It is a smallish feline, the females weighing perhaps $8\frac{1}{2}$ to 10 pounds, while the larger males scale in at 10 to 15 pounds. Monstrous-sized European wildcats are sometimes recorded. One caught in the Carpathian mountains is reputed to have weighed in at 33 pounds, but such sizes are uncommon in Britain. From the wildcats I have seen and caught in Eastern Europe, I am half inclined to believe that they are a distinct species, or perhaps a sub-species of *Felix sylvestris*. Most are tawny in colour with distinct tabby markings, though specimens similar in colour to the Abyssinian variety of the domesticated cat have been taken in the Carpathians. The head of the true wildcat is broader and more powerful than his domesticated cousin, and the canasial teeth are longer and stronger. The tail is also shorter, thicker and more bushy than the tail of a house cat. Perhaps the most interesting feature to the biologist (though the fact may be of doubtful interest to the hunter) is that the gut of the wildcat is only three quarters the length of that of his domesticated relative. In spite of these differences, the wildcat will hybridize with the house cat and produce fertile progeny. I am of the opinion that most of the motley collection of house cats one sees have at least a dash of the blood of this savage creature.

The domesticated cat is a descendant of the African wildcat, an easily trained and remarkably tractable feline, so tractable, in fact, that the Egyptian tombs depict paintings of nobles hunting water fowl with them. Trade with the Levant brought these cats to Britain. At first they were highly regarded (probably because of their scarcity in Britain), and Howell Dda (Howell the Good) put the compensation to be paid for the killing of a cat at the amount of grain it would take to cover up to the tip of the cat when it was hung head downwards. I believe these cats were very biddable, but by wandering in the English countryside they mated with the savage, untrainable European wildcats and produced the aloof, intractable cat with which we are all so familiar.

The Scottish wildcat lives primarily on small rodents, though it finds little difficulty in catching and killing rabbits and both blue and brown hares. Birds are also taken, and feather often forms the bulk of the faeces of many wildcats. Pennant, writing in 1776, refers to the animal as the British tiger, and states that 'it is the fiercest and most destructive beast we have, making dreadful havoc among our poultry, lambs and kids'. There is little doubt that they will take fawns and even grown lambs, and their method of dispatching them is interesting. The cat leaps upon its prey, gripping with its teeth the neck or shoulders and delivering a series of rapid and very strong disembowelling hind-leg kicks. The lacerations are astounding. C. St John, writing in 1845, states that he was quite amazed at the strength and ferocity of this creature. Fish are sometimes taken, and game chicks are fair and easy prey. Domesticated fowl up to the size of a small turkey are quite easily slain by wildcats. In Poland, one hill farmer once complained that a nearly fully grown nanny goat had been attacked by a wildcat, and although not killed, was so badly lacerated that she had to be destroyed.

This really is a ferocious creature, dangerous to stock and man alike, and no account of the wildcat would be complete without a description of the famous cat and man fight at Barnburgh in South Yorkshire. During the eighteenth century a young man was riding to his home along a rather lonely stretch of road. A wildcat, probably with kittens near by, was infuriated by the presence of the man and attacked him savagely, dragging him from his horse. He vainly tried to drive off the furious cat, and then, blinded by the wounds she inflicted, desperately sought to strangle his attacker, who retaliated by disembowelling the youth. The pair staggered into the church near by, and both died in the porch. The church still bears the name – the cat and man. Keepers in the Grampians frequently tell stories of cats tangled in rabbit snares who, on the approach of men, have torn out the snares and attacked their tormentors. Truly, this is a worthy, valiant and extremely dangerous adversary for any terrier.

The wildcat breeds twice a year, the male and female coming together for a brief and noisy courtship in March or June. Four or five kittens are born after a sixty-three day gestation. The African wildcat and the Siamese have a slightly longer gestation period.

Hybrid wildcats and tame cats often breed a third winter litter. Normally the female nests in disused rabbit burrows, hollow trees or rock clefts, and avoids the kitten-eating male, driving him off with great fury should he seek to enter the lair. At four to five weeks the kittens leave their nest, but do not usually accompany their mother on hunting expeditions until they are about three or four months old. It is during the rearing of these kittens that the female will take larger prey, including lambs, kids or fawns, perhaps driven by the hunger caused by the problem of rearing such a litter. Metz, a noted Eastern Europe hunter and naturalist, is not of this opinion, however, for he believes that such large prey are attacked and killed because the female believes them to be a threat to her litter. Many European hunters will attest to the fact that a wildcat returning from a night's hunting and accompanied by her litter will fearlessly attack both man and dogs. Jan Grabotsky, a Polish refugee, once told me he had seen a smallish female wildcat attack a large domestic pig who had the temerity to go too near her kittens. Any farm cat will be utterly fearless and dangerous in defence of her young, so the reader can easily gauge the savagery of a wildcat defending her litter.

Wildcat hunting requires a particular type of dog. While some dogs learn to rush in and kill these cats, it can be an expensive education to both man and dog before a terrier acquires such skills. Eyes, ears and entrails are often mutilated if a terrier decides to tangle with a wildcat. Early Cairn breeders (the working Cairn breeder, not the show breeder) often favoured dogs with well-furred faces and with hair overhanging the eyes, as they believed the fur took the blows from the cat's claws, thus saving the eyes from damage. Nevertheless I have seen several Lakelands and Russells that were reputedly able to dispatch wildcats without too much trouble. The knack seems to be to rush straight in and engage the cat at close quarters, inflicting a crushing bite or two the moment the battle commences. A terrier who fences for a hold with a wildcat is hopelessly outmatched and soon *hors de combat*. Some Airedales, particularly dogs of the Oorang strain, learn the same knack of disposing of bobcats and living to tell the tale, but many a dog is likely to be killed or mutilated before one is acquired which learns the skill of killing either a bobcat or Scottish wildcat.

Of course, the safest way of killing wildcats is to use a terrier that will stand back and give tongue like thunder, enabling the digger to delve towards the source of the din. Few wildcats live in deep earths as they usually rely on the mining activities of rabbits and never dig their own lairs. They are easily dug to, and their presence can be detected not only by the barking of the terrier, but by the nauseous stench that exudes from an angry, cornered wildcat. Wildcats that bolt – and many will if they do not have kittens in that particular lair – can be shot, or sometimes taken by lurchers or greyhounds. Those dug should be dispatched as soon as their heads become visible, as not only does this rapid destruction prevent unnecessary suffering on the part of the cat, but many will fly at the digger and his dog and inflict considerable damage.

Taking such a creature alive presents a problem, however. I have heard many boast that they can catch a live wildcat with bare hands, but I have never seen anyone attempt the feat. The problem of releasing a frightened tame cat from a net or snare is trouble enough and very dangerous; to handle a live wildcat is courting disaster. I have never used a tongs to draw badger, but I would not contemplate drawing a wildcat without one. They should be bagged as soon as possible, and the person with the unsavoury task of holding the sack should wear thick gloves or gauntlets. When the naturalists began to realize that the true wildcat was becoming rare and being replaced by a hybrid wildcat/feral cat, I caught several wildcats for private zoos and animal collections. Without exaggeration I may say that they present great problems if they are to be taken alive. Treat stories of them being taken by hand with a large pinch of salt, and never attempt to do it.

The kittens are equally fierce, though they obviously lack the strength of the adults. Even before they open their eyes they will spit and threaten when handled. True wildcats never become tame, even if taken very young. The noted naturalist, Frances Pitt, reared several that were impossible to tame, and always very fierce if she attempted to take any liberties with them. Even the hybrids between house cats and wildcat males will be unapproachable and wild. Some people have succeeded in breeding these cats in captivity. I have never been so successful, for some accident or other has always dogged my footsteps when I have attempted to rear Scottish wildcats. Such cats are not only difficult to handle, prone to sulky behaviour and almost paranoid in their shyness, but they seem to have absolutely no immunity to cat flu and the deadly feline infectious enteritis. In short, they do not make satisfactory pets – and that is a blatant understatement.

Terriers used to hunt these cats should have considerable experience with foxes and badgers before being tried to cat. On all occasions they present a fearsome foe to the working terrier.

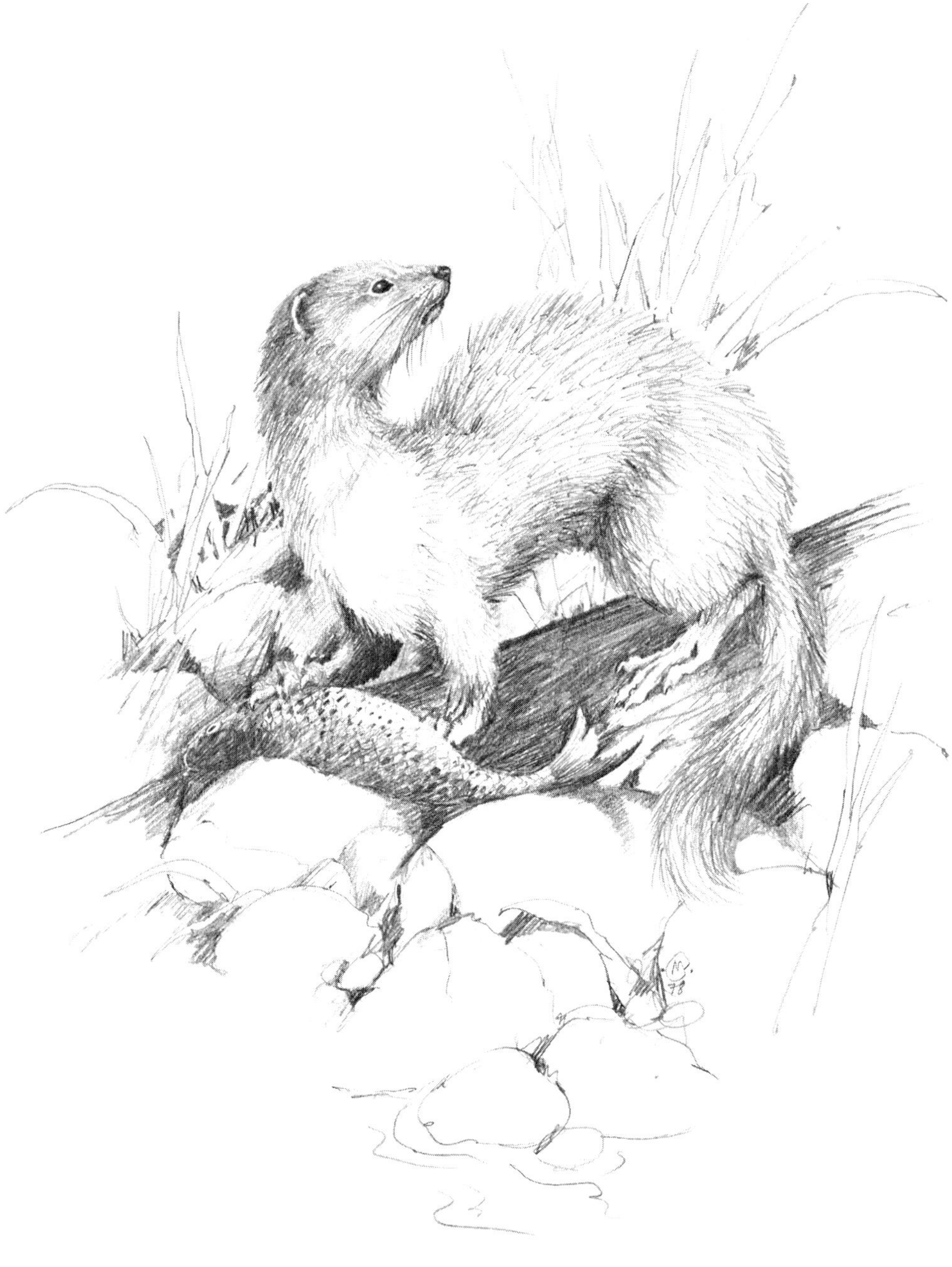

MINK

The mink is not a native of Britain and, like all introductions, has turned into a problem since it became established. Mink farming had been practised in Britain since 1929, and early escapes were common, but it was not until 1957 that there was any record of mink having bred in the wilds in these islands. Some small colonies were found in Devon during the 1960s and were treated as a rather interesting conversation piece, but in the last few years large numbers of mink have been recorded in most counties and they are now being regarded as a serious pest. Many otterhound packs, having perforce forsaken their original quarry, are now hunting mink, and several trap-making companies have patented mink traps.

Mink are roughly the same size as ferret. The female is almost identical in size to a jill, and the male is roughly twice as big. A good-sized male will weigh up to about 3 pounds. Although many different colours of mink have escaped from time to time, it is interesting to note that litters bred in the wild have invariably reverted to the dark brown colouring of their American ancestors. The pelts of these feral mink are of questionable value and tend to lack the quality of both wild American-caught pelts and the skins of mink bred in captivity. White mink are rarely found in the wild, even though many are farmed, as not only does the colour make them an obvious target, but, through some genetic mishap, most white mink are stone deaf – hardly a quality to assist the survival of an animal.

Mink rarely stray far from water, and invariably nest in the enlarged holes of rats or water voles. They are solitary creatures, coming together for a brief and violent courtship some time between February and April. At other times, the male is quite aggressive to the smaller female. The young are born some thirty-nine to fifty-two days after mating. Never sell any mustelid (stoat, weasel or otter, etc.) short for courage, for in spite of their small size, the stoat family are exceeedingly brave and, apart from the badger, usually lightning fast. Peter Robinson, a mink-farmer neighbour, once told me that he had seen mink apparently asleep when a rat raced across the wire top of their cage. They had literally galvanized into action and pulled the squealing rat through the wires. The whole action had taken place in a split second.

I always doubted this story until I attended a course on mink diseases at Penkridge. At the meeting I boasted of my speed of sleight of hand, and against Peter's advice foolishly offered to grab a live mink. It was white and looked so much like a jill ferret that I ignored his advice. After all, I had tailed rats and they were considerably faster than a ferret. I reached down to pick up the spitting, arch-backed creature waving my left hand just above his muzzle while my right hand darted in for the tail. I will never forget my surprise, as it all happened so quickly. Both hands were badly bitten before I could say 'knife', and five neat sets of punctures manifested themselves on my hands. Since then I have had a great respect for all kinds of mustelids.

I have only once been asked to deal with mink, and then only when a batch of six escaped from a mink farm. Legislation regarding the keeping of mink is now highly stringent and all compounds have to be escape proof. Many farms run ducks or geese in the compounds, as not only do they eat the food that falls through the wire-floored mink cages, but, when a mink escapes, they are literally sitting targets (sitting ducks, you might say) for the ruthless fugitive. The escapee slays a duck or so, and the remainder make such a din that the mink farmer realizes he has a break-out. Brutal, but absolutely necessary. Anyway, on this occasion the six mink did stop to kill the ducks but escaped from the compound. It was upsetting enough to lose £450-worth of breeding mink, but the local papers had a field day. To cap it all, one of the mink reputedly bit a child and the local rag went berserk. If the public had believed half the paper had written, the whole of Yorkshire would have declared a curfew and been placed under martial law.

The farmer, sensing future troubles, asked me to hunt down his six miscreants. Stories of mink being able to fight off a dog the size of a Labrador and putting whole packs of dogs to flight didn't really impress me, and I took three of my Jack Russells and hunted the surrounding brooks and rubbish dumps. I killed four of the six escapees and the owner never saw hide nor hair of the others. Although my terriers had numerous punctures on their faces, they were not in any way over-matched by even the largest male we caught. One female dived into a rat hole, and I foolishly put a jill ferret in to flush her out. Unlike stoats, who will usually make a bolt from a ferret – though several hunters near Bristol have vouched for the fact they have bolted mink while ferreting for rabbit – this mink did not, and drove my badly bitten jill out of the hole. I dug the mink with a spade and terriers, and dispatched her quickly. This, I confess, has been my only hunt for mink.

Mink can become real pests. Not only do they kill poultry and game birds with the same ferocity as an escaped ferret, but they swim with the dexterity of an otter and cause terrific damage in fish hatcheries. Norway and Sweden have been greatly troubled by feral mink that have wiped out salmon in certain areas. In Iceland, ground-nesting birds have been greatly reduced by the ravages of escaped mink. A farmer near Bristol stated that he had over a hundred ducklings killed in one night when a feral mink invaded his poultry yard. Brooks in whose banks mink have taken refuge are usually devoid of any forms of water birds, for mink hunt by night and find sitting water birds easy prey. It seems likely that if this creature ever becomes generally established in Britain, it will alter the fauna and subsequently the flora of our islands. It is fortuitous that otter-hound packs have begun hunting this creature now that the otter has become a protected animal.

In 1977, however, I judged the terrier class at the Monmouthshire County Fair, and saw some interesting terriers that the Chapman brothers had bred and which had been used for mink hunting. Eddie Chapman, who is terrier man for the hunt at Gobion, had mated his Jack Russell dog on to a crossbred Bedlington/Fell terrier bitch. The offspring resembled very leggy, narrow, black Fell terriers with the linty coat of the Bedlington granddam. These, I was assured, had done considerable work in mink hunting, and while no terrier was able to creep into the lair of a mink, they were much at home in water and admirable digging dogs. The docked puppies were very attractive, but the undocked adults looked decidedly mongrelly. Still, handsome is as handsome does, and the dogs had won an excellent reputation among local huntsmen.

Before leaving the chapter on mink hunting, I really must relate the story of a friend who, dissatisfied with his ferrets repeatedly jibbing rats, bought a kit mink to use as a ratting ferret. Sergeant's book, *Mink on My Shoulder*, had inspired this madness, and madness it was. True, the animal would enter a rat hole when it decided it was suitable, but in spite of its speed and agility, it suffered bad maulings at rat and 'jibbed' them, as would a ferret that had been badly bitten. When upset it was a tigress, and after a tussle with a rat was impossible to handle. It was also more than just prone to lie up once it had killed its prey. At rabbiting, it moved like lightning and never once gave a bunny a chance to bolt. Other mustelids have been tried in the place of ferrets. In the late nineteenth century, London rat catchers were tempted by the exotic imported Egyptian mongooses, but they, too, had little success with them. Advice to hunters: stick strictly to ferrets and forget about mongoose and mink.

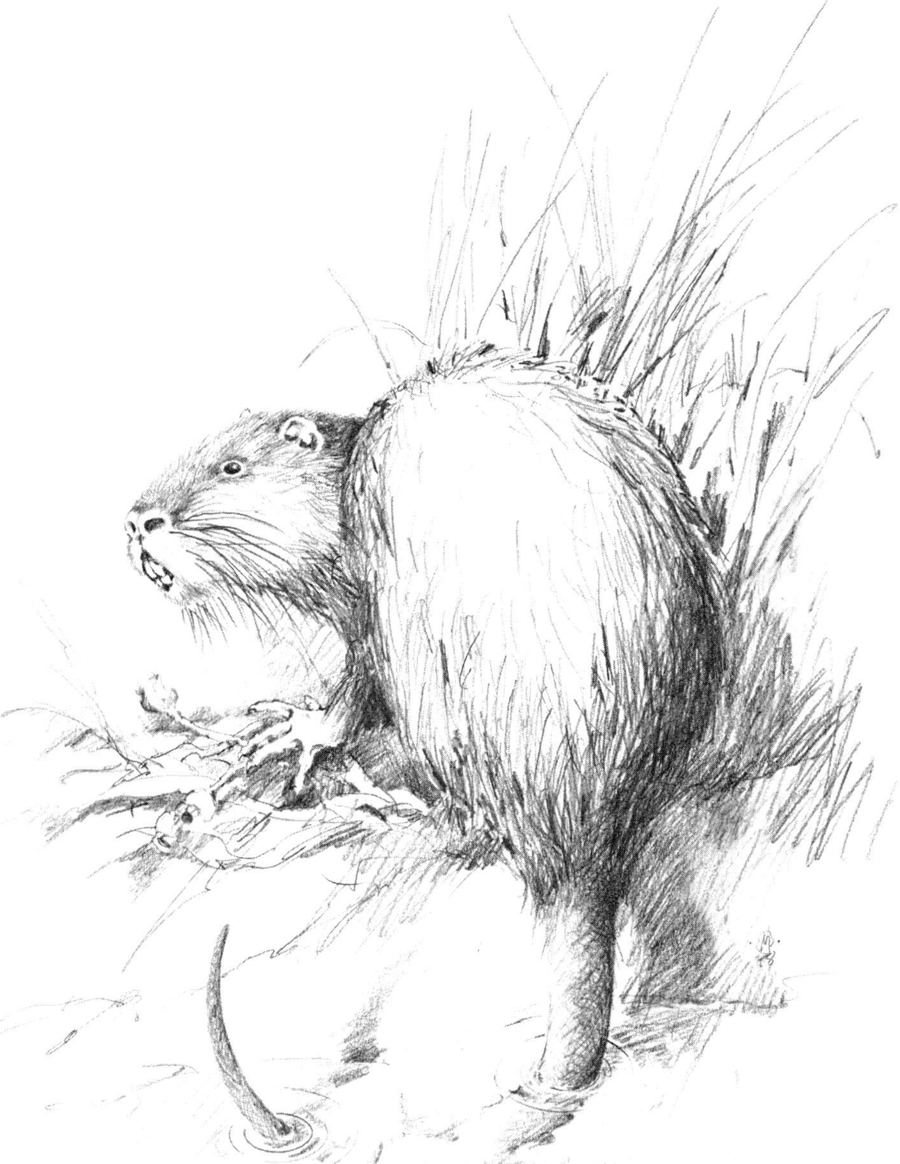

COYPU

I rather like coypu; they are, perhaps, the least offensive of the rodent family, and certainly one of the most intelligent, in spite of their ponderous, slow movements and their stupid expressions, made even more asinine by their huge orange incisors. My first encounter with a coypu was during my childhood, some twenty years before I hunted them. A rather tatty fair-cum-circus arrived in our village, and, in addition to the bored elephants, the scrawny lions and a mangy bear, the sideshows boasted the biggest rat in the world, caught in a London sewer after it had done some horrendous work gnawing workmen to pieces, according to the publicity. It turned out to be a gentle coypu, so tame that it would eat grass from one's hand. I was already besotted with rodents and shouted, 'It's only a coypu, not a rat,' and the manager of the stall immediately looked so pained and angry at the revelations of a precocious eight-year-old child that my mother hustled me out of the tent, from whence I went to annoy the lions.

Coypu are not natives of Britain, having originated in the marshes of South America. They are said by naturalists to be the principal food of some puma and jaguar. They are rarely found far from water, and swim and dive with the grace of fish. Coypu are one of the largest rodents, and specimens well in excess of 20 pounds have been recorded. Originally they were imported into Britain and bred as fur animals, for nutria (*nutria* being Spanish for otter) was a popular fur of the 1930s. Sooner or later escapees were inevitable, and as we have few predators capable of dealing with a 20-pound rodent, they began to breed in quantity. At first their arrival, like that of the mink, was greeted with mild curiosity. One article that appeared in a rural newspaper stated that the coypu was actually a useful creature as it kept the waterways clear of reeds and sedges and that great pest, the Canadian waterweed. They certainly caused little trouble during the wartime years, but in the 1950s the habits of the coypu changed. They tended to stop eating waterweed and started to cause a fair amount of damage to kale, cabbage and corn crops. Furthermore, they now tended to burrow into banks at the sides of the dikes, rivers and drains of East Anglia. A high tide penetrated some burrows and flooded adjoining fields. In 1962, the Ministry of Agriculture and Fisheries declared war on these creatures that had by now spread from the broads of East Anglia to the fenlands near Peterborough, and the public, alarmed by newspaper articles predicting 20-pound rats coming up the sewers, became decidedly anti-coypu.

Coypu are rather more nocturnal than they are diurnal, and become decidedly active after dark. Lurcher men, lamping the waterside fields in East Anglia, used to report large numbers of coypu feeding on sugar-beet crops. The females usually breed two or three litters in a year, and up to ten are found in each litter. What is exceptional is that the coypu produces young after an astoundingly long pregnancy of 132 days, where the usual rodent gestation period is very short (by comparison, rats have a twenty-one-day gestation period). There are compensations for such a long pregnancy: the young are born fully furred and can move around and swim a few hours after birth. The teats of the female are high on the flank, so suckling usually takes place while the mother is in the water.

The onslaught on the coypu population was entirely successful, and perhaps a little unnecessary. The fearsome winter of 1962 wiped out large numbers of them, and further culling has driven them deeper into the broads. Far from being a scourge of the countryside – the super-rodents, like something out of H. G. Wells's *The Food of the Gods*, that the popular press predicted – they are now becoming quite rare, even in East Anglia, and are never seen in any other part of the countryside. During their culling, however, they provided numerous terrier keepers with an interesting and out-of-the-way sport. My own team of hunters hunted them for several months, as did several members of the Border Terrier Club. Two hunters with pedigree Norwich terriers actually wiped out a colony that was becoming well established in Buckinghamshire. However, in spite of the hunting, trapping and shooting, there seems little chance of the species becoming entirely wiped out in Britain, for they now inhabit some of the less accessible parts of the Norfolk broads.

Coypu are not particularly exciting animals to hunt. Their burrows are large and not especially deep, so there is little chance of a dog getting trapped while hunting them. Furthermore, the coypu is reluctant to fight and much prefers to bolt if it encounters a terrier. Bites from coypu are never really serious, though pieces of the incisor sometimes break off and remain in wounds, causing sepsis. Wounds are rarely more than skin deep, for, in spite of its rat-like appearance, the coypu is unable to mete out the savage wounds of which the brown rat is capable. A rat the size of a coypu would be a tremendous foe, well beyond the capabilities of any terrier, but the coypu can scarcely be regarded as a sporting animal. A peculiarity of the animal is that, when swimming away from an attacker, it will hum quite musically. When really distressed, either by harrassment from terriers or by being trapped, they gnash their huge orange incisors so fiercely that pieces of teeth actually break off. This tooth-gnashing action is probably a protective mechanism meant to frighten off a would-be attacker, and it certainly makes the coypu sound extremely fierce. When a hunter goes to take them alive, they move at surprising speed and squeal loudly. I have received several minor bites from coypu I have tailed, but unlike rat bites, which invariably fester, wounds from coypu bites rarely seem to go bad.

Perhaps as a sporting quarry 'twixt rat and fox, the coypu has a place, but a terrier usually out-matches him. Only on one occasion have I seen a dog that could really be called damaged by a coypu. I once stayed with a terrier breeder just north of Norwich, and his hunting companion had a lurcher whose wounds made the dog look as if it had been hit by an express train. Some of the wounds were obviously fox bites, but, he assured me, the others were caused by the dog 'fielding' coypu while out lamping.

The pelts of British wild coypu are not of any commercial value as our climate is apparently not conducive to the production of first-class quality skins. In 1965, I took twenty-four reasonably sized coypu, ranging from young females weighing 12 pounds to a large husky male weighing $18\frac{1}{2}$ pounds. I set to skinning them, 'sleeving' the bodies as I would a rabbit, but no furrier would touch them, as the nutria, or fur of the coypu, is from the belly of the beast, not from the dorsal skin as in most fur-bearing animals. On tanning my pelts, most of the guard hairs and quite a few of the undercoat hairs fell out, and the resulting hides looked decidedly moth-eaten. Yet there is little doubt that the fur farms of the 1930s produced profitable pelts. It was, in fact, the war which altered fur fashions and, let it be whispered, probably caused several small fur farmers to turn loose their stock in the broads.

During the late 1960s, a television programme mentioned that a London restaurant was serving coypu meat to its customers – not quite as ludicrous as it sounds when one considers that bird's-nest soup, an expensive delicacy, is made from the spittle of swallows. Coypu meat never really caught on, which is perhaps a good thing as animals regarded as delicacies soon become extinct – nothing is quite as species-destroying as a rampaging gourmet. Coypu meat is really a little like bland rabbit flesh – in fact, all rodent meat is closely similar in taste, be it rat, squirrel or coypu. I fed a great number of them to my ferrets, but, for no particular reason, did not myself really fancy eating them in quantity, though they were no more disease-ridden than the average rabbit. It seems that the public felt the same, as coypu no longer appears on the menus of London restaurants.

Regarding the taking of young coypu – and I will re-emphasize that no wild animal ever makes a satisfactory pet – the hunter will need a Home Office licence before he is allowed to keep one. I doubt whether such a licence would be refused, though the powers-that-be might certainly require certain safety precautions to prevent the creatures escaping, and may possibly even require the males to be sterilized. Rodents are fairly low in intelligence and usually tame fairly well, particularly if taken young. Drabble actually had a very tame brown rat. Coypu are no exception, and become remarkably tame. The specimens at Riber Park would take grass from the hands of visitors, though few people would consider putting their hands too close to those huge, orange-coloured teeth. Breeders who used to keep nutria ranches tell me that some coypu became as tame as dogs and would actually come to the whistle. Although they are extremely tame as young, buck coypu become very fierce if forced to live a solitary existence. Sociable animals often suffer greatly when isolated from their own kind.

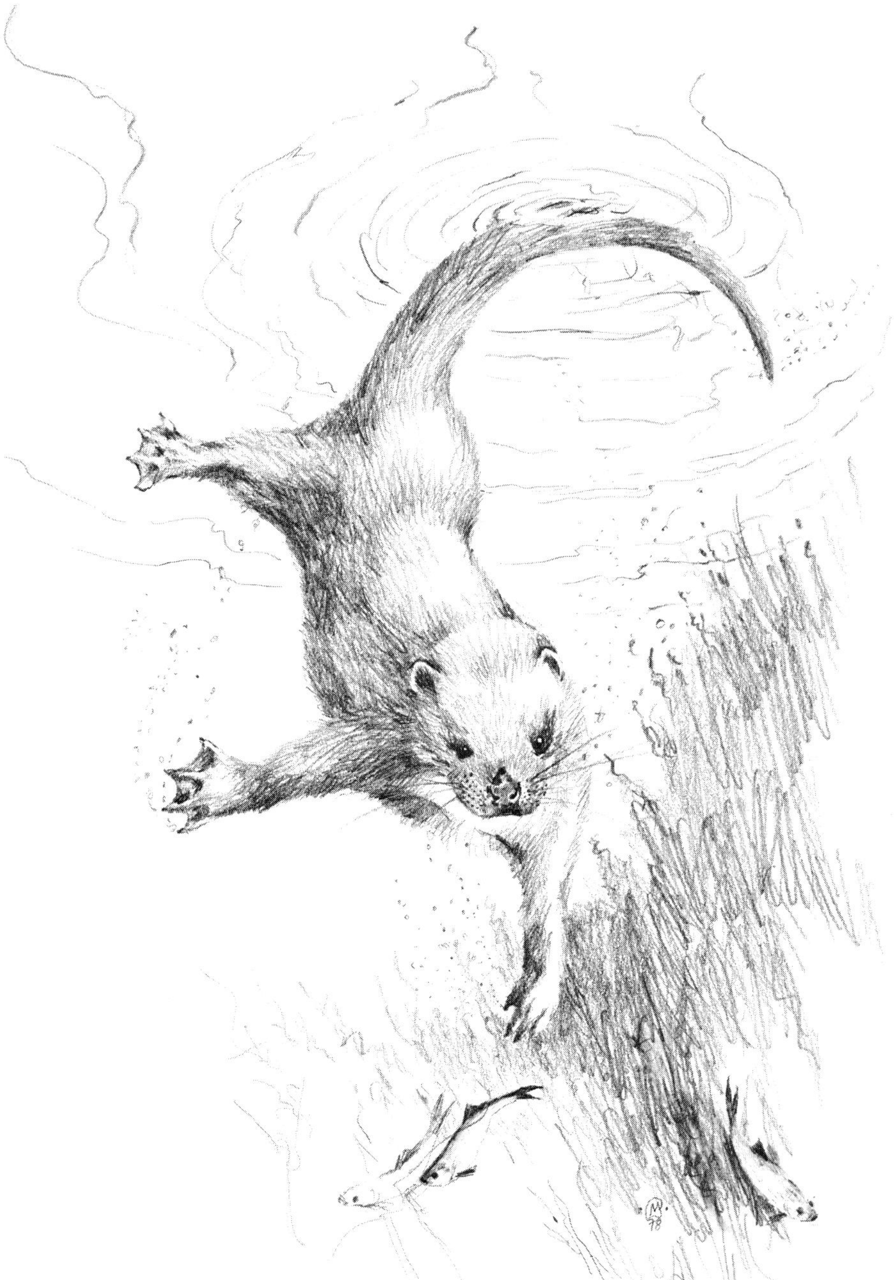

THE OTTER

(*Publisher's note:* Since the writing of this section, the otter has, as the author predicted, been placed on the list of protected species in England and Wales.)

Mark well this prophecy: this is the next animal to be placed on the protected list. It is true that more otters exist than most people imagine. They are seldom seen, however, as they are inclined to be rather nocturnal and rarely stay in one place very long. Maurice Burton believes that they are fairly common and cites several instances of them appearing on the outskirts of London. I am not at all happy about the accounts of otters in cities indicating the species to be fairly numerous. Far too many flat dwellers own exotic and unsuitable pets, and I have often been asked to supply otter cubs to bed-sits in London. When these people discover that an otter is not an aquatic dog, and not at all at home in a two-roomed flat as they were in Gavin Maxwell's cottage, they reject their pet, leaving it to try and make its own way in a rather hostile world. (The huge otter discovered wandering in the middle of Birmingham a few years ago, turned out to be a specimen of the marsh otter, found only in the Middle East.) I am not happy about statements to the effect that this creature is not uncommon. Not only has it been hunted by organized packs, but it also has to put up with the problems of pollution, and the effect of chemicals on its food – fish – is too well known to mention. Our streams and rivers are rapidly becoming poisoned, and the otter is bound to suffer as a result. He will certainly be the very next animal to be protected by law.

Otters, as mustelids, are cousins of stoats, weasels and mink, and like all these animals are both courageous and formidable fighters. An average-sized male is about 4 feet long, the tail accounting for about 15 inches of its length. Burton gives the record length of an otter as 5 feet 3 inches, but this measurement was taken from a skin and is just a little suspect. A healthy male will weigh between 20 and 25 pounds, but specimens taken by northern hunters have reached over 28 pounds in weight. Again, Burton quotes 50 pounds as the record weight for an otter, but again I am doubtful about this gargantuan beast. Was it really a British otter, or was it something that was imported and turned loose? A glance at Maxwell's book, *Ring of Bright Water*, will convince any reader that quite a few foreign species of otter do find their way to this country via livestock importers, and since all mustelids are difficult to keep under lock and key, they often make their escape.

The otter is typically musteline in shape: its body is long and lithe, and its tail, which is thick at the base, tapers to a point at the tip. Otters are designed for aquatic life, for not only is the body streamlined for swimming, but the ferret-like paws are webbed. The fur is a rich brown, and though some fur-bearing North American otters have brown underfur, the guard hairs of the British otter are dark brown but the underfur is a pale grey. There is little variation in the colour of the pelts of British otters, which is curious, for mustelid pelts are extremely variable.

The evolution of the otter is interesting, for it is only in comparatively recent geological times that it has taken to water. So recent is the move to an aquatic way of life, though the adult otter is very much at home in water, the cubs show a marked reluctance to leave the security of the land. What is also curious is that while most of the mustelids are solitary, the opposite sexes meeting briefly to mate before going their own ways again, the dog and bitch otter, having mated, stay together during the pregnancy and each help to provide food for the growing cubs. As soon as the otter cubs are capable of taking care of themselves, the dog otter leaves the bitch to seek another mate. Henry Williamson's fascinating animal novel, *Tarka the Otter*, is essential reading for every naturalist, and so far as I am concerned, reveals a far deeper knowledge of otters and otter behaviour than any scientific treatise yet published.

Whether or not the otter can in any way be classed as a pest is very much open to debate. The otter is certainly a wasteful feeder, and when fish are plentiful will merely take a bite out of the shoulder of the fish, play with the carcass awhile – as a cat plays with a dead rat – and then amble off to hunt a new victim. They are true mustelids, and kill far more than they need. Burton states that crayfish are a favourite food, but quantities of eels are also taken, which is something of a blessing to the angler, as eels are the bane of most fishermen. Many surveys have also noted that the principal food of otters usually consists of sick, injured or ailing fish, and that an otter in a well-keepered fishing water probably helps to keep down piscean disease by killing off the unhealthy specimens.

Otters will also take quite a few land animals, such as rats, moles and mice. Rabbits are sometimes taken, though I feel that these would have to be ailing to be caught by an otter. Water fowl are, of course, easy meat for a hunting otter, and I have twice seen sizeable cygnets taken from under the very nose of a parent swan. Riverside poultry keepers rarely complain about damage by otters, though there are several authenticated accounts of otters getting into poultry houses and, true to their stoat-like heritage, creating absolute carnage. An old sporting diary I have in my possession makes mention of the fact that one poultry keeper on an estate had several game fowl killed by an otter during the winter of 1847, and that when the miscreant was caught it was found to weigh 54 pounds. At one time I doubted the story, and treated it as an exaggeration, though the diary is clearly very precise in what it records. Since then I have found that many diaries note otters of record weight being taken during the nineteenth century. What has happened to the otter? Were the reports of huge otters greatly exaggerated, or were eighteenth-and nineteenth-century otters larger than their modern descendants?

The scarcity of the otter – and in spite of what most natural history books state, the otter is quite scarce – has rather limited the would-be otter hunter. Most otters are found on rivers and districts where hunting by otterhound packs has been regular. It is necessary to explain this bewildering statement. Rivers not hunted by established otterhound packs have usually been open house to anyone with a terrier or lurcher that is entered to otter, and the otter, which breeds all the year round, was afforded no protection from the amateur hunter. He thus either migrated, or quite simply became extinct, in these districts. In districts hunted by established otterhound packs, however, first, the otter was hunted only during the summer months when conditions were reasonably pleasant for the foot followers; and secondly, most hunts have gone out of their way, particularly in times when hunts have been rapidly losing support, to 'woo' the landowners. In return, not only have these landowners allowed the hunts to work the land and river banks, but they have also prevented trespassers from trying terriers and such like at otters. This has at least given the otter a breathing space, and allowed him to go in peace for most of the year. It must also be stressed that while some foxhunting packs are lethal on fox and kill great numbers in a year, otterhound packs have often gone a whole season without a single kill, or even, to be devastatingly honest, without sighting an otter. Thus otters have actually been on the increase in some otter-hunting areas.

The terrier owner who wished to try his terrier to otters has had to join an otterhound supporters' club to get even a slight chance of seeing the otter, let alone trying a terrier to one. A matter of a hundred years ago, nearly every otterhound pack was made up of huge, shaggy-coated, oily-furred hounds, descended, so Lucas believes, from the French Griffon Nurvenais. These dogs were wonderfully aquatic, possessed good noses and wed quite easily to otter. They were, however, fearsome fighters, and won a well-earned reputation for being savage with people. One otterhound master had the somewhat unwanted distinction of being eaten by his own hounds. In recent years, however, draft hounds from foxhound packs and some staghounds were used (Henry Williamson's Deadlock, the arch-enemy of Tarka, was a draft hound from a staghound pack who had lost his speed as a result of being disembowelled by a stag), and the old-fashioned shaggy monster hound has tended rapidly to become a thing of the past. Some hunts have continued to maintain a pack of pure-bred otterhounds, but Sparrow, in his famous book *The Terrier's Vocation*, states that not only are the foxhounds more easily obtainable, but they do the job better than the old type of otterhound. Lucas suggests that if a newly formed hunt was short of funds, a suitable pack could be created by mating a bloodhound stallion hound on to an Airedale bitch (Airedales were reputedly bred from an old-type otterhound); he goes on to say that not only do these hunt as well as otterhounds, but that they have the same fiery temperament as the old, shaggy hounds. Photographs of such hybrids show an animal that closely resembles a purebred otterhound.

A curious fact about both terriers and hounds that have been used to hunt otter is that it is reputedly quite difficult to get either dog to enter to otter. Parson John Russell, of terrier fame, was once said to have changed his fox-hunting hounds to otter for a season and to have hunted 3,000 miles of river without so much as finding an otter. He was then given an entered hound by a neighbouring pack, and within a few weeks his whole pack was hunting otter with great enthusiasm. This may be the case with hounds, and though Sparrow states that it is difficult to enter a terrier to otter, I did not find this to be so. While there is no natural enmity between dog and otter – a natural enmity that is often furiously manifested between dog and cat – neither is there natural enmity between dog and fox, yet dogs enter quite well to fox when properly trained. A terrier who realized that the otter was not forbidden quarry, usually entered with the same enthusiasm displayed when hunting badger or fox.

Otters are mighty fighters and can bite with great speed and force. Sparrow states that the bite is far more wounding than the bite of a badger, but I have never found this to be so, though it is worth mentioning that the punctures put in by an otter bite are capable of penetrating both flesh and bone. It is the speed at which an otter fights that makes it a dangerous opponent for a terrier, and it has always been wise to remember that an otter is simply an oversized, aquatically orientated stoat, with a fighting power proportionate to the increase in size.

During a hunt the otter would often take refuge in a holt or lair, which might be among rocks (which made the work of a terrier very difficult), or among waterside tree roots. Often the entrance to such a holt might be three parts under water, making it useless to try a dog that was reluctant to get his feet wet. The Dumfriesshire Otterhound Pack used Border terriers at one time, and these were amazingly good in watery conditions. Old-timer otter hunters frequently made a point of ratting their terrier puppies along dyke sides to get the terriers used to wet working conditions. This early ratting programme was obviously of great use to a dog that was to be used for otter hunting. Sometimes a hard-pressed otter might take refuge in an old fox earth, badger set or suchlike close to the waterside and in such places could give a terrier a fair amount of trouble, even though quite easy to bolt from these alien earths.

Upon land, the otter is a savage enough fighter, but its fighting prowess is greatly increased when he is in his natural element. Sparrow quotes Varndell, a former master of the Crowhurst Otterhound pack, who stated that he had twice seen hounds drowned by otters. The reader will remember that the formidable hound, Deadlock, went to his watery grave after a duel with Tarka in Williamson's book. Whether or not an otter will intentionally drown a hound is a little questionable. I believe that the hound dies after being overmatched in an alien environment, but then I am always reluctant to attribute human guile to animals.

Terrier packs have frequently been used to hunt otter. Alys Serrell, in her famous *With Hound and Terrier in the Field* (1904), gives some interesting accounts of grim fights between otters and her working fox terriers. Lucas also makes mention of a hard-bitten little pack of Border terriers that did very well on otters, though the most fascinating account of otter hunting with terrier packs is certainly to be found in Lucas's little known book, *The Sealyham* (1922). These intrepid little dogs gave their owner great service to otter, and in spite of the fact that their cloddy build made them more suitable for badger digging, they took impressive hauls of otter for Lucas. It is worth mentioning that Lucas never allowed his dogs to finish the otter unaided, for such actions smack of brutality and pointless cruelty. It always was a precept among otter hunters that otters taken by terriers should never be baited but dispatched immediately.

Before leaving this chapter, I really should mention in more detail the craze for keeping otter cubs as pets. In 1957 I caught two cubs when on leave from military service. I found some difficulty in selling them to a pet shop for £2 apiece, and some four months later the pet-shop owner was still stuck with his now almost fully grown cubs. After

Ring of Bright Water was made into a film, I found myself being offered £40 a cub from the same pet-shop owner, who assured me that he would buy every cub I could get, no matter what its age. Frankly, the whole thing had been reduced to absolute madness. Otters are not suitable as pets; they are expensive to keep and, being stoats, are so curious that they will wreck the average domestic house in a few days. Otters are impossible to housetrain, and will nearly always retaliate when chastized by fouling carpets, rugs or any other furnishings to hand. Furthermore, the diet of the otter is principally fish, and the faeces will leave its owner in no doubt as to this fact. I will now leave the subject of otter cubs as pets with a true story.

I once knew a delightful young woman who was both beautiful and intelligent – a rare combination in woman, I have found. Sadly, her character had a tragic flaw: she was a little bit of an exhibitionist and insisted on keeping the most strange, exotic and undesirable pets. Hearing I could possibly obtain an otter cub for her (she'd seen *Ring of Bright Water* three times, I believe), she was always at my kennels in the hopes of persuading me to get her one. One day, Alan Ryder, a close friend and amateur terrier man, turned up at my house with a cub inside his jacket. Too late, my lady friend had begged the damned animal. The cub was still blind and about four or five days old, I estimated – difficult to obtain, but very difficult to rear. Still she persisted and sat with the creature night after night, even taking it to her modelling engagements (she worked for a noted London fashion photographer). Within a month or so the cub was ambling around and just starting on its career of havoc. By the time it was six months old it had wrecked the flat, chewing cushions, demolishing lamp-shades, biting through electric wires and twice creating an expensive fire, the consequences of which the insurance company refused to pay for, though I doubt whether there was a clause to cover otter damage in the contract. The stench from its dung corner made the place smell like Billingsgate, but still she refused to sell the damned creature. She would take it for occasional walks along the streets of Chiswick, and numerous dogs who had never heard that dogs were reluctant to enter to otter went berserk to attack it, and she would be forced to hail a taxi to take her spitting fury home. When upset, the creature would bite like a ferret, and twice she needed plastic surgery to repair the damage to her arms. I lost contact with her a few months later, but I was told that she eventually had a nervous breakdown, no doubt inspired by her thoroughly undesirable pet.

An early medieval reference to the otter states that, as food, it should be regarded as fish and eaten on Fridays. While I would refrain from eating otter if I possibly could, I must confess I would sooner eat one than keep one as a pet. Wild animals are not suitable as house pets, unless one has the skill and patience of a dedicated naturalist like Phil Drabble.

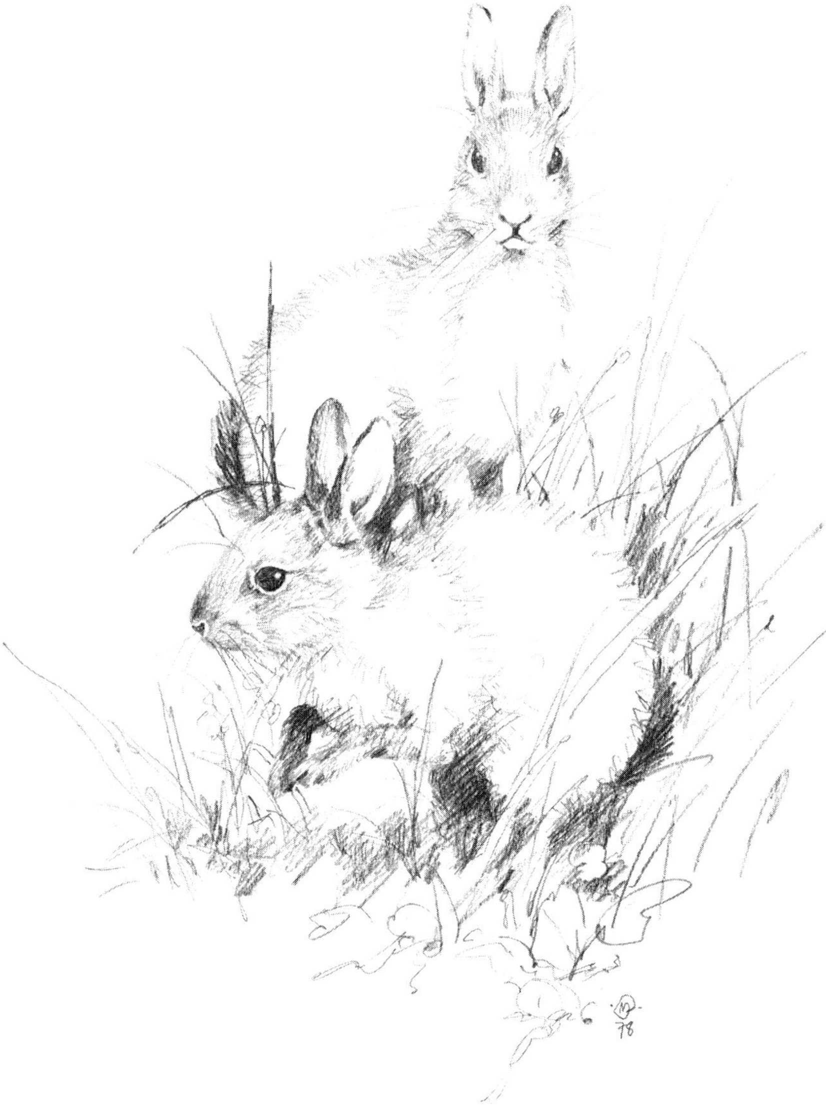

RABBIT HUNTING

No purist terrier man will allow his dogs to hunt rabbit. It does, indeed, teach a terrier all manner of evils. A dog that is not steady to rabbit will, more often than not, go to ground on a fox or badger, and bay like thunder at any rabbit lying up in the same earth. There are people who say that a dog tackling a fox or badger will roar and rage at a formidable quarry, but merely bay half-heartedly at a rabbit it is trying to dig to. This may be true, but it does not alter the fact that a dog that regards rabbit as fair game will not give of its best at fox or badger. Many old-time fox-hunting men made sure that their terriers would walk past a rabbit. Any hunt terrier men would still be advised to make sure that their dogs are stock steady to a rabbit, for there is nothing more foolish than when the pack of hounds is held back, the hunt followers are grouped round the dig and six tons of clay have been shifted by sweating diggers, only to uncover a terrier baying frantically at a cornered bunny.

Still, in a country where fox-digging by laymen is frowned on and where a terrier is kept for entertainment and interest rather than merely for fox digging, rabbit hunting is perfectly permissible; and I must admit, being no purist, that it is also damned good fun. Furthermore, a terrier can prove an invaluable aid to the ferreter and rough shooter, for there is no finer dog than the terrier for working rough cover to evict rabbits. I enjoy rabbit hunting, but would not use a rabbiting dog to hunt fox or badger. Thus any purist would do well to skip this chapter and avoid its contents.

Few terriers, except the Bedlington, could catch a rabbit on the run, and even most Bedlingtons would find it very hard to do. But in cover, where a rabbit sometimes becomes boxed in between roots, sticks and other hazards, some terriers can be very deadly. About eleven months before writing this chapter, my best rabbiting dog, a Russell-type terrier bitch called Set, died. In her brief three-year life she accounted for 400-odd rabbits, killed primarily in cover. She was an extremely noisy bitch and gave tongue on most quarry, be it rat, fox, badger or rabbit, but she was superb at taking rabbits in cover. Many experts in canine behaviour believe that the dog's bark, far from alerting quarry to danger, actually confuses it and leads to it being taken. While this would explain why hounds bay while hunting, it should also be pointed out that wolves, who are very efficient hunters, are in fact very silent.

Terriers make useful ferreting dogs provided one is prepared to put in the work to train them. A dog required for ferreting requires far more training than does a dog who is only required to go to ground and bay at fox or badger. First, the terrier needs to be thoroughly broken to ferret – so well broken, in fact, that it regards the ferret as an ally. This breaking to ferrets is childishly simple, but breaking a terrier to nets is considerably harder. If a rabbit hits the nets after being driven out by a ferret, no terrier should touch the enmeshed bunny; but should it slip through the nets and try to escape, the dog should nail it in a trice. A terrier that attacks a netted rabbit is a menace, for not only is the rabbit either badly damaged or given a chance to escape, but the nets become as tangled as the Gordian knot. It is essential to hold a young terrier when a rabbit hits the nets, and smack him as he lunges at the tangled bunny.

Some dogs take quite a time to learn the difference between a netted rabbit and one bolting from an unnetted hole, but if a dog is worked with ferrets regularly (and this is *the* most important thing), he will soon learn the difference. Unlike the rough-cover worker, the ferreting dog must not only be silent, he must also be capable of remaining stock still. A rabbit will often try to creep out of an unnetted hole and hop almost silently to safety. If a dog remains stock still, the rabbit will try and make a bolt for it and can be nabbed as it leaves the hole. But the dog that lunges at the rabbit as it approaches the mouth of the warren is quite the most useless creature to have, for not only will he fail to catch the rabbit, who slinks back below ground, but he will awake the rabbit to the dangers above ground. The prey will now refuse to bolt a second time, even allowing the ferret to kill it below ground rather than face the combined force of terrier and nets. The whole art of training a ferreting dog is to take him out as often as possible. I have owned a few excellent ferreting dogs, but not one could hold a candle to Rory, a Border terrier owned by a midland ferreter, Nap Johnson. Nap (short for Napoleon – oh, how his parents must have hated him) was a retired mechanic and obtained the rights for ferreting the railway embankments between two midland cities. Such places are havens for rabbits – I must confess I have poached embankments quite shamelessly.

Nap's dog was a pedigree Border, bred, I believe, from the handsome champion, Maxton Matchless. Rory, unlike his illustrious father, was no oil painting, but he was a superb work dog. He would crouch above any unnetted hole like a wiry-coated cat, his only movement being a quiver of anticipation. Once the rabbit hit the nets and was secured, he would ignore it, but should a rabbit try to sneak off from an unnetted hole, he was dead in a trice. I once netted an embankment with Nap one winter day when my hands were scarcely warm enough to peg a net. I had hurriedly netted several holes when the Border terrier started tapping my leg with his head. At first I thought that the dog was either demented or simply suffering from very bad ear canker, but on investigation realized he was simply trying to get me to net an earth I had overlooked. I did so, praising his sagacity, and when the ferret was inserted, sure enough a rabbit bolted from that very hole. There was no need for a ferret 'bleeper' with Rory (though detector kits can be quite invaluable). If the ferret killed below ground, Rory would mark the exact location of the kill and, within a few shovelfuls of soil, we had our rabbit. Rats are a curse on railway embankment warrens and lie up in the same holes as rabbits (Liverpool is notoriously bad for rat-infested rabbit warrens, by the way), but Rory would simply let them pass through the hole and escape. Though at other times, if Nap and I were hunting rat, Rory killed them with almost hysterical fury. He was a superb ferreting dog, though he would put his tail down and run at the smell of a fox. ('Each to his own' is probably as true of terriers as of man.)

After rat hunting (which, as the reader must be fully aware by now, is a passion of mine), hunting rabbit in thick cover with a small pack of terriers takes some beating. The speed of the sport is fantastic, and the chance of kills so small that it is exceptional to finish up a day with a haul of ten rabbits. The problem of running rabbits with terriers is, of course, that few rabbits feed more than a yard or so from the hole during daylight hours, and at the slightest sign of danger race back to their warrens. Since myxomatosis, many rabbits nest in thick cover rather than below ground. These give a far more sporting run, and only when they are hard pressed do they go to ground. Furthermore, one can obtain permission to hunt these scrub rabbits in the most unlikely places. I have had some incredibly good runs on tipping land in Swinton, Yorkshire, and how the rabbits scraped a living from that grassless rubbish dump I will never know. Yet I caught nine rabbits there in one season – not a large number, by any standards, but it is the quality of the runs not the bag which counts when one is hunting rabbits with a terrier pack. Lucas cites an instance of a rabbit who gave him many runs before the dogs actually caught it. It is always a little saddening to kill a rabbit, fox or rat that has given good value in sport. I once hunted a rabbit in Rotherham for nearly two months, and each time it made a home run by disappearing down a gap in the electric cable trench covering along the railway line. One day I saw him run in the direction of the railway track and was prepared to find my dog snorting down the drain entrance, but was surprised to see the dogs take him. Railway workmen had just finished repairing the cable trench cover.

This cable trench provided me with incredible sport during my time in Rotherham – illegal, but incredible. Rabbits abounded in areas where the top paving slab was cracked or broken. It was perhaps a foot from the top to the bottom of the trench, with nine inches between the sides. Henry Rodgers and I simply netted an area where the top slab was broken and put a dog into the trench as much as a mile away, allowing him to drive towards the nets. Once I netted near Tinsley and allowed the dog, a Russell-type terrier called Hellion, to enter the drain in Rotherham. I walked along the track listening to him bustling the rabbits towards the nets. I underestimated the rabbit population of that three-mile stretch. Two hit my nets, but fifteen large rabbits and eleven youngsters bolted after them. It was like shooting ducks in a barrel, and not really sporting, I must confess. The concrete sides of the trench had also rubbed the dog's shoulders to the flesh, so I never tried it again.

Holmes (Rotherham) embankment common, on the other hand, rendered me great sport but few kills. Rabbits were fairly common, as were stoats, and the land was filled with hollows, piles of stones and broken concrete blocks. I would put up the rabbits and they would give me a fair run before hitting cover or diving into the minute crevices in the concrete or stone piles. I hunted them for several months, running my team of terriers nightly, before I made a single kill, but I had great sport. Just before I left Rotherham, myxomatosis hit the district and in one rather nasty hunt I killed twelve crippled, blinded rabbits. The men who allowed this disease to be brought to Britain deserve life imprisonment. I knew most of the carcasses as lively healthy rabbits that had once provided me with endless fun. It was a sad sight to see the area reduced to a desert.

Of course, to get bumper hauls of rabbits using a terrier pack one must make sure that the rabbits are sitting out, not crouched in their burrows. This can be done quite simply by making the warrens less attractive. They can be ferreted early in the morning, and after the rabbits have bolted the holes can be blocked – a little like earth stopping. Alternatively, the warrens can be tainted with some noxious-smelling chemical that rabbits find abhorrent. Creosote is useful, as is burning sulphur, and this will keep the rabbits out for weeks. Paraffin is another substance that neither rabbits nor badgers can stand. Alan Bryant, of Bryant's Rabbit Catching Equipment, Surbiton, still sells quite a few chemicals for stinking out rabbits.

Barry Dainty, the former terrier man for the Warwick Hunt, used to hunt rabbit with his terrier pack. I think he had eight or nine, and he used them at night, driving across the fields in his Land-Rover and keeping the rabbits in the headlights while his terriers ran them.

RABBIT HUNTING

This demands a fair amount of practice and training if it is to be an efficient form of hunting, but if one has one or two whippets to run with the terriers, the sport can be fast, furious and very lethal to rabbits. One night, however, Barry's pack ran a badger, and the old boar turned and took out the throat of his best dog. At one time he also ran an ancient Collie with his terriers, and this bobbery pack had a fair number of kills to its credit.

Terriers work well with lurchers and whippets, but there can be problems in using this combination. Sometimes a lurcher will field and catch a rabbit that the terrier has bolted, and the terrier may regard it as his kill and attack the lurcher retrieving the rabbit. At the very least this will result in the lurcher becoming somewhat reluctant to retrieve, and at worst it can result in a very dead terrier, for some lurchers, especially collie/greyhound crosses, are particularly jealous about their kills and will readily retaliate if a terrier tries to rob them. I once worked a large, shaggy lurcher of unknown origin with my terrier pack, and he was a priceless acquisition to the team. He would watch every movement of the pack, and not only took a great number of rabbits, but also quite a few hares. Lucas used this lurcher/terrier combination to hunt both hares and rabbits.

Let the purist scoff and the professional terrier man shake his head in despair – to the terrier owner who wants a general all-round terrier rather than an exclusively fox and badger dog, rabbiting is great fun and a sport which never palls.

IV

The Care and Showing of Working Terriers

CARING FOR A WORKING TERRIER

The working terrier is a tough little dog, both in temperament and constitution, but it is likely to encounter more infectious diseases than any other breed of dog. Not only does it come into contact with foxes, which can harbour most canine diseases, but it is also used to hunt rats, which are the source of some of the most deadly infections known to the bacteriologist. While this is not meant to be a chapter on illness, the working-terrier man must understand the diseases that can attack his dog. Here and now let me express the view that it is absolutely essential to inoculate a dog before it is taken hunting. While a dog that is not inoculated may survive a year or so of regular rat hunting, it is certain that it will not do so for longer. During 1977 my team of ratting terriers took an incredible three tons of rat, and we had not had one outbreak of lethal leptospiral jaundice, or Wiel's disease. This was not the result of any magical remedy, miracle of stockmanship or country-remedy peppermint mouthwash, but was entirely due to the fact that my dogs are regularly inoculated against leptospirosis. Within my own group of friends, we will not allow any dog to hunt with our ratting team unless it has been recently inoculated.

The usual inoculation advised by most vets is for protection against the following diseases:

1. Distemper.
2. Hardpad.
3. Canicola fever.
4. Leptospirosis.

Distemper is a real killer, and although it can affect all dogs at any ages, it is normally young stock which will suffer most from this commonest of canine diseases. It is an insidious disease, the infection usually manifesting itself as the dog becomes listless, perhaps off colour, and a slight discharge of pus appears from its eyes and nostrils. The temperature then rockets and the dog becomes decidedly ill. The saddest part of the disease is when a dog apparently recovers from the early stages of the infection, but one day suddenly develops a thrashing fit that is the precursor of similar epileptic turns, the dog becoming so distressed and damaged that it is a kindness to put the poor devil to sleep. Some epidemics of distemper are of a particularly mild nature, and while most young puppies succumb to the virus, most adult dogs shake off the infection. Laidlaw and Dunkin (1958) divided distemper into three categories:

1. Virus A: a particularly virulent form of the disease, fortunately quite uncommon.
2. Virus B: a very uncommon type of the disease.
3. Virus C: a mild form of distemper, and actually quite common, far more so than most people realize.

Frankly, there is little one can do to cure this infection. Once the disease has started, all one can do is to keep the dog warm, feed a light diet, and hope for the best. No patent remedies or antibiotics have any effect on the virus. The answer is, of course, to inoculate your puppy against the disease, and the best time for inoculation is at about twelve weeks of age.

Hardpad is merely another type of distemper. It broke out in Britain in 1948 and had such devastating results that people thought it was an entirely new type of disease. In some cases the skin of the nostrils and pads thickened and hardened – hence the term 'hard pad'. Treatment is roughly the same as the treatment for distemper, and also just about as ineffective. Should a dog contract a mild form of the disease, then he may recover, though dogs that recover are frequently crippled as a result of damage to the nerve endings by the invading virus. If the dog contracts a particularly virulent form of the infection he will probably die or be permanently and hideously crippled by it. Inoculation is the answer, and though it may not be one hundred per cent effective in preventing damage by this virus, it is nearly so. Very, very, few dogs that are inoculated contract distemper.

Hepatitis is another killer disease and strikes so suddenly that a dog can be hale and hearty one day and very dead the next. Old hunt kennel staff used to remark that if a dog was alive forty-eight hours after the infection manifested itself, then the animal would recover. Hepatitis causes the breakdown of the functions of the liver. Symptoms are very variable, and death is usually very rapid once the liver ceases to function properly. Early indications of the disease are a high temperature, wasting, vomiting and a very weak pulse can be detected. Sometimes the breakdown of the liver is such that symptoms resembling those of jaundice manifest themselves. Keratitis or 'blue eye' may occur about a week after the onset of the illness, and internal bleeding may take place.

Occasionally antiserum injections and glucose and vitamin K may help, but treatment is usually fairly unsatisfactory and inoculation is the only answer. It is also wise to realize that most lamp-posts, so beloved by dogs walked on leads, are real infection points for this disease. Very few lamp-posts in Britain do not have traces of this deadly virus.

Leptospirosis

This disease is the dread of all rat hunters, for it is deadly to both man and dog alike. In man it is known as Wiel's disease, a lethal infection that must strike terror into the heart of every sewer cleaner and refuse dump worker, or anyone who has to work in places where rats abound. It was once known as 'the rat catcher's yellows', and families who supplied rats for the notorious rat pits owned by Jimmy Shaw and others were often decimated by this infection. To add to the alarm I should have created, may I also point out that Monlux established that above fifty-five per cent of the rats in this country are carriers of Wiel's disease. Furthermore, it can be transmitted from dog to man and from man to dog as well as from rat to both man and dog.

Once seen, the disease will never be forgotten. The dog develops a listlessness, a couldn't care less attitude and starts to pass putty-coloured faeces. The eyes, gums and belly turn bright yellow; some rise in temperature is experienced, and the dog quickly wastes away and dies. Death can be quite rapid – I have seen dogs waste away to jaundiced skeletons and die, all within the space of eight days from the onset of the disease. Some cases may respond to antibiotics, but most do not. Also the dog remains infectious, both to man and dog for months. Treatment is rarely satisfactory, and is always very, very costly. It is far better to have a dog inoculated against the disease. Reinoculation once or even twice a year is quite essential, for any dog regularly hunted to rats in quantity is going to encounter the infection. No dog, I mean *no* dog, that is not inoculated should ever come in contact with rats.

Another killing disease that is all too common is *Canicola fever*. Heptospirosis and Canicola fever victims sometimes recover, but their systems are so devastated – I think blitzed would be a more accurate word – that they are little use as hunting dogs. A survey conducted in Glasgow showed that forty per cent of street dogs had, at some time or other, been infected with Canicola fever.

Again symptoms are variable, ranging from a high temperature to marked thirst and vomiting, from loss of weight to ulceration of the tongue and jaundice. Damage to the kidneys and subsequent illnesses are usually experienced, and sometimes the dog passes into a state of coma and dies. Some animals recover with the aid of antibiotics, but are often so damaged as to be little further use as hunting dogs. Again, inoculation against the disease is the only sensible method of ensuring that your dogs are not infected.

Mange

If one intends to hunt regularly it's dollars to doughnuts that you will experience this nasty, unsightly infection attacking your dog. Briefly there are two sorts of mange – Sarcoptic and Follicular. Follicular mange is unlikely to be picked up while hunting (and does not usually respond to treatment), but sarcoptic mange is very easily contracted. Fox earths abound with mange parasites, usually a rather resistant mite called sarcoptes communis, while rats, once mature, are invariably infected with another mange mite – *Sarcoptes scabii* – the mite which causes the most maddening of human maladies – namely scabies. Dogs infected with sarcoptic mange scratch madly and soon become denuded of hair, the skin becomes torn with the scratching and often suppurates. Condition plummets and the dog looks decidedly sorry for itself. If left to run its course, this mite will cause such a scratching that the dog becomes completely bald. Also the skin of such an animal is literally lacerated by the scratching. Furthermore, the mite can easily leave the dog and infect people, and having been a scabies victim, I can assure you that it is a most unpleasant and embarrassing condition.

Mange is fairly easily cured, though it is often a lengthy job. Old remedies suggest that mutton fat be heated up until it is molten and flowers of sulphur stirred in until it becomes a creamy paste. The mixture is now rubbed on to the dog, and though it looks messy it is often extremely effective. The dog looks unhappy about being anointed with such a mess, but it is an exceedingly soothing, albeit a smelly mixture. A more modern method is to dip the dog in a solution of liver of sulphur (potassium sulphide), and though the liquid gives off the odour of rotten eggs, it certainly sees off the mange parasite. Furthermore, this pungent chemical, used regularly, seems to produce a gleaming, glossy coat on the dog. Liver of sulphur is absorbed (in small quantities) through the skin and excreted via the kidneys, so do not be surprised to see your dog passing sulphurous smelling urine a few days after using this substance. One snag, however, is that it is quite difficult to find a chemist who stocks liver of sulphur, and for some reason chemists find it quite difficult to obtain. It appears that while it is possible to buy the most lethal substances such an aldrin and dieldrin and warfarin with great ease, the sale of this innocuous but foul-smelling chemical is subject to an odd quirk of legislation. The name, liver of sulphur, incidentally is due to the fact that the blocks of this substance resemble pieces of jaundiced, and very unhealthy, liver. If such a substance can be obtained then it needs to be kept in sealed tins, as it tends to become a little unstable and wet. Still this is a very useful, though old fashioned, mangicide and if it can be obtained is quite effective in the control of mange.

Another chemical that is highly effective as a controller of this unpleasant complaint is benzyl benzoate – a creamy white emulsion that is sometimes prescribed by doctors as a scabicide (scabies is human mange). I say sometimes prescribed, as this chemical, although very effective, is also a skin irritant and causes unpleasant rashes when used on some people. As a mangicide it is very useful, very effective, and rarely causes problems. Rub one half of the dog with this emulsion one day and the other half the next day, and repeat this treatment a week later. It will certainly see off even mange caused by the fox mite (sarcoptes communus).

Gamma BHC or benzene hexachloride is also useful as a dip or emulsion and proves highly effective as a mange killer. It is a very stable chemical and a dip in BHC solution will usually give the dog resistance to further infections for about a month. Many hunt kennels dip their hounds in this substance four or five times a year as a preventative against mange. Some dogs react to the substance strangely and fall into thrashing fits, but very few dogs are allergic to properly diluted BHC.

Last, but not least, is the more modern chemical monosulfiram, sold under the trade name of Tetmosol. This is a very effective treatment if the maker's instructions are obeyed to the letter, but beware: if this chemical is used in a careless manner, it can be very, very, dangerous indeed.

Wounds

Few working terriers go through their lives without being bitten by their quarry, so unless the terrier owner wishes to spend a fortune in vet's fees, it is as well that he should learn a little canine first aid.

Rat bites are very devils for festering, and anyone who hunts rats will find that their dog gets bitten from time to time. Should any reader be inclined to scoff at the damage an ordinary brown rat might inflict, may I suggest that he examines the incisors of a fully grown rat. Rat bites are not only very deep and wide, for a rat's lower incisors spread out when they enter the flesh of a foe, but a number of very dangerous bugs are introduced by the wound. Not only can a rat bite introduce the deadly Wiel's disease (though it is more often spread via the urine of the rat), but also another unpleasant infection called rat-bite fever. This disease is caused by one of two bacillus, the names of which need not concern us here. It often only manifests itself about two weeks after the bite, when the dog becomes lethargic, develops a high fever and loses weight rapidly. Sometimes a rash that resembles a distemper rash breaks out on the belly of the dog, and in some cases fur falls out in patches. Cleaning any rat bite with disinfectant can minimize the chances of a dog developing this disease, but as soon as a dog is bitten by a rat a wise precaution is a shot of antibiotic such as penicillin. Oxytetracycline is another useful preventative, taken in tablet form.

Fox bites, being another prolific source of infection, almost invariably 'go wrong'. Slashes usually cause little trouble and as a rule respond to simple salt-water washes, but punctures, as I have stated, are another matter. These need great care if they are not to lead to massive infections of staphylococcus. Old huntsmen used to advocate soaking the bitten portion in neat whisky, which certainly has an antiseptic effect, but is inefficient as well as expensive. Antiseptics such as Dettol, TCP or Milton are far more effective, and if one has access to antibiotics in tablet form, then by all means use them. The punctures inflicted by an otter are also of a type that can cause serious trouble unless treated immediately.

Few deaths are caused by fox bites in comparison to the number of deaths that occur as a result of kennel fights. A piece of advice: never kennel more than two terriers together. They may live in harmony for years, but sooner or later a fight will break out and the results of such three-cornered battles are often frightful. While one dog works on the victim's face, the other dog creates mayhem on the victim's unprotected belly. Such wounds can be fatal, for, if the gut is punctured, peritonitis and death are inevitable unless the terrier man gets his dogs to a really good vet rapidly. It is also worth mentioning that, after a hard dog *v.* dog fight, shock and pneumonia can carry off the healthiest animals. Early manuals on dog fighting are useful guides to the treatment of such consequences. Immediately after a fight, Wilcox, a noted pit fighter of the 1840s, is reputed to have covered up his dog in his thick overcoat and to have kept him in a warm place – excellent advice, though a little hard on overcoats, perhaps. Shock and pneumonia frequently follow a severe mauling and cause a very rapid death. A dog that has been involved in a fight should be kept quiet and placed in a warm place (preferably under a heat lamp) until the owner has a chance to treat him. I have had many kennel fights and, I confess, a few deaths, but such treatment has saved many a dog's life in my kennels.

In passing, may I mention that dog fights are common among sapling puppies up to a year old, but once a dog is given a chance to work, this aggression burns off. My own stud dog, Vampire, had a very bad (and justly earned reputation) for fighting until he joined my rat-hunting squad. Within a week or so he had 'put away childish things' and was working well enough alongside other stud dogs. Lucas mentions the story of a Border terrier that caused havoc by fighting and stock slaying. As soon as he was entered to quarry (in this case otter), he quietened down and became a most docile but efficient animal. Lucas also suggests that a few rats tipped into terriers will invariably quieten them down — but while this is true, it could also put the terrier man in court for contravening the baiting laws. By all means, take an aggressive young terrier out ratting, for it will certainly have a very quietening effect on him and help to stop his fighting. By far the greatest cause of kennel fighting is boredom. A dog that is given outdoor work is rarely any problem in kennels.

THE FELL AND MOORLAND WORKING TERRIER CLUB

Next to the four diseases for which inoculation is recommended, the greatest problem the working-terrier man can encounter is to have his terriers trapped below ground while hunting fox or badger. Nothing can be more distressing than to lose a dog in the bowels of the earth; the terrier man is beset by doubts — is the dog injured, or trying to get out? Is the dog walled in behind a layer of loose soil, or is he already suffocated and dead in one of the narrow subterranean passages? Perhaps the saddest fourteen days of my life was when I fruitlessly tried to dig through to two terriers trapped in a noted nightmare earth in Wall, near Lichfield. What at first appeared to be a one-eyed set turned out to be an earth ninety feet deep with holes up to a half a mile away from the start of the dig. Needless to say, I never recovered my dogs; even after seven years I am still unable to pass that earth without a strong twinge of regret.

In 1966, Cyril Tyson of Egremont, together with twelve other interested and practising terrier men, met with a view to forming a rescue scheme to dig out trapped terriers. What originally started as a tiny gathering of friends, prepared to dig out each other's dogs, has now developed into a national club. It is, without doubt, the best working

THE CARE AND SHOWING OF WORKING TERRIERS

The Fell and Moorland rescue service in operation: above, digging out, below, a successful ending.

terrier club in Britain, and its aims are purely humanitarian because it is not in any way profit-making. It has branches nearly everywhere, but particularly in the north of England. No practising terrier man, be he amateur or professional, can afford not to join this club, for not only will a cry for help produce club members ever ready to dig for a trapped terrier, but, in times of emergency, the club is prepared to pay for earth-moving equipment to rescue dogs. Annual membership of this admirable club costs, at the time of writing, a mere fifty pence. Some of the rescues read like sagas, and I now quote from the 1977 year book:

Pennine Area
Delph Quarries, Pudsey, Leeds.

On Saturday, 8th February, two Lakelands were sent to ground in a rock tip at approximately 8 a.m. One a dog called Sam, the other a bitch called Rusty, owned by Les Davis. Les rang me on Saturday evening explaining that the fox had bolted, seen him and gone back into the pile. After waiting until 11.45 p.m. he then blocked most of the holes until Sunday morning when rescue attempts would start. On arriving at the tip we started to try to locate the dogs by hand digging but this was quite impossible. After lunch it was decided to hire a J.C.B. to dig pilot holes some twelve feet deep hoping to locate the trapped terriers, but this was unsuccessful.

The holes were again blocked and checked twice a day for six days but still there was no sound. On the seventh day a bigger machine was hired from Scotts of Pudsey, a Poclaine. This machine it was felt would dig the tip right out into the big rocks below, which we felt held the terriers. After extensive digging some 20 ft deep and 30ft into the tip moving some very large rocks, the terrier bitch appeared in a shocked condition although unharmed. After digging for two more hours the dog dropped from a crack, to a great cheer from the lads. It became apparent that the terriers had gone far in the huge rocks and were unable to get back up the pile.

Whilst in the process of digging the terriers out a member of a shooting club came over enquiring as to how much this would cost the club. He was told and no more was said. A few days later a donation of £10 was received by me from the Gibraltar Wildfowlers and Roughshooter Association. May all sportsmen be as good when others are in need. Many thanks to all the lads involved in this rescue for being very helpful and the team effort was terrific.

Members present:
    Gary Allot (Machine Organiser)
    Eddie Harding (Machine Driver)

Peter Rushworth
Ernie Wademan
Irish Bob
Dave Weston
Les Davies
Frank McGuire
Ronnie Davis
Paul Holmes
Harry Imerson
Selwin Kershaw
Brian Swain
Mick Rawson
Mrs Horsley
A. Johnson (Area Representative)
    Cost to Club   £157.32
    Less Donation   £10.00
                                £147.32
                  Signed A. JOHNSON

Not all the digs have such a happy ending, however.

Saturday evening, January, I received a call from Glyn Slater of Barnsley to say that his pal, Mr Shaw, had lost a terrier in a local drain and they were concerned for its safety. The terrier had flushed a fox from a thicket and had chased it into a drain. I went down to have a look on Sunday morning and found that the drain had been dug in several places by the local members on the Saturday but they had been unable to trace any branch pipes or junctions. The farmer had been consulted and said that the pipe was a single line, terminating in a pond at the field bottom. This was correct and after efforts to partly drain the pond the dog's owner, stripped to the waist, submerged himself under the ice which covered the pond and located the drain end, removed a large stone which was partly blocking it and after another dive he reported feeling a dead animal wedged in the drain end, then promptly collapsed in a heap and had to be revived by a brisk rubbing down. He again collapsed and was quickly thrown on to a tractor and rushed home where, I am very relieved to say, he recovered quickly. After this episode and after making sure there was no hope of rescue, it was decided to let the pond subside for a day or two. The following Tuesday waders were sufficient to get to the drain and the dead terrier was recovered. The fox had squeezed past the stone blockage and was found drowned under the ice. As a footnote may I thank the lads who helped in this attempt, the farmer for his time and the machinery for draining, and the dog's owner who entered into the bitterly cold water and showed the best spirit of the Fell and Moorland Working Terrier Club, making sure of his terrier's fate before his own discomfort.

Dave Ramsden

Yet another dig was of epic proportions and is worth recording.

Lintz Ford, Rowlands Gill

On Sunday, the 11th of April, together with Charlie Anderson, Joe Eddy and Walter Carr, I was hunting fox at Tollgate Wood, Lintz Ford, Rowlands Gill.

At 11 o'clock we entered three dogs into a huge set on the bank side. Nothing was heard for half an hour, after which two dogs emerged, one slightly bitten. The third dog, belonging to myself, a cross Lakeland named Brock, did not appear and no sound was heard of him. As darkness approached we still heard nothing so we put up sticks at the holes and decided to come back at first light.

The next morning (Monday) with other members, I returned to the set but the sticks had not been moved. After informing John Winch, extensive hand digging was carried out but no sign or sound of the dog was heard. A halt was called at darkness.

On Tuesday we were back at the set and after viewing the operation John Winch decided to bring in a machine. The machine arrived, and after much difficulty which included fording the river, the loss of a door and both headlamps, it reached the set. The only way it could approach it was to pull itself up with the aid of chains, but once in place great progress was made with the excavation. The set proved to be tremendous and by the Wednesday a depth of 19 feet or more was reached but still no sign of the dog.

It was decided to dig on until midday on Thursday by which time the machine had dug almost the whole of the bankside away, but tubes extended into the hillside.

After hearing no sound of Brock since Sunday it was decided to backfill as everything had been done which was possible.

Many thanks to all members for their efforts.

Members present:
  J. Eddy
  W. Carr
  R. Short
  J. Johnson
  T. Martindale

THE CARE AND SHOWING OF WORKING TERRIERS

C. Anderson
J. Winch
T. Amber (Digger Driver)
Fred

E. FORSYTH

I repeat: no terrier man can afford not to be a member of this estimable club.

WORKING TERRIER SHOWS

Working-terrier shows, so long as they are not taken too seriously, can be great fun. Sadly and absurdly, they often are taken too seriously, and some quite nasty scenes involving angry and disillusioned competitors are only too common. Such shows are hardly ever judged to standard, and often the most unqualified people judge, so strange decisions are reached as well as sometimes amazing and obvious chicanery being practised. The prizes are so pathetically small that I am bewildered to know why spectators should regard these shows as anything but a day out. Regard these shows as a get-together where hunters can meet to discuss terriers and perhaps choose a suitable stud dog to use on their bitches, and you will generally enjoy a day's recreation. Regard these shows as a be-all-and-end-all, your reason for living, and you certainly will not enjoy your day out, and what is more will make enemies among people who could have been useful friends or contacts. Frankly, I avoid these shows because far too many people go there with the express purpose of winning at all costs.

The working-terrier shows were originally staged by hunt supporters' committees for a bit of fun, and also as a means of raising funds. The idea soon caught on. Exemption dog shows started putting on hunt terrier classes. In the early 1970s, so popular had the hunt terrier class become, that most gymkhanas were also staging working terrier shows. In the early days of hunt shows, classes of over 100 were not uncommon and the shows proved to be great fund raisers. Various clubs staged their own shows: the Midland Working Terrier Club put on some excellent shows in these early days, and the then newly formed Fell and Moorland Working Terrier Club was already drawing record crowds and exhibits. In recent years, however, the number in the various classes has fallen off, and where we once found over 100 exhibits there are today only a few dogs in these classes. Furthermore, the quality of the exhibits has dropped considerably.

The reader may well ask the reason for this declining popularity, and to be honest it is possible only to guess at the reasons for the decline of the hunt terrier show. It is certainly not that hunt terriers are falling from popularity – far from it, for the Jack Russell must certainly prove to be the most popular breed in Britain. Nor is it the fault of the hunts, for the shows are usually very well organized – far better organized than they were in the halcyon days of the early 1970s. I would attribute the decline to various things. First, to the fact that the shows are as a rule very badly judged, usually by huntsmen from neighbouring hunts, who know little about terriers; and secondly, to the extraordinary lack of sportsmanship in the working terrier owners who show their dogs. It seems ludicrous to think that grown men will fight over the relative merits of their terriers, but this has become a not infrequent event. It is this appallingly bad sportsmanship that is proving the death of the working terrier show.

Should the terrier man still wish to attend such a show – and many can be, I admit, exceedingly entertaining – they can be found advertised in *Horse and Hound*, the *Shooting Times* or similar magazines. Some of the working-terrier clubs actually prefer to use *Exchange and Mart* to advertise their shows, and such is the circulation of this magazine that these shows are usually very well attended. At most working terrier shows, some hunt supporters' secretary will be circulating handouts for such and such a hunt terrier show, so the reader can usually bet that there will be a working terrier show within thirty miles of where he or she lives during the summer months. Most shows are staged on a Saturday or a Sunday, but the Great Yorkshire Show, one of the better supported affairs, is run during weekdays and still has an astonishingly large entry. One or two club shows are run during the evenings, but these are usually shows that are not expected to have large entries, and are usually staged indoors.

Theoretically, almost any breed of terrier can be shown at these shows, for the prizes are awarded to the most suitable terrier to work fox or badger, or, formerly, otter. Perhaps only an Airedale terrier is unsuited for working this quarry, so in theory any terrier small enough to get to fox or badger could win in these shows. In practice, however, only Borders, Lakelands and the white-bodied terriers known collectively as Jack Russells are usually placed in these shows. Cross-breed terriers, hybrids between Borders, Lakelands and Russells, are occasionally placed. Norwich terriers and Norwich terrier crosses sometimes win, and some of these cross-breeds can be both striking-looking dogs and also excellent workers. In the midlands and south, Russell-type terriers are the most commonly exhibited breeds, but further north, the Lakeland or Fell terrier make up the bulk of the exhibits.

During the hey-day of the working terrier shows, certain hunt shows put on classes for Norfolk terriers, but these classes now seem to have been dropped. This is a pity since this type of terrier can be a very useful worker and if sufficient numbers of the breed or its prick-eared brother, the Norwich, could be attracted to the hunt shows, they could make up an interesting class of terrier. As it is, breeders sometimes slip one into the Border/Lakeland cross-section, for huntsmen judges rarely know much about the various breeds of terrier, and breeds like the Norwich and Norfolk tend to pass unnoticed in the cross-breed classes.

There are classes for puppies under six months, and sometimes for puppies under a year old. Many of these are quite obviously older than they are supposed to be, and this can quite often become a bone of contention among the exhibitors. Judges should acquaint themselves with the skill of telling dogs' ages by dentition. This skill will help to alleviate the bitterness of some of the exhibitors, who find that their puppy has been beaten by a dog that is certainly not a puppy. Puppies under six months are usually easily recognized, but it is not so easy to determine age with a dog slightly over a year old. I have, more than once, seen a noted exhibitor show two-and-a-half-year-old bitches in the puppy classes and win. Judges need to be quite firm about throwing out dogs that are obviously over age.

Some shows, particularly the Warwickshire Hunt Show, put on under 10-inch classes for small terriers. These classes are sometimes well attended. I once showed in such a class that had over 100 exhibits, though several, including the winner, were well over 10 inches. Most shows who stage such classes insist on exhibits being bridged, or measured, before they are allowed in the class. Some exhibitors become exceedingly adept at chicanery in pushing their dogs under the 10-inch bar. One can, of course, complain to the judge that this practice is going on, but there is little point in doing so if you regard such a show as merely a day out. These under 10-inch terriers rarely go on to become 'Best in Show', as it is quite difficult to breed a really good-quality small terrier.

Most hunt shows stage working certificate classes for dogs and bitches who hold a certificate (signed by a pack master), stating that the dog has been worked with the hunt and is dead game. Many such certificates are simply informal letters from masters. Some certificates are quite elaborate and attractive; I have heard that the Atherstone Hunt issues a very ornate working certificate. Working-certificate classes are rarely well represented, not because few terriers have actually seen work at fox or badger, but quite simply because few terriers actually see service with hunts. Most hunts employ their own terrier men, and these are frequently reluctant to allow an outsider to try his terriers. Sometimes masters behave so autocratically that they will refuse to sign certificates stating that a particular terrier has worked with the hunt. This is rare these days, however, when the hunts need all the support they can get if they are to withstand the troubled times which lie ahead for them.

Veteran classes for dogs over six years old (sometimes the age qualification is nine years old and over) are sometimes quite well attended. Some ten years ago some excellent Jack Russell terriers were being shown, and these dogs, now well and truly veterans, are often of better quality than the present-day youngsters. There are few dogs shown today that are of the same quality as those champions of the early 1970s. A glance at the veteran's class is frequently well worth while. Today a large number of Jack Russell terriers are obviously part fox terrier, and some considerable quality has been sacrificed to create a tall, leggy, fox-terrier type of Russell. The dogs of the late 1960s and early 1970s really did take some beating.

Some shows put on classes for child handlers, and small children, sometimes as young as two or three years, parade their dogs around the ring. It is always a pity that some of these mites have to lose, but most clubs make sure every child who enters gets a rosette or suchlike.

A Typical Show Schedule

Class 1: Puppy, any breed, dog or bitch under six months old.
Class 2: Puppy, any breed, dog or bitch under a year old.
Class 3: Rough dog over one year.
Class 4: Rough bitch over one year.
Class 5: Smooth dog over one year.
Class 6: Smooth bitch over one year.
Class 7: Border, Lakeland, or Cross over one year.
Class 8: Veteran dog over six years old.

Class 9: Working certificate dog or bitch.
Class 10: Best dog or bitch handled by a child under fourteen years old.
Class 11: Best brace (or matched couple).
Class 12: Best in Show, to be made up from winners of each class except classes 11 and 10.

The time will come when a terrier man will be asked to judge a terrier show. At first it will appear a great honour, but in practice, the experience may begin to pall a little. If the reader is ever asked to judge, may I suggest that he adopts the following code of practice:

1. Acquaint himself with the Border, Lakeland and the recently formed Jack Russell Club standard and judge to these standards *to the letter*.
2. Request that his friends do not show under him. This will reduce the chance of ill feeling from friends and acquaintances whom he does not place and also reduce any criticism he may run into for favouring certain individuals.
3. Explain to exhibitors why he has placed certain dogs and not others. Quotes like, 'It's really not what I'm looking for today', or 'It really didn't catch my eye', are a sure sign that the judge isn't up to the task, and furthermore, such statements tend to aggravate or infuriate exhibitors.
4. Learn to keep a book during the judging. Not only will this enable the judge to write a sensible and coherent account of the show, it will also reduce the chance of placing dog (a) first in one class and dog (b) second, and then reversing the positions in the next class. This looks very amateurish and sets the exhibitor wondering whether the judge knows his job.
5. Not be swayed by exhibitors who tell him that such and such a dog won first prize here last week, and that a particular dog has never been beaten. Judge to the standards, and disregard the comments of exhibitors.
6. Not allow himself to get angry at the ringside hecklers, all of whom would be able to do the job better than the judge. This is difficult, and I for one, tend to become very riled at such back-chat. Try not to be.
7. Remember that the judging of a show requires considerable stamina. A judge can be on his feet for up to six hours when judging a large show, and it can be really tiring, even to a man who has dug badger for years. An entirely different type of stamina is called for when judging a show.

Terrier Racing

This is frequently offered as a side-attraction at hunt terrier shows, and is so ridiculous that I am baffled when people take the business in any way seriously. It is meant to be a joke, but some treat the matter with deadly earnestness. Briefly, a fox brush is dragged around behind a horse and rider, or powered by a bicycle wheel, and the terriers are slipped at it. Some clubs in the north treat terrier racing with deadly seriousness, and the judge may ask any exhibitor to withdraw a terrier if he suspects that the dog has whippet blood in it. It is a joke event basically with ridiculous prizes. I would never, ever, enter a terrier in such an event, as some dreadful fights can break out when one of the terriers grabs the brush. My dogs are bitten enough at legitimate quarry, and further bites during a flippant and irrelevant event are not what I am after. The fact remains that terrier racing is quite popular with the hunt-show fraternity.

WORKING TESTS AND TRIALS

It is now virtually impossible to stage a working terrier test in Britain without contravening some of the regulations imposed by the various anti-baiting laws. This may, at first glance, seem something of a restriction on human liberties, for our country is grossly over-governed by any standards, but a close examination of our laws prove them to be both sensible and humane. To test the courage of a terrier involves one of two actions:

1. For a party of people to wander the countryside over many days to find suitable quarry in its native environment and to test the courage of the dogs on this quarry.
2. To capture a suitable quarry and test the terrier on the said quarry in an environment that is both terrifying and bewildering to the animal concerned.

The first method is frankly unsatisfactory, as it would often involve many a long and fruitless journey for judges and witnesses before the hunter actually found quarry at home. The second method involves a violation of the baiting laws, and not only would such violation warrant a stiff fine or imprisonment, but the publicity resulting from the action would give field sports a very bad name and provide a great source of ammunition for the anti-blood sport people. Only recently some American terrier owners obtained numerous rats by trapping them around the farms. They were then tipped alive into a box, and terriers were tried out on them. This was a procedure that was perfectly acceptable maybe sixty years ago, and was certainly practised when a writer like Drabble was a boy, but the action caused such a furore in the American press that I doubt whether another rat-killing contest could ever be considered. Do bear in mind that this tirade of disapproval was in the United States of America, where the baiting laws are nowhere near as strict as they are in Britain.

Our animal baiting laws are remarkably sensible, and it would be a sad thing if we ever allowed our standards to drift back into the barbarism of the days when baiting was regular sport. I would certainly hate to see the return of the days when it was quite acceptable to cut the legs off a bulldog to prove that it would not release its hold on a bull, even in the face of such excruciating agony. Nor would I like to see trials of courage such as described by Alken where various breeds of bulldog and terrier were required to draw badger from a barrel *ad nauseam*. At one time the All Ireland Blue Terrier Club staged working terrier tests of courage that also bordered on the sickening and were decidedly reminiscent of the days of Alken. Here the dogs were required to draw a badger but not to kill it. Immediately the dogs had drawn Brock, the badger was released, whereupon it ran back to the sanctuary to allow dogs to draw it once more. Dogs that succeeded in this sport, and I use the term 'sport' with my tongue very firmly fixed in my cheek, were awarded the 'Teastas Mor' or great test certificate, while dogs that slew rats and rabbits were awarded the 'Teastas Beg' or little test. While it is commendable to maintain the courage of working terriers, tests involving the baiting of live animals are to be deplored. Those who would like to see a return to these lamentable practices should remember that dogs have to bite a badger quite hard to be able to draw it, and that even a creature as leathery-hided as a badger must experience great pain when bitten by a terrier.

American Working Terrier Club working certificates are considered to be of controversial value by the hunting fraternity. To obtain these working certificates, a hooded (and tame) white rat is caged, and the cage placed at the end of a long tunnel. A terrier is now required to go to ground and bay at the caged rat for a set period of time, and a working certificate is awarded to successful dogs. This is a curious sort of test, devised to circumnavigate the regulations of the American Society for the Prevention of Cruelty to

WORKING TESTS AND TRIALS

Animals, who are opposed to allowing the use of a wild animal for dogs to bait. One member of the American Working Terrier Club has made a very valid point that a dog which has been hunted to legitimate quarry will not bay continuously at a rat in a cage, but will merely endeavour to find a way into the said cage. It is also of interest to note that it is doubtful if the caged rat finds the experience particularly pleasant, even if the dogs are unable to get through to him. I hasten to add that such confrontations would not be legal in Britain.

I am told by two working-terrier men from Kerry that the Glen of Imaal Terrier Club has succeeded in producing a working-certificate test that does not contravene British baiting regulations. Glen of Imaal terriers cannot become full champions without a working certificate or 'Misnaec Teastas'. To obtain this certificate, and to avoid the stigma of baiting, the owners of Glen of Imaal terriers walk many miles to try their terriers in natural earths against quarry in its natural environment. The quarry is invariably badger, for the Glen of Imaal is a little large for fox hunting. I should imagine that the club performs a commendable service in providing such tests, but there is little doubt that the RSPCA must keep a very close watch to make sure that the club does not violate the baiting laws.

Early in 1976, the newly formed Jack Russell Club of Great Britain debated the instituting of a working-terrier test to ensure that the working qualities of the Jack Russell terrier should be maintained and, if possible, improved. The laws applying to the running of such a trial were thoroughly investigated, but while it was suggested that it would be possible to arrange rat hunts and fox digs for limited numbers of members of the club, it would not be possible to arrange any form of more general trial without breaking the law. Subsequently, the proposed working terrier tests were not implemented. At the time of writing, I believe Alan Thomas of Nantymoel Working Terrier Club is carring out a thorough investigation into the possibility of implementing some form of working test for terriers, but his task is not an enviable one. The British laws regarding cruelty to animals are rightly very strict, and are likely to become even more so in the future.

Appendices

JACK RUSSELLS WORKING IN AMERICA

Ailsa M. Crawford

The Jack Russell in the United States is a relatively new breed, but one that is fast becoming known for its working ability in the field of small game. These alert, fast, intelligent little working machines, possessed with stamina, guts, loyalty and determination, are entered to woodchuck, mouse, rat, rabbit, squirrel, muskrat, raccoon, fox, coyote and even upland birds in this country. No matter what one chooses to work a Jack Russell to, you can always be assured of an excellent day or evening of sport, providing, of course, the terrier has been trained properly from an early age and not asked to do too much too soon.

It would be impossible for me to cover in one chapter the working abilities of the Jack Russell to all the small game mentioned, so I will attempt here to pick but one that I feel is the most unusual and common only to this country. I must also preface this by saying that, in working the terriers to raccoon, I am speaking only about my working experience, for most hunters in this country do not use terriers to raccoon, but rather larger hounds bred for that purpose. In doing so, I will first give you a brief rundown on the animal itself, so that you will better understand what the terrier has to cope with.

The raccoon is the animal I have picked to tell you about. Many times over the years, I have pulled a terrier from a drain over a fight with a raccoon, and this I will explain a bit later on. The raccoon or 'coon', as it is sometimes nicknamed in America, is a carnivorous North American mammal, which feeds upon small birds, mice, eggs, turtles, frogs, fish, insects, nuts, fruit, maize and sometimes poultry. They are nocturnal animals, although I have seen them, upon occasion, come out to feed in the late afternoon. They haunt the banks of ponds and streams, and find much of their food in these places. The animal has a curious habit of washing its food in water before eating it, apparently because it lacks saliva glands, and wetting the food before eating naturally makes it go down easier.

The typical coon is a well-built animal, about three feet long, with a tail about ten inches and a coat of long, coarse, greyish-brown hairs, short ears and a bushy black and white ringed tail. He has black, mask-like facial markings, making him look like a person dressed for a masquerade party. He extends over the whole of the United States and into southern Canada, and goes as far south as Mexico, where he attains his maximum size. He is a good swimmer, but he is unable to dive or pursue prey under water. He is very clever, and has feet in the front that are almost like human hands in the way he can use them, with very sharp long nails. He also possesses needle-like small teeth that can chew their way out of most anything. The raccoon makes his home high up in the hollows of large trees, preferring a dead limb to the trunk itself, and he hibernates during the severest part of the winter. Their families usually range from four to six young and they stay with their mother for about a year.

John James Audubon spoke about the raccoon as being a cunning animal, quite dextrous in the use of its forefeet, ready to steal from anyone at the drop of a hat. So, you see, we have here a wild animal of good size, who can defiantly hold his own, and one who usually gets his way and has the upper hand. He is not unlike the badger in his defending abilities. He may even be a bit more forceful and bold when it comes to being the instigator, and there is no way that, one for one, or even two to one, for that matter, a terrier could get the better of him. Raccoons are hunted in the United States mainly for their pelts, and coon hunting at night has been a sport for many, many years. In the southern states, blacks and whites alike take great pride in raising 'coon hounds', and, just to give you an idea of what type of a dog they raise for this sport, a coon hound is about the size of a foxhound, maybe even a bit larger.

What about the Jack Russell then? Where does he come into the picture, and why is coon *versus* Jack Russell a fun sport? I can only answer this from my own point of view. Number one, because these two animals have much in common, i.e. fortitude, stamina, agility, and are both quick to react and very clever, it makes the meeting of the two very exciting indeed. It is, in fact, a battle between the minds, rather than one to kill, for, you see, the Jack Russell soon finds out that he could never have the upper hand with a grown coon. So it becomes a matter of manoeuvring, pride and strategy as to who gets who out of a drain first! Once the coon has been bolted, he is then treed, and the terrier's job, of course, is to mark the spot by giving tongue. What happens after that is up to the hunter at hand.

How does one train a terrier to raccoon? Well, the beginning training is the same as it would be to train any terrier to work. You must, first of all, have a well-adjusted, outgoing, healthy animal who accepts you as his friend and who has full confidence in you. Starting at an early age, from three months on, you should devote part of your day to the pup, playing with him and getting him used to going into things, i.e. going after a cookie, ball, etc., in a boot or drain pipe, log or the like. At about four months, he can start to go out into the field, preferably with older experienced dogs, for short periods of time. He can also be introduced, at this time, to a caged rat, which will get his adrenalin going, and then, when you take him out into the field after that, he will be more eager. I always start my puppies off with older dogs. It is much easier and safer that way, and they are quicker to learn. The one thing that one always has to be careful of is not to overface a young dog for, once he has been frightened, the damage has been done and it takes forever to undo it, and sometimes is never accomplished at all. Also, one has to be careful not to get discouraged or give up on a young dog, thinking that he will never be any good. Give him some time; some of the best working terriers I have had have been very slow to start.

I remember how one time, to give you an example, I was called up late at night to bring some terriers over to a friend's field, where his Jack Russell had gone to ground in a drain after a full-grown bull raccoon. After quite some time, when my friend and his Jack Russell seemed not to be making any headway bolting the coon, he called me up and asked me to come right over. I took with me one of my best working bitches, Hamilton Pim, and along with her her son Kipper, whom I had quite frankly given up on, hunting-wise, but thought it was a good opportunity to give him one last chance. We arrived on the site to hear the sounds of confrontation coming from both my friend's Jack Russell and the coon. Naturally Pim, shaking with anticipation, excitement and eagerness to get down the drain, bolted out of the car door before I could grab her and was gone! This was the worst, because what in fact happened was that she entered the opposite end of the drain from the one the other Jack Russell belonging to my friend had gone into, and thereby cornered the coon, making it impossible for him to bolt. Under conditions such as this, the coon was naturally forced to attack and really get down to brass tacks.

I soon sensed that Pim was in trouble and, putting a flashlight and my head to the ground, was able to see inside the drain pipe. There was my best working bitch, unable to do anything with the raccoon latched on to her neck. It was quite evident that something had to be done, and quickly, for her air supply, although not completely cut off, was very limited and the Jack Russell at the other end had regained his strength and was only making everything worse in his excitement by attacking the coon. I think anyone owning a terrier will agree that no matter how much training in obedience the dog has had, when things get to a fever-point like this, it is almost impossible to call a dog off. Try as he would, my friend was unable to call his dog back for quite some time. At this point we had two options: start digging and try to break up the drain pipe, or send another terrier down, hoping it would distract the coon for a moment so that he would let go of Pim. We tried the first briefly, but soon realized that the pipe, a large sewer-type, was too big and strong for us to break through with the tools at hand. I then put Kipper to the test and asked him to go down the pipe. He entered a few feet, became frightened and backed out. I tried a second time, the same thing happened and I was ready to crown him, when all of a sudden, as a result of the coon's more advanced tactics and anger, Pim cried out with a shrill cry of obvious pain.

That was it: Kipper, hearing his mother in trouble, entered the pipe and went full force to it. I think that what happened finally was that Kipper pushed his way partly past Pim to the coon and an unbelievable fight ensued. Pim was freed and backed out, and the other dog, having had enough by that time, came out too, leaving Kipper and the coon to face each other. It was not long before the coon bolted out and, with three terriers in hot pursuit, managed to enter a near-by stream, where he dumped all three terriers and took off, leaving his pursuers to fend for themselves in the water. Confusion reigned for a bit, and then all were gathered up and dispersed for the night. The terriers were the worst for wear, as all had been cut up, especially Pim, but the coon loped off, tired yet ready to do battle another night.

The exciting part of the whole evening was the fact that, finally, after attaining two years of age, Kipper had proved his worth and had been entered for the first time. From that day until this he has been the star Jack Russell to coon! It is amazing to see him work. He is cautious, quick, has perfected his strategy and manoeuvres and, above all, enjoys the sport and has gained guarded confidence – the most important factor of all, I feel, in a good working terrier. He is the only terrier I have ever seen who, when confronted with a coon or ground-hog in a drain or earth (where the opposition is fairly close to the entrance, or when the animal has been cornered in a stable yard, or under a car, etc.) will enter the earth, head towards the coon, on his belly, with front legs tucked well back and to his side to prevent the coon from grabbing hold of them. Kipper has truly learned by experience, and learned well, and he is a delight to watch while working. He will enter a drain, will work the coon back until he gets to the widest part of the pipe, will then manoeuvre himself behind the raccoon and, at this point, will start working the coon back towards the entrance.

It is not, of course, quite as easy as I put it here. The raccoon, being the animal I have described to you, is not pushed about as easily as all that, but rather fights very hard to gain the upper hand and, in most cases, does. Naturally it proves little to exhaust the terrier beyond the point where he no longer considers it sport, but is in fact truly fighting for his life; and that is where I come in, and take charge. In most cases, one can get the terrier out by distracting the coon enough to let the terrier pass him and then reach the entrance of the drain. In my years of experience, I have not, thank heaven, lost one terrier to this type of sport, but have usually been with them whenever they have gone to ground. In the few cases when I have had a terrier go off by itself, and it has not returned within a matter of an hour or so, I will go out searching until I find it and, once found, with the help of other members of the family will proceed to excavate!

So, you see, starting a young dog with older, more experienced ones, can be beneficial. If I am going to work a terrier to raccoon, I make the decision after carefully watching the pup work in the field and with other dogs. For this game, I would only pick the most aggressive, cocky, confident and eager youngster out of the lot, one built with good bone, strong jaw and shorter leg. I would then introduce him to a raccoon in a humane trap. You can tell a lot by this, for coons are not silent, and when trapped are as aggressive and vocal as ever. Depending on how the pup reacted to that situation, I would then make my decision. From that point on, it is truly a matter of gaining experience, and working the terrier to any small game is beneficial. One day, when he is asked to check an earth, he will get his chance to confront the big one!

The United States offers such a lot to those interested in working their terriers. North, south, east and west all have different terrains with different small game available. I have a file with letters from all parts, telling stories of Jack Russells working, and it is very encouraging indeed. The American Working Terrier Association is an organization started quite a few years ago in this country to encourage all breeds of terriers to work, not only Jack Russells; and they organize and hold trials throughout the country, giving certificates of gameness and recognizing working ability in any terrier. So, as in Britain, this country has those people interested in working their terriers for fun and sport, as well as those interested in working their terriers for a purpose, i.e. to keep farms rodent-free, to keep fields free from woodchuck holes that livestock could fall into, and to keep rabbits out of a garden growing vegetables commercially, just to mention a few. I have also had a letter from a man in the west who tells me that his Jack Russell is excellent on snakes. Another mentions working Jack Russells to coyote, and how successful the Jack Russell is at keeping this wild dog out of their living and farm area, and yet another from Florida talks about working his Jack Russell to armadillo. The Jack Russell has indeed been introduced to many and varied species on the hunted list in this country, and, from all reports that I have received, terriers and owners alike are enjoying themselves, sharing together their hunting experiences.

Aside from working these terriers to game, a great amount of success has been attained by owners taking their dogs through obedience training. Jack Russells seem to like the routine and discipline of going to class, and all that I have known who have done so have done extremely well, and usually ended up showing up the rest of the class by graduating with honours at the top. Many of those that I speak of have been young pups, eight to twelve months of age, all combined into a large class with various breeds, including that of Alsatian and Doberman. Another new type of work which Jack Russells are entering into in this country is that of tracking. This is the work which Bloodhounds have been used for for many years by the police department. One does not normally think of the smaller breeds when it comes to this type of work, but there are studies being done now in this country, through the army, with terrier breeds being used to track down explosive devices. So the terrier is once again coming into its own and being used as a working dog, which is a gratifying development indeed, and hopefully one which will continue.

Many of our well-known Foxhound kennels in the country use terriers to bolt, and have them living right in the kennels with the hounds. When the hunt leaves the kennels in the morning for a day of sport, the terrier will either ride in the hound truck, following the hunt that way until he is needed, or ride in the saddlebag of a huntsman or field member, waiting to be called on if the need should arise. In the United States, we do not yet have a so-called terrier man, whose job it is to work the terriers prior to the hunt going out, but it would not surprise me to hear of this job being carried one of these days.

The future of working terriers in America looks very good. More and more people are becoming interested in working them to new and varied game, and likewise, more people are amazed to find out that the terrier, is in fact, a good working dog. Much will depend on these people, interested in sport, as to whether the working terrier will advance in this field or be ruined by inbreeding and the show ring. Certainly I have been working very hard to prevent the latter, and will continue to do so as long as I am able, for I believe strongly that these super little dogs are worthy of more than that, and that they should continue to do the work for which they were intended, and which they love and do so well.

THE AMERICAN WORKING TERRIER ASSOCIATION

Patricia Adams Lent

Since my childhood I have enjoyed different kinds of sport with terriers, but it wasn't until I was out of college as a young adult that I became cognizant of, and concerned about, what was happening here in America to the grand little sporting dog I had always loved and respected for the irreproachable hunter he is! At that time I was living in the ruggedly beautiful, mountainous state of Vermont in northern New England. Steep and rocky terrain, long snow-covered winters, the almost imperceptibly short growing season best describe life in Vermont, and trying to farm was, at best, difficult. We worked hard to make a living from Jersey cattle, Dorset sheep and draft horses. The bright spot was the abundance of hunting I enjoyed with my terriers.

We spent many happy hours hunting rats on farms throughout the rural community, and ridding farm ponds of the dam-destroying muskrats. The terriers were expert at these endeavours, and soon word rang out among the local gentry of their competency, whereupon I received calls asking for the service of my terriers. Away we would go, eager to lend our assistance!

The scourge of every farm and to every farmer was the woodchuck, which dauntlessly and persistently dug its dens in the best pastures and meadows where it had access to the succulent food. The woodchuck not only enjoyed the farmers' grass and hay, but his dens were hazards, both to animals and equipment. Left alone, this rodent soon multiplies, and where there were only one or two dens previously, the pastures and meadows were soon riddled with them. The farmers waged war, mostly using poison, but the woodchucks were undeniably the victors.

In one season my terriers completely rid our farm of the pest, after which we sallied forth to put things right on other farms. It was great fun which provided sport for the terriers and much needed help for the farmers.

When not employed at these more serious tasks, I enjoyed hunting rabbits, squirrels, grouse and woodcock with the terriers. From firsthand experience I knew what a superb little sportster the terrier was, and

THE AMERICAN WORKING TERRIER ASSOCIATION

how useful he could be to the farmer, and I worried that he wasn't getting his chance. Farms all over America were besieged by various vermin, yet very few working terrier breeds were being used to help with control.

I kept asking myself, why? Why were the small terriers being deprived of their chance to help? A terrier small enough to go to ground could do a sizeable clean-up job with rats, opossums, muskrats and woodchucks – the most common farm pests. What, if anything, could I do to bring attention to the terrier's hunting ability and versatility?

For several years I pondered the possibility of putting on terrier trials by constructing and using an artificial earth. I conceived the idea of having an American Working Terrier Association whose purpose would be twofold: to bring attention to the breeders and owners of terriers that terriers are hunters; and to sponsor terrier trials to test for willingness to go to ground and apparent gameness. On 5 June 1971, with help only from my sons Trevor, 15, and Jeffrey, 11, I staged the first American Working Terrier Association trial in Penn Yen, New York. That first trial was an overwhelming success! More importantly, it marked the beginning! Growth and expansion have been continuous from that time, until at the moment of writing, November 1977, the AWTA sponsors trials in all parts of the United States and will hold its first Canadian trial in 1978.

Since its inception, the AWTA has attracted all the American Kennel Club recognized breeds as well as dachshunds and Jack Russells. It has been of interest to observe the various breeds while judging trials during our seven seasons. Within each breed varying degrees of performance are easily detected. Some individuals do not hesitate to enter the artificial earth, and these travel straight through the earth quickly, and upon reaching the quarry begin to 'work' the rats after a brief cursory investigation. Others potter about the entrance to the earth, obviously enchanted by the scent, but lacking the initiative to follow the scent into the dark passage of the earth. Some simply show no interest or actual acknowledgement of the earth. Far and away the most outstanding trial performances are by terriers who are used for hunting. These whistle flawlessly through the test. Next in line of performance are the terriers which have been trained specifically to work in an artificial earth. (My book, *Sport with Terriers*, details how to train for trials.) But perhaps the most interesting to watch are the terriers from show or pet homes which have never before seen an earth, artificial or natural, and have not been exposed to any type of hunting. Here is where an inherent instinct to go to ground can be witnessed.

I can honestly say that no one breed out-performs the others. It is all within each individual's character and/or training. I've judged outstanding first-trial performances by Norwich, Cairns, Borders, Scottish, West Highlands, Bedlingtons, Lakelands, Smooth and Wire Fox, Welsh, Jack Russells and Dachshunds. And I've judged individuals of these same breeds which have appeared to be deficient of the native instincts of a working terrier; this lack of aptitude can almost always be attributed directly to the terrier's background environment.

During these past seven years of observing and judging the small terrier breeds as they performed at the trials, one thing has been clear. The working instinct is discernible in the different terrier breeds today, which is reason to exert every effort to broadcast their attributes as hunters. Not only do terriers excel as vermin extinguishers, they are excellent little flushing dogs for bird hunting. Nobody can expect a terrier to equal the style of a pointer or setter, but nevertheless a terrier demonstrates a technique unto itself, and retrieves with alacrity. Terriers love hunting rabbits and squirrels and take to both like a duck takes to water.

The AWTA has received a growing support, generated from the trials. Trials initiate the neophyte into the outer fringe of hunting, thus serving as a stepping stone into the hunting field itself. While the AWTA recognizes a working terrier as one which hunts its quarry underground, we actively promote the use of terriers for above-ground hunting as well. There is so little chance for terriers to go to ground here in America where the small dens require a terrier of 10 to 12 pounds. However, the woodchuck, fox, muskrat and opossums can be hunted with great success in above-ground conditions. Because earth work is considered the epitome, the AWTA issues working certificates to its members' terriers for work in a natural earth. Understandably, the working certificate is highly coveted and is not to be confused with the certificate of gameness, which is issued for work in an artificial earth at a trial.

The AWTA trials have classes for Novice, Open and Certificate dogs. Novice is for inexperienced dogs. Their test is performed in a 10-foot earth, and, if necessary, this class is used for training with points deducted accordingly. Here a dog is allowed two minutes to enter the earth, during which time the handler may encourage him in any way, except by force. The Open class is for dogs with hunting experience, or when a dog has scored 100 per cent in Novice. The earth is 30 feet long and the dog has thirty seconds from its release (dogs are released 8 feet from earth's entrance) to reach the caged rats. At no time may the handler offer any kind of encouragement. Once it reaches the quarry, the dog must react positively to the rats and sustain for a full minute. This reaction can be growling, barking,

NOVICE EARTH

OPEN AND CERTIFICATE EARTH

Entrance

Caged rats

Removable door for judge's viewing and for removal of dog

Entrance

Caged rats

Removable door

whining, biting or lunging at the cage, or any combination of these. A dog scoring 100 per cent in Open is issued a certificate of gameness. Thereafter it is eligible to compete in the Certificate class against others of the same breed. The breed winner is the one which reaches the quarry with the fastest time.

The accompanying diagrams show what the liners, used in constructing the earth, are like. They show the wooden liners, which are three-sided, 9 inches across and 9 inches deep and roughly 10 feet long. One liner is used for the Novice, while three are used for Open and Certificate. A scent line (using muskrat, fox or raccoon scent) is run along the earth's floor, the liners are placed in an 18-inch-deep trench and then covered with earth, making it all, especially the entrance, look as natural as possible. Only the removable door directly in front of the quarry is left uncovered, providing an observation point for the judge as well as a means of removing the dog from the earth. The artificial test indicates a dog's willingness to go to ground and a desire to get at the rats. It's hard to say whether the dogs or the people enjoy a trial more!

My hope in founding the American Working Terrier Association was to draw attention to the small terrier's intended and original role, and by so doing make people realize fully what a terrier is, what he was bred for, and how he can be used as a versatile little hunting partner. The AWTA wants all terrier breeders and owners to know these things. It emphatically encourages breeders to preserve the terrier's character so that it may always remain in the sporting ranks.

The American Working Terrier Association is proud and full of hope because its trials and publicity have generated an interest among people to use their terriers for hunting, and many breeders now look for homes where their puppies can enjoy sport.

We feel that all is not lost for the working terrier breeds here in America.

Happy hunting! With a terrier, of course!